SOCIAL MEDIA
MARKETING
BASICS

This is a **FLAME TREE** book
First published 2015

Publisher and Creative Director: Nick Wells
Project Editor: Polly Prior
Art Director and Layout Design: Mike Spender
Digital Design and Production: Chris Herbert
Screenshots: Richard N. Williams
Copy Editor: Anna Groves
Technical Editor: Rob Buckley
Proofreader: Sally Brigham
Indexer: Eileen Cox

Special thanks to: Gillian Whitaker

This edition first published 2015 by
FLAME TREE PUBLISHING
Crabtree Hall, Crabtree Lane
Fulham, London SW6 6TY
United Kingdom

www.flametreepublishing.com

15 17 19 18 16
1 3 5 7 9 10 8 6 4 2

© 2015 Flame Tree Publishing

ISBN 978-1-78361-398-4

All non-screenshot pictures are cour   photographers: 1, 7 (a)   o; 3 jurgenfr;
5, 8 Eugenio Marongiu; 28 Nagy-Bag   hpann; 38 Gozzi   reedom; 48 Ivein Radkov; 72   eridis Vasilis;
74 spaxiax; 88 Bloom   110 Jack Frog; 120 StockLite; 126 michaeljung.

EVERYDAY GUIDES
MADE EASY

SOCIAL MEDIA
MARKETING
BASICS

RICHARD N. WILLIAMS

FLAME TREE
PUBLISHING

CONTENTS

SERIES FOREWORD 5

INTRODUCTION 6

GETTING STARTED 8

For those new to social media, this chapter explains what social media
is and how to set up an account.

SOCIAL MEDIA AND BUSINESS 28

For all you budding entrepreneurs out there, this chapter will show you
how social media can help your business.

SOCIAL NETWORK MARKETING 48

Here we look at the major social networks and how they can help
you achieve your business goals.

CREATING YOUR AUDIENCE 72

In this chapter we will explain how you can build up a following and obtain
those coveted 'Likes', 'retweets' and other interactions.

GETTING THE MOST OUT OF SOCIAL MEDIA 88

Here we go into more detail about social media promotion, using blogging
and measuring the effectiveness of your social media strategy.

ADVANCED SOCIAL MEDIA MARKETING 106

How you conduct yourself is critical for success. In this chapter, we also
explore how you can further your social media efforts.

USEFUL WEBSITES AND FURTHER READING 126

INDEX 127

SERIES FOREWORD

Word of mouth still remains the ultimate sales and marketing tool. Get people talking about you and your products, and you can expect your profits to soar. But in the age of the internet, those conversations needn't take place just on the high street or over coffee – they can be between millions of people who have never actually met, in different countries, in different languages.

Social networks are the key to spreading this digital word, whether it's happy customers chatting on Facebook, celebrities tweeting on Twitter, reviewers writing on blogs, professionals exchanging recommendations on LinkedIn or fans showing off videos and photos on YouTube, Flickr, Instagram and Pinterest. But joining or even starting these conversations can be difficult – venture where you're not wanted or come on too strong, and before you know it, everyone *will* be talking about you... but for all the wrong reasons.

This guide to social media marketing will help you navigate the conversational pitfalls of social media. From the basics of how to create persuasive profiles on all the important social networks and seeing who's saying what about you, through to the subtleties of netiquette, the law and dealing with trolls, this book will show you, through simple, easy-to-follow steps, not only how to use these powerful new tools but also to get the most from them and boost your sales. Follow its advice and it'll become your new best friend on the internet – one that could potentially make you a lot of money.

Rob Buckley
IT and marketing journalist and editor

INTRODUCTION

Social media is here to stay, and if you are not onboard it is time to start, especially if you have a business or something you want to promote. While it can be daunting at first, the great thing about social media is that it is accessible to all, which makes it a highly powerful marketing tool.

GETTING INVOLVED

Social media has changed the way people communicate. While you are probably familiar with a few social networks, such as Facebook, Twitter, LinkedIn and the like, there are literally thousands more. There is so much choice it can be quite bewildering to know where to start

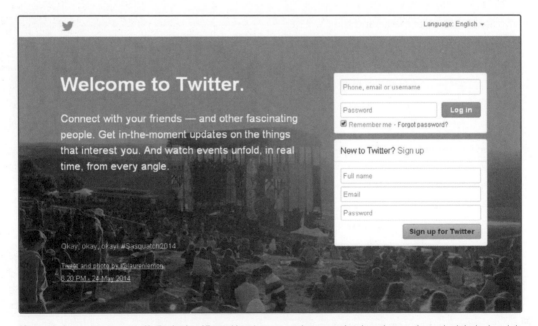

Above: Whether you are new to sites like Facebook and Twitter (shown) or want to take your social media marketing to the next level, this book can help.

and how to get involved. This book has been designed to help you find your way through the social media landscape, guiding you through the range of social media, from social networks and forums to blogs and video- or photosharing sites.

YOUR GUIDE TO SOCIAL MEDIA MARKETING

This book has been designed to provide a useful resource for both those new to social media and the complete novice. You can read the book from cover to cover, or just use it as a reference for when you need help using social media whether for personal use or marketing.

Easy Explanations

Where possible, we have tried to cut through the jargon and technical explanations, providing you with an easy to understand guide. Throughout this book, you'll find there are many step-by-step guides that take you through the exact actions you need to follow to accomplish certain tasks.

Hot Tip

Look out for Hot Tips throughout the book, which provide quick and handy information on the way to get the best from your social media. They also highlight many shortcuts and quick techniques, which will help you become an expert user.

GETTING STARTED

WHAT IS SOCIAL MEDIA?

We are, by nature, social animals. Social media builds on that instinct by enabling us to connect and share with people. It may be our ideas, news, photos, videos or opinions – anything and everything about our life that we want to let others know about.

WHAT SOCIAL MEDIA COVERS

Social media has become the way to communicate information between people, wherever they are. It is, in fact, an umbrella term that covers any site that connects people and shares information, and includes:

Below: Facebook is by far the most popular social network on the Internet.

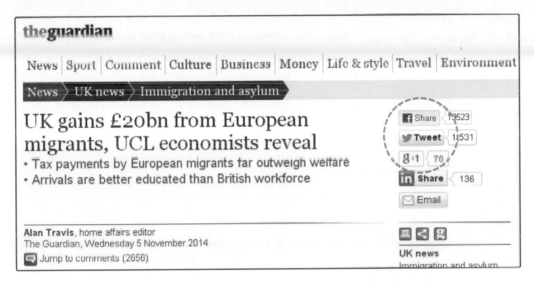

Above: Mainstream media websites, such as the Guardian, allow you to share news stories through social networks.

- **Social networks:** These include Facebook (facebook.com), the original and best-known.

- **Blogs:** Online journals for individuals and businesses, but also technically includes microblogs such as Twitter (twitter.com).

- **Video- and photo-sharing:** Instagram (instagram.com), Pinterest (pinterest.com), YouTube (www.youtube.com).

- **Other sites:** These include social bookmarking, news sites, online reviews, music networks, social games and virtual worlds.

> **Hot Tip**
>
> Most newspapers and broadcasters run blogs, written by their staff, to which you can add comments. Try these out for yourself and get used to how they work before you launch your own blog

Active Interaction

What distinguishes social media from regular sites is that you – and the other people in the community – are actively involved in generating the content.

Your Voice

Social media communication is two-way. You write the blog, make the video or recommend a travel destination, and others can comment on it and make their own suggestions. Even if the source of the original content was a news site, or some other form of traditional media, it is still interactive – you can add your voice to it, comment or give feedback and create something new. What's more, it can all happen instantly.

WHAT YOU CAN DO WITH SOCIAL MEDIA

Typically, social media can help you:

- **Communicate with people you know:** Social networks let you connect with the people you know, allowing you to share updates about what is going on in your life with family and friends.

Above: Friends Reunited specializes in connecting you with people you used to know.

○ **Find new people to communicate with:** You can extend your network to include friends of friends or move outside of your existing circle by following an event – such as a music festival or book launch – or join a group of people that share your interests.

○ **Find people you've lost touch with:** Several websites are designed to reunite people who have lost touch, such as finding old school friends or work colleagues.

○ **Find or set up a group:** Whatever your interest, there is likely to be a group that you can join or you can start your own, allowing you to connect with like-minded people.

○ **Keep in touch with what's going on:** Social media helps you keep track of news, whether from friends and family, world news, your interests or celebrity or sports gossip

Above: Social networks, such as Twitter, are great for keeping track of the news as stories often break on there first.

ORGANIZE EVERYDAY LIFE

Some avoid social media for fear that it is too distracting and will take up all their time. In fact, rather than being excessively time-consuming, social media can help you organize your time and live life to the full.

ORGANIZE YOUR SOCIAL LIFE

Arranging an evening out? This is when sites like Facebook come into their own. It's the perfect way for a network of friends to stay in touch. If there is a change of venue or date for an event, it's easier to post details on Facebook, where everyone can see, rather than phone people individually.

Entertainment

There is so much going on, at the theatre, on the TV, in the cinema; how do you decide what to go and see? You are also able to read in one place what all the critics say, read other people's views, as well as access entertainment forums to view the ratings and comments that others have given.

Events

Social media lets you send the invites, gather the responses, update the venue and correspond with everyone through a single page to make sure everything goes smoothly.

Left: Sites like Rotten Tomatoes have all the critics' reviews in one place to help you decide if you want to see a film or not.

Travel

You can read reviews and comments about holiday destinations on sites such as TripAdvisor (www.tripadvisor.com), allowing you to judge whether a hotel or resort is worth staying at. While some companies play the system by posting fake reviews, you can usually get a good consensus of general opinion.

Hot Tip

As well as the destinations, comments by TripAdvisor users can also be rated for their helpfulness. Beside the review, you'll see a rosette showing how many users have voted it helpful.

Above: Although they can offer helpful advice on an unfamiliar destination, remember that opinions aired on such sites as TripAdvisor are purely personal.

ORGANIZE YOUR WORKING LIFE

Business is just as social as your personal life. Many social media tools are designed to help you in your career – whether it's finding a new job, developing your skills or promoting your business.

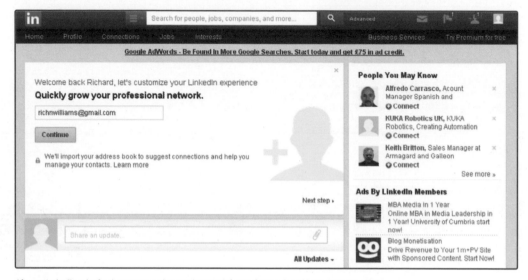

Above: LinkedIn is by far the most popular social network for professionals and business networking.

Promote Yourself

You can go a long way to create 'Brand You' by adding your profile and developing a rich network of connections on sites such as LinkedIn. LinkedIn is the major business social network that allows you to connect to people in your own field as well as suggesting jobs you may be interested in based on your profile. It also provides recruitment managers with the search tools to headhunt people who match their requirements.

Promote Your Business

As well as personal branding, many social media sites enable businesses to build their profile and promote their brands. Social media can complement traditional press and TV advertising campaigns and, in many cases, be just as effective.

Connect With Other Businesses

Social media sites provide a global forum in which to share experiences. Sites like LinkedIn offer industry groups a place where people can exchange views on current issues. Many professional and trade bodies run their own communities and groups to bring like-minded professionals together.

INBOUND MARKETING

Using social media to connect with customers is known as 'Inbound marketing' and can be more effective at bringing customers closer to the brand compared to direct advertising, which is known as 'outbound marketing'.

Above: You can find all sorts of trade and professional forums on which to discuss your business or profession.

TYPES OF SOCIAL MEDIA

There is such a variety to social media, with new applications emerging all the time, that it is hard to categorize them. There is also a great deal of overlap. For example, most social networks allow you to share photos and videos, which is the main focus of media-sharing sites like Flickr and YouTube.

SOCIAL NETWORKS

These are the most familiar type of social media, thanks to the great popularity of Facebook and LinkedIn. Social networks let you connect with people who have a common background and shared interests.

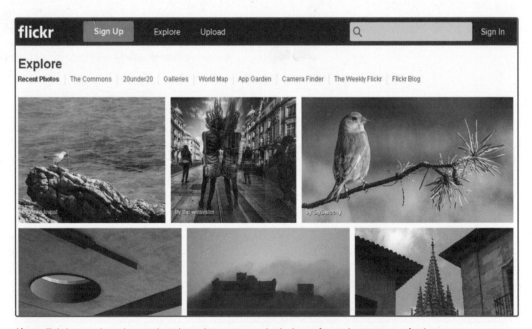

Above: Flickr lets you share photographs with people in your network, whether professional pictures or just family snaps.

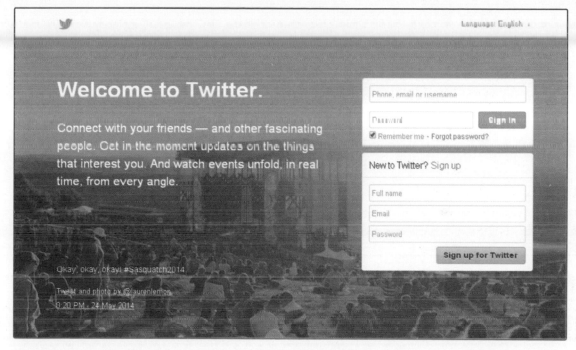

Welcome to Twitter.

Connect with your friends — and other fascinating people. Get in the moment updates on the things that interest you. And watch events unfold, in real time, from every angle.

Language: English

Phone, email or username

Password

Sign In

☑ Remember me · Forgot password?

New to Twitter? Sign up

Full name

Email

Password

Sign up for Twitter

Okay, okay, okay! #Sasquatch2014
Tweet and photo by @laurenlemon
8:20 PM · 24 May 2014

Above: Twitter has over 250 million regular users and is by far the most popular microblogging site in the world.

MICROBLOGGING

This is virtually synonymous with Twitter, which is by far the biggest microblogging site. You can read and post very short (micro) blog posts – less than 140 characters on Twitter – as well as discover new people to follow.

BLOGS

A blog allows you to publish content online. A blog can be about anything. The best blogs encourage feedback and debate by allowing comments.

Hot Tip

Tweets have a very short lifespan. If you see one that you want to keep and refer back to, save it as a 'Favorite'. Hover your mouse over the tweet and click the star icon. This also lets a tweeter know that you liked their tweet.

FORUMS

Online forums enable members to debate questions. Whatever your interests, you should find forums that suit you among the hundreds of millions available online.

SOCIAL BOOKMARKING

Sites like Delicious (delicious.com) allow you to save and manage bookmarks – or links – to web pages and other resources you come across on the internet. As it's easy to amass hundreds of bookmarks, you can also tag them with keywords, which makes them easier to search and share. When you view someone else's bookmarks there's usually a description and sometimes an opinion about the site, which can help you decide if you want to visit.

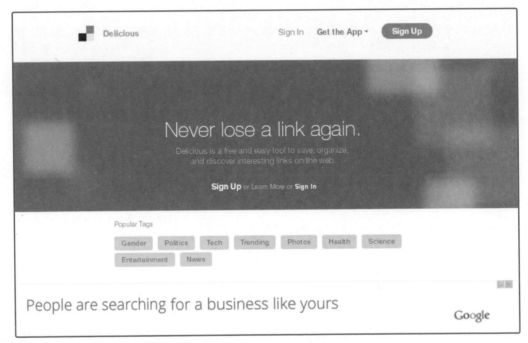

Above: Delicious enables you to save and share links and bookmarks to interesting websites with your friends.

SOCIAL NEWS

These services post news stories and blog posts, or links to them, for you to vote on. The most popular, that is those that get the most votes, are displayed more prominently and for longer. Among the main social news sites are Digg (digg.com) and Reddit (www.reddit.com).

MEDIA SHARING

Upload your photos or videos and share them with family and friends or open them to public viewing, as you prefer. Among the most popular sites are Dailymotion, Vimeo and Instagram. These sites also allow you to add a profile and invite comments on your photos and videos.

LOCATION-BASED NETWORKING SERVICES

These allow you to see recommendations for places you can go locally, such as restaurants, hotels and places of interest.

Above: Digg provides a one-stop place for news stories, which you can share with your friends and followers on other social networks.

SPECIAL INTEREST SOCIAL NETWORKS

If you have a particular passion – such as music or travel – you can probably find a niche social networking site that is targeted to your interests. Often they link in with other social networks, like Facebook, so they can show you what your friends recommend.

Social Virtual Gaming

Some online games act like social networks. You can play in a virtual world, such as World of Warcraft, where you can connect and meet other gamers, or through a social network, like Farmville, which tens of millions of people play through Facebook.

Social Virtual Worlds

Places such as Second Life offer picturesque worlds, which you inhabit in 'real time' with other users. Your character is represented by an avatar that interacts with the others.

Above: You can socialize in a totally virtual world in Second Life.

SIGNING UP AND CREATING PROFILES

Most social media sites follow similar processes when it comes to setting up a new account. This will typically involve creating a profile, so you need to consider how much personal information to share.

GETTING STARTED

Most social media sites let you explore the site without becoming a member so you can be sure that it's right for you. However, there will come a point when you will need to register. While each individual site has its own specific requirements, most will include:

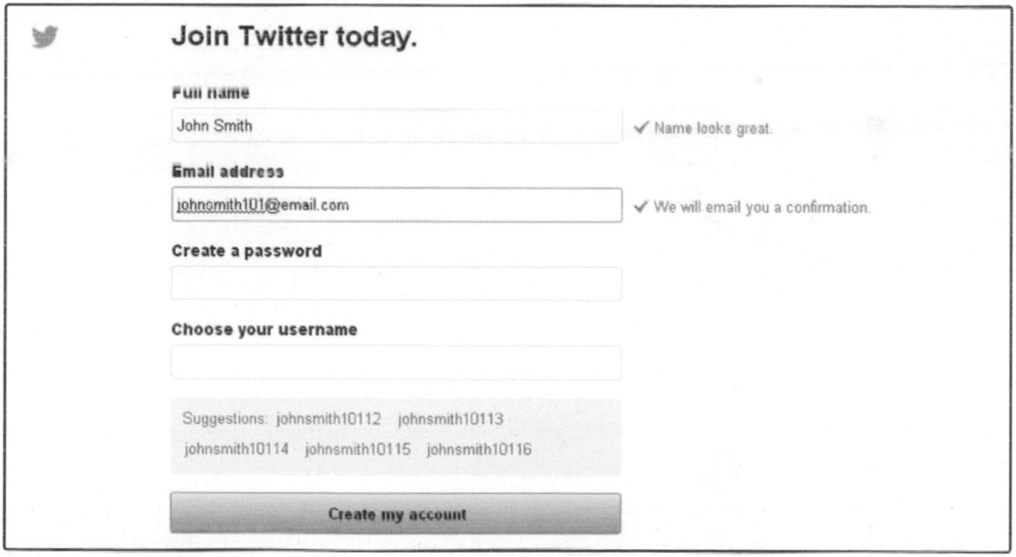

🐦 **Join Twitter today.**

Full name

John Smith   ✓ Name looks great.

Email address

johnsmith101@email.com   ✓ We will email you a confirmation.

Create a password

Choose your username

Suggestions: johnsmith10112   johnsmith10113
johnsmith10114   johnsmith10115   johnsmith10116

Create my account

Above: You will need access to an email address and also create a username for nearly all social media websites.

Above: Passwords help keep your social media accounts secure.

- **Email address:** This is usually used for logging in as well as notifying you when someone has commented on what you've written, and to pass on messages from other users.

- **Username:** This has to be, for obvious reasons, unique. If your first choice is not available, the site will usually suggest various options based on it. Be careful to make this something you are comfortable with, as it will become part of your online identity.

- **Password:** This is usually between six and eight characters; often requiring a combination of letters and at least one number.

- **Date of birth:** Often used to return more relevant suggestions for friends or people you may know. Some sites use it publicly, though if you're self-conscious about your age you can choose to leave off your birth year, or not publish it at all.

- **Security question**: This is to check that it is a person and not a spam robot that's trying to join. Sometimes, you need to fill in the letters and numbers in the image – called a CAPTCHA (Completely Automated Public Turing test to tell Computers and Humans Apart).

- **Activation email**: Once successfully registered, you'll usually be sent an email to the address you entered. You'll need to click on the link in the email to activate your account and show you have a working email address.

> ## Hot Tip
>
> When filling in your profile you can decide who this information is shared with, through the privacy settings. If you are at all worried, leave personal details out, as you can always add them later.

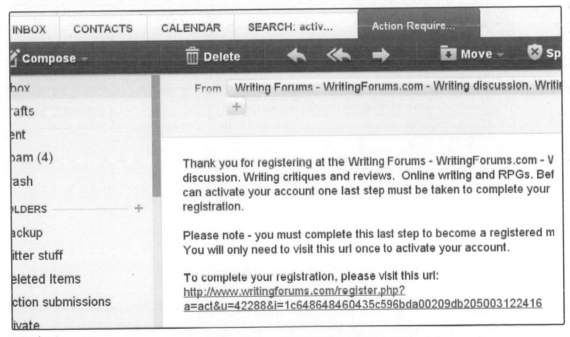

Above: When you sign up to a social media website, you will probably have to activate your account by clicking a link in an email.

SETTING UP YOUR PROFILE

Your profile is possibly the most important aspect of any social media site, as it will fundamentally shape how useful it is to you. Recommendations for friends and people who share your interests will largely depend on your profile.

Hot Tip

The information you put here will be shared with other people on the site. In most cases, the same information or a shortened version of it will appear in search results on Google or Bing, etc.

TWEETS 12.6K   **FOLLOWING** 647K   **FOLLOWERS** 49.2M   ⚙   +2 Follow

Barack Obama ✓
@BarackObama

This account is run by Organizing for Action staff. Tweets from the President are signed - bo.

Above: Your profile is what other users will see. Even presidents of the United States have their own social media profiles.

Personal Information

Generally, you will be asked to fill in details of where you live, where you were educated, what you're doing, what your likes are and so on.

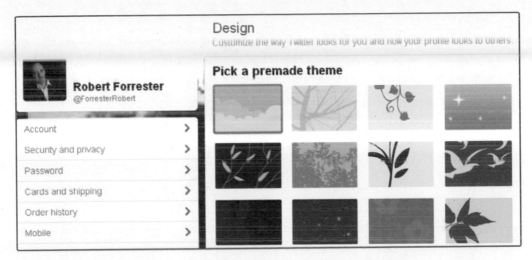

Above: Many social media websites, such as Twitter, let you customize and personalize your profile page.

Profile Elements

Your profile is what will attract other users to connect with you, so you need to ensure your profile is visible and as appealing as possible. Social media profiles often have several elements to help you attract friends and followers:

- **Name:** This can be your real name, a fake name or a username.

- **Picture:** If you want to be noticed, a profile picture is essential.

- **Biography:** You need to tell people who or what (if you are setting up a business page) you are and what you are about.

- **Location:** It doesn't have to be specific, but at least explain what country you reside in.

- **Background:** Many social media sites let you customize your profile page to look as appealing as possible.

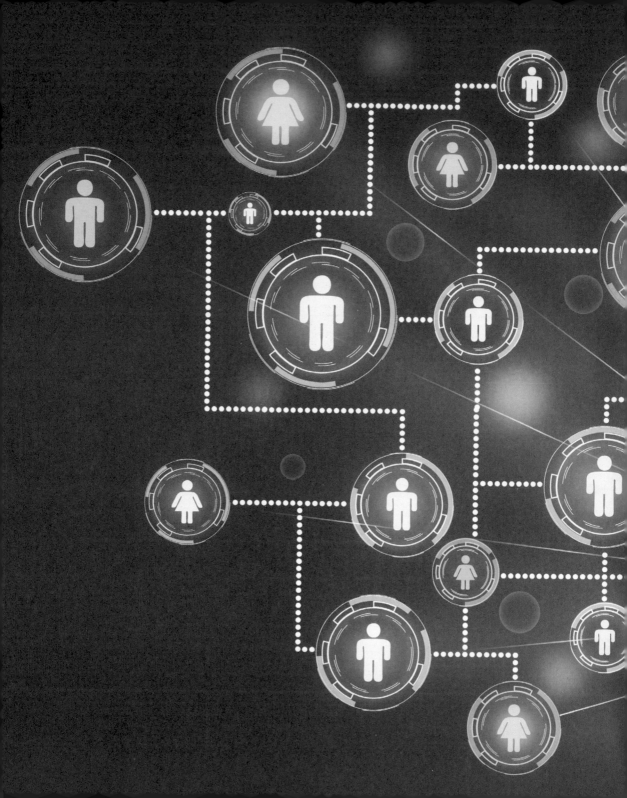

SOCIAL MEDIA AND BUSINESS

HOW SOCIAL MEDIA CAN HELP YOUR BUSINESS

Social media is changing the way companies promote their products and services to us. In this era of immediacy, it is very powerful, if used well. Used badly, it can just as quickly destroy a brand.

RIGHT HERE, RIGHT NOW

Given that so many of us use social media it's not surprising that businesses have realized it can be a much more effective way of reaching consumers than straightforward advertising. Many of us, even if we don't do it consciously, block out ads. That's why businesses are using social media, in much the same way individuals are.

Above: Tesco is among a growing number of big businesses that now use social media to connect with their customers.

Reputation Management

The immediacy of social media provides an instant communication channel with customers. If your systems have crashed, let your customers know that you're doing something about it rather than wait for the flood of tweets from unhappy users, poisoning your reputation. And keep them in the loop. Social media can be instantly updated, so make sure it's used to send out the latest information. After all, no one likes to feel they are being left out of the conversation.

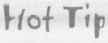

Hot Tip

If you want to know what's being said about you, there are a number of social media monitoring services that alert brands to problems so they can respond quickly.

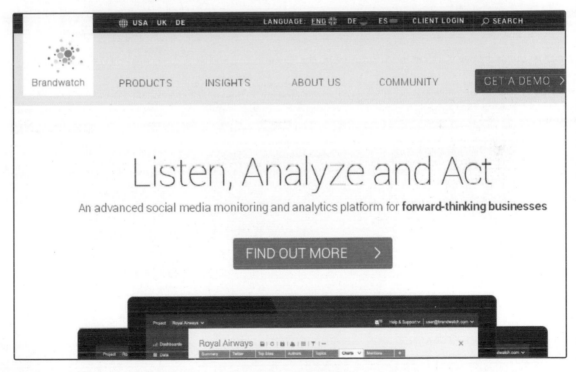

Above: Tools like Brandwatch can help you monitor what is being said about your business.

Communication

Social media can help you communicate with people connected to your business.

- ○ **Business to customer:** Whether you sell to other businesses or to consumers, social media provides a channel of communication. Online ads, blogs, video channels, Twitter and Facebook pages can all help you reach your customers.

Above: Social media can get the message out – fast and direct.

- ○ **Consumer to business:** Previously, the problem was getting feedback from the consumer. Now, social media allows your customers a way of getting in touch with you directly.

- ○ **Consumer to consumer:** Word of mouth is perhaps the most powerful marketing tool available to you, and review sites, forums and discussion boards allow you to create a buzz about your products.

REACHING PEOPLE

The way people use the internet has changed dramatically in recent years. Mobile devices mean we spend much more of our time online and can access the internet almost anywhere.

Nanotargeting

Social media marketing can be more fine-tuned than any other platform, helping you to reach specific audiences. Social media sites can match adverts to those who are most likely to respond, providing a more targeted approach to marketing.

Pay By Results

Many social media sites operate advertisements through pay-per-click (CPC) or pay-per-thousand impressions (CPM) models, so you only pay when someone is interested enough to click on your ad or when it has been viewed by a thousand people. These can be cheaper and more effective than the scattergun approach of traditional marketing methods, such as mail shots and print advertisements. See information on LinkedIn ads on page 69.

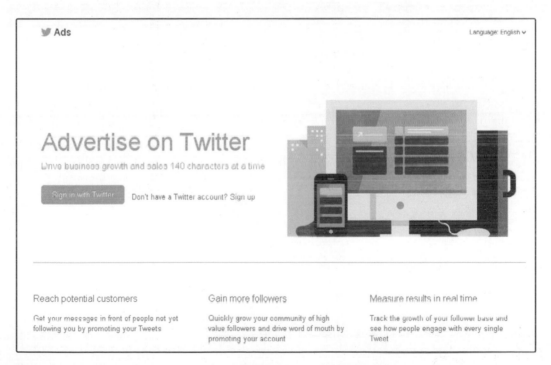

Above: Social media advertising only charges by number of followers reached, or clicks or likes obtained.

CREATING A BRAND

A brand is not just your name, but can be anything that identifies you and your business. A brand is not necessarily something you have full control of, as it is often what other people perceive about you, but social media can help you build and maintain a positive brand image.

Above: A brand is more than just a business name; it is how people perceive a company.

GETTING KNOWN

We all know of successful brands. These are the companies that become synonymous with what they do: Coca Cola, Apple and McDonald's have brands famous the world over. Brand building is about getting people talking about your business and your products, and few methods are as effective at brand building as social media is.

CUSTOMERS AS A COMMUNITY

The best way to develop a brand is to stop thinking of your customers as just people who buy your products but think of them as a community.

Encouraging people to actively engage on social media and talk about your business and products is the perfect way to get your name known. To encourage this, you need to create an atmosphere that enables interaction, engagement and commentary, and social media is the perfect conduit.

Starting a Community

One way to encourage interaction is openly to ask for opinions in your social media pages, blog posts and tweets, and rather than use just social media to promote your products, provide your community with the information they want, such as news or opinions related to the subject of your business.

Above: Companies like McDonald's use social media to talk to their customers, respond to their concerns and conduct competitions.

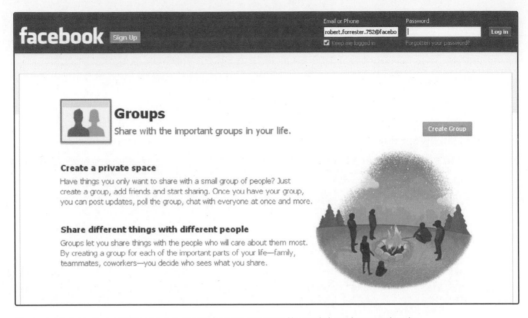

Above: Joining groups, or creating your own, is a great way to connect to like-minded people on social media.

Become Part of the Community

You cannot expect people just to start talking about you, so you need to be part of the community you are trying to build in the first place. This means you need to be active in places where the community hangs out. There are various ways to do this.

- **Blogs:** Post regular comments on other people's blogs.

- **Forums:** Become an active member of forums related to your business topic and make regular contributions.

- **Social media groups:** Join groups relating to your topic area.

Building a Following

If you want people to engage with you, the key is to show your knowledge in a practical way rather than just shamelessly promoting yourself. Offering promotional content alone is as likely to turn off customers. If it's seen as advertising dressed up as content, it will be treated as spam and there's a danger your account will be blocked or deleted.

Human Interaction

The main trick with social media marketing is to remember it's a conversation. People do not like interacting with faceless corporations, so while you want to act as professionally as possible, remember to be human. Talk to people and draw them into conversation.

Below: Monitor who is sending you messages on Twitter and Facebook and respond.

SOCIAL MEDIA STRATEGY

If you are using social media for business or promotion, you really need to establish a clear strategy. Working out your goals, and how best to achieve them, is the first step for any successful social media marketing campaign.

TIME IS MONEY

Social media networks, especially Facebook or Twitter, can eat away at your free time. Because of this, you do not want to approach social media marketing without first coming up with a strategy, working out what you want to achieve and how best to achieve it, otherwise you could be wasting an awful lot of time.

Below: Knowing your goals is important for any successful social media campaign.

ESTABLISH YOUR GOALS

Before you begin marketing on social media, it is worth establishing what you want to achieve. You goals will affect the rest of your strategy, such as the type of people you will connect with and the sort of content you will produce for your Twitter or Facebook pages. All goals need to be realistic, achievable, and measureable. For instance, if you would like 10,000 followers on Twitter, set a time when you want to achieve that number.

Social Networking for Business

You need to remember that social networks are not sales tools, but they can be useful for marketing in several ways:

○ **Brand building:** Social networks are great for raising brand awareness and boosting your profile.

○ **Customer engagement:** Social networks can provide a platform for customer communication.

Above: If your goal is to get a certain number of friends, likes or followers, set a date when you want to achieve this by.

○ **Promotion:** Announcing new products, news and information, as well as bringing traffic to your website, can all be done through social networks.

RESEARCH

Once you know what you want to achieve on social media, you need to do your research. Firstly, you need to identify who your community is. This should not just be your potential customers, but also other people in your industry that may be worth connecting with on social media. If you engage with people on social networking platforms, it could encourage them to follow or friend you.

Hot Tip

To assist in your market research, you can include a form on your website for customers to complete.

Above: Following people on Twitter or sending a friend request on Facebook are easy ways to engage with people on social media.

Customer Needs

You should also do market research on customer behaviour and ask what they want from businesses like yours.

- **Buying influence:** Ask your customers what encourages them to buy products from companies such as yours. Is it price, quality or something else?

- **Reputation:** Before you begin using social media to boost your brand, you need to establish what people already think about you. Are there things you need to address? What are your strengths and weaknesses?

- **Competition:** Do not just ask about yourself; ask how people perceive your competition. Establish what they are doing that you are not.

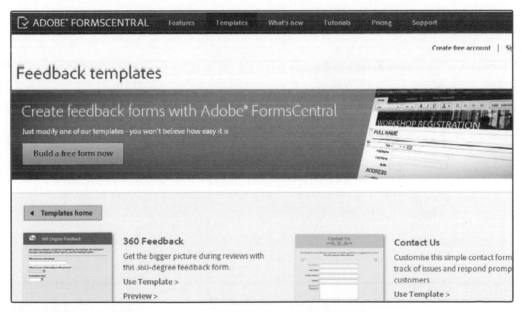

Above: To help with market research, use feedback forms such as these provided by Adobe FormsCentral (www.acrobat.com/en_gb/products/formscentral/templates.html).

PROMOTE YOUR SOCIAL MEDIA PROFILES

You cannot expect people suddenly to stumble upon your Twitter profile or Facebook page. You need to let people know you are on there. This may mean including your social networking details on your website, blog or even your correspondence to customers and suppliers. Some businesses include their Twitter username (commonly known as 'handle') and Facebook page with the rest of their contact details, as many people now prefer using social media rather than email or other traditional forms of communication.

CONNECTING WITH PEOPLE

Your goals will affect the types of people you will connect with on social media. You also need to be selective. People may judge you by the accounts you are connected with. Following pop stars or humorous tweeters may not set a good impression with your potential customers.

Above: All big companies, such as Tesco, now include share buttons on their websites.

Above: Most trade organizations and news outlets have social media pages that you can connect with.

Who to Connect With

For businesses, you want to restrict the people you connect with to several categories.

○ **Customers:** When customers follow or friend you, follow or friend them back as this provides positive engagement.

○ **Business associates:** Partners, suppliers and contractors all make for good people to connect with.

○ **Trade organizations:** Connecting with professional bodies associated with your industry is a good way to keep up to date with new rules and guidelines.

○ **Professional networks:** Follow and friend people you know who run other businesses, even in different fields, as their advice can also be useful.

○ **News outlets:** Information can be gleaned by following trade journals or websites associated with your industry.

BUILDING SOCIAL INTO ECOMMERCE

A lot of buying and selling is done online these days, and as well as promoting your business, social media can be used to help create and grow your own ecommerce efforts.

WHAT IS ECOMMERCE?

Ecommerce is simply the name given to buying and selling online. The simplest way to do this is to sell directly through your own website, but you can also sell products through established ecommerce sites such as Amazon and eBay. This has the advantage of saving you from having

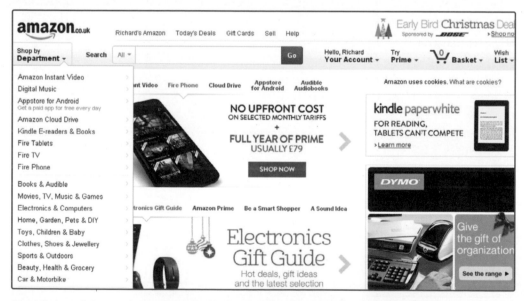

Above: You can sell almost anything on Amazon, from books and media, to TVs, lawnmowers, toys, clothes and car parts.

to build your own website and take payments, and you can use social media to promote your items, linking directly to your Amazon or eBay pages.

Social Ecommerce

Online stores like eBay and Amazon are inherently social. They are built around marketplaces, and people buying and selling, but customers can make suggestions and share their likes and dislikes with others. The use of reviews, recommendations, communities and forums, and sharing buttons, provides customers with a much more social experience.

Public Profiles

If you sell items on sites such as Amazon, you can also create your own profile page, which acts like a type of social media page, listing all your products and lets you include information about you and your business.

Right: It takes just minutes to add your Amazon store to your blog or website using aStore.

Hot Tip

Add your own Amazon store (aStore) to your blog or website. It takes just a few minutes and no technical knowledge is needed (astore.amazon.co.uk).

aStore for amazon associates

Would you like to have your own store featuring Amazon.co.uk products? And would you like to have this store up and running in minutes? aStore by Amazon is the solution.

Build an aStore Now

Don't have an account?
Join Associates

What is aStore?

aStore by Amazon is a new Associates product that gives you the power to create a professional online store can be embedded within or linked to from your website, in minutes and without any programming skills.

Feature Amazon Products

Create a dedicated shopping area on your website in minutes.

- Keep visitors on your site longer as they shop
- Select the Amazon products to feature
- Include all Amazon products, or display only the categories you choo
- Customize your store's look and feel

Offer a Shopping Cart

Affiliates

Ecommerce sites, e.g. Amazon, provide the ability to add affiliate links onto your blog or website – also known as referral marketing – where you are paid a small percentage of any purchases made by people referred by your website. This can help generate additional income, especially for those in service businesses, such as writers or musicians, who can link to their music and books. The more people spend after clicking the affiliate link, the more you can earn.

Ecommerce Apps

There are apps that will let you add your ecommerce store direct to social media sites.

○ **Set up your own eBay storefront**: This can feature on your Facebook page with Facebook eBay Items app.

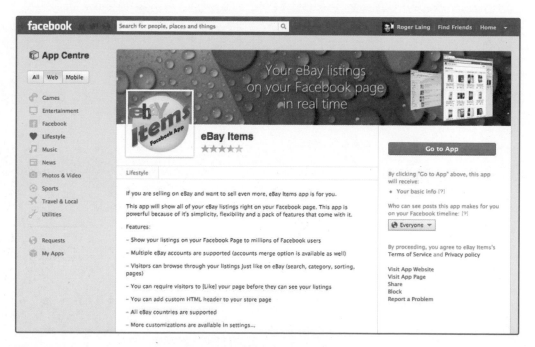

Above: Apps like this eBay one will help you set up your own storefront on Facebook.

- **If you have your own store**: Apps like SocialAppsHQ (www.facebook.com/socialappshq) let you sell an unlimited number of products direct from Facebook. It can be set up to increase your fanbase by encouraging people to Like the page in return for exclusive content or by using the invite-your-friend feature.

Hot Tip

If you are selling items through Amazon or eBay, make sure you include links to your sellers' page on your social media profiles.

- **For Facebook shopping**: Hosted platforms, like Bigcommerce (www.bigcommerce.com) and Volusion (www.volusion.co.uk), create social stores, which in effect produce photo galleries on your Facebook page (or eBay) that link back to the main site to complete the transaction. Other solutions, such as Ecwid (www.ecwid.com), let users check out from the store without leaving Facebook.

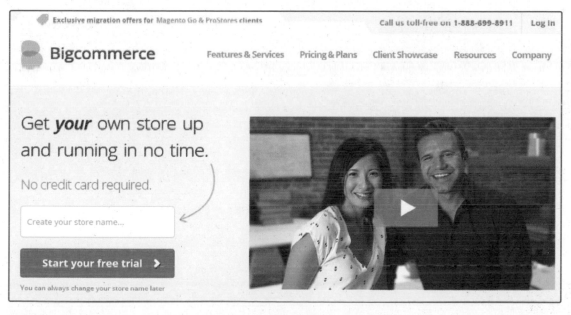

Above: Hosted platforms like Bigcommerce make it easy to set up your own ecommerce store.

SOCIAL NETWORK MARKETING

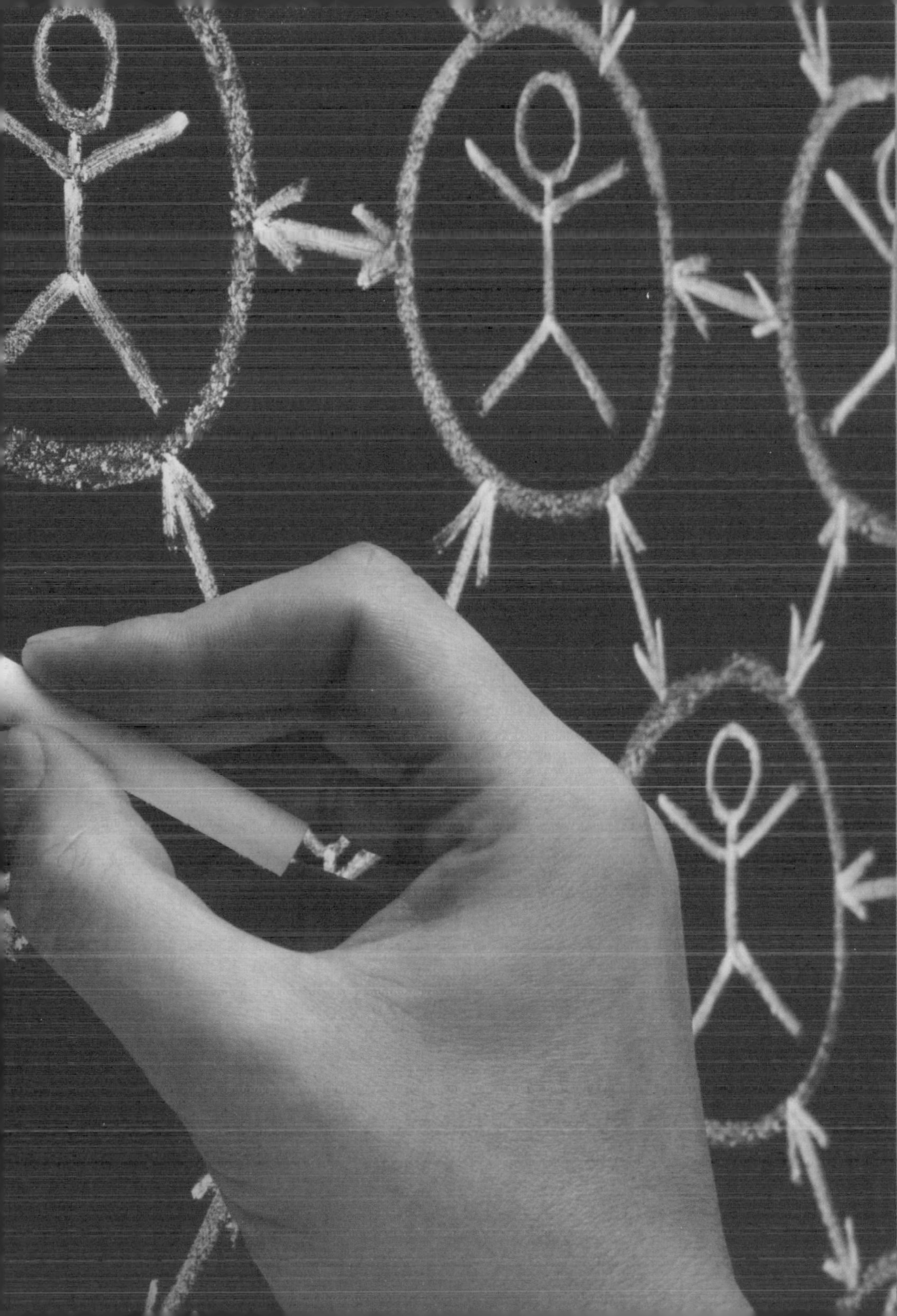

FACEBOOK FOR BUSINESS

> Facebook is by far the world's largest social networking platform. Even if you have your own personal Facebook page, you'll want to set up a separate business page.

FACEBOOK PAGES

These provide a way for businesses to communicate with potential customers so they can learn about their products and services. Setting up a Facebook page is relatively simple.

Below: It's easy to set up a Facebook page for business so communication becomes a two-way thing.

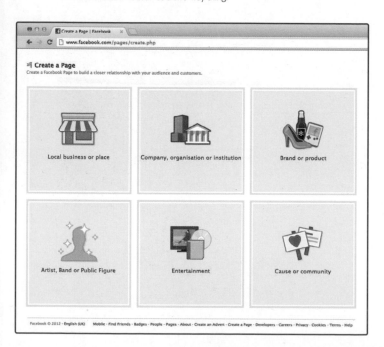

1. Go to www.facebook.com and click the Create page option on the left-hand side.

2. Select the page that's closest to your needs, such as local business or place, large company or institution, product, brand or artist, band or public figures, entertainment or causes and community.

3. Supply the other details, agree to Facebook's terms and click the Get started button.

BUSINESS TIMELINE

What follows is very similar to setting up your personal account, as business pages also follow Facebook's Timeline concept.

- **Timeline cover photo**: A unique image that illustrates your business. The inset profile picture can be a logo or product image.

- **About section**: Add a description of your company in up to 155 characters. The place for the company history is elsewhere.

- **Post**: Add a story to your timeline. You'll notice that it's set to Public viewing by default.

- **Milestones**: These have to start with when your company was founded but after that, it can be anything from a new product launch to your first sale or industry award.

Above: Facebook business pages use the same Timeline concept as your personal Facebook page.

PROFILE

It is up to you how complete your profile is. Remember, fans have to get something from visiting your page, especially if you want them to Like it.

Hot Tip

Just as you can use Likes to track activity on your page, you can use them to check how well other businesses are engaging with their customers too. Likes appear under the Profile photo of any business page.

LIKES

Likes are the trading currency for business pages. You need more than 30 to turn on Insights, which is a basic form of analytics that tracks activity on your page. If someone Likes your page, they will receive updates in their feeds and their name will appear as a supporter of any ad you create when it appears on their friends' pages.

Above: You can track the number of Likes your page receives by going to the Admin panel.

AUDIENCE TOOLS

There are various tools to help you attract Likes and monitor the success of your page.

○ **Build Audience:** Located at the top of the page, this lets you invite email contacts to Like your Page. Select Invite Friends, then choose the file and email service to use.

○ **People Talking About This:** Under the Likes tab, this shows the number of unique users who have mentioned your page in a News Feed, a post, Liked it, shared, or commented on it in the last week.

○ **For your eyes only:** This count for individual posts is only visible to you and shows the number of users that have generated a story by liking, sharing or commenting on the content.

> ## Hot Tip
>
> **Some businesses offer a reward – a gift, donation to charity or a return Like – for people that Like their page. Use this approach cautiously: you may end up with too many fans, attracted by the reward, who have no real interest in your business.**

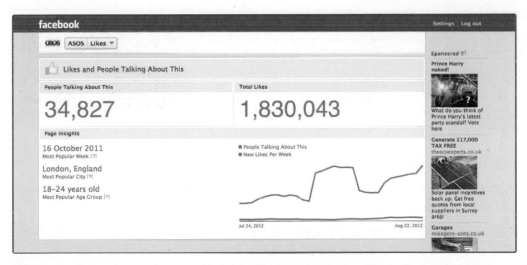

Above: Page Insights give various stats about page activity, including the most popular week, the main location of users and the largest age group of users.

ADVERTISING ON FACEBOOK

One of the simplest ways of getting people to your page is by advertising. Done correctly it doesn't need to cost a lot of money because you're effectively paying by result. You can target your ads very precisely, based on users' gender, age, location, interests, or a combination of these. You can also target fans, friends of fans or even users who have certain words in their profile.

Above: Facebook advertisements charge by result and you can set limits on how much you want to spend.

Getting Started with Advertising

1. Go to the Build Audience tab and select Use Adverts Manager. Click the Create Advert button.

2. Select what you hope people will do when they see your advert under Choosing Your Objective. Responses can vary from Send people to your website to Boost your posts.

3. Select the images you want. You can have up to six at no extra cost.

4. Write your ad, including headline, and choose where anyone clicking the ad will land. Typically, this will be your Timeline.

5. Choose where you want to place it in your desktop and mobile news feed.

Right: Choosing your objectives for an advertising campaign.

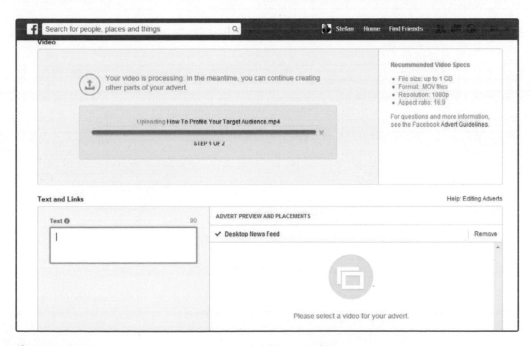

Above: As well as images you can select video, just text, and include links in your advert.

Choosing Your Audience

You can target who gets to see your ad in several ways.

○ **Location:** If yours is a local business, this can be as specific as a postcode.

○ **Age and gender:** Put in the range of those you want to target.

○ **Interests:** Reach people who mention this interest in their Timeline in some way. Putting a hashtag before the keyword opens it up to similar interests.

○ **Behaviours:** Reach people based on past purchases or intent, the devices they use and so on.

○ **Connections:** Filter the audience further so the ad is only shown to those who do (or don't) have connections to your page and their friends.

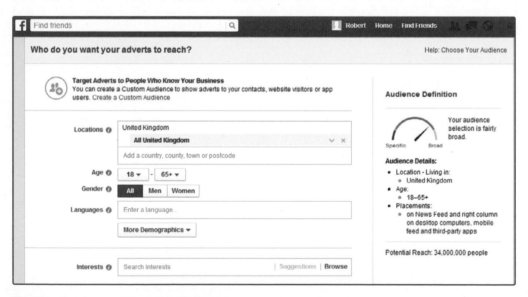

Above: Targeting who you want to see your advertisement.

Fix Your Budget

Setting a campaign budget is important to prevent any nasty surprises. Choose an amount you're comfortable with. Once the charges have reached that limit, your ad will no longer be displayed.

Bidding and Pricing

On bidding, you can choose to optimize for meeting your objective (such as Page Likes) or clicks or impressions. Pricing can be automatic, where Facebook optimizes your bid to get the maximum response, or manual. If you choose manual there is a suggested maximum bid for clicks (CPC) but you can change that.

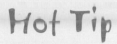

Hot Tip

You can choose to pay less than the bid price Facebook suggests but your ad will not appear as frequently and this is likely to affect responses.

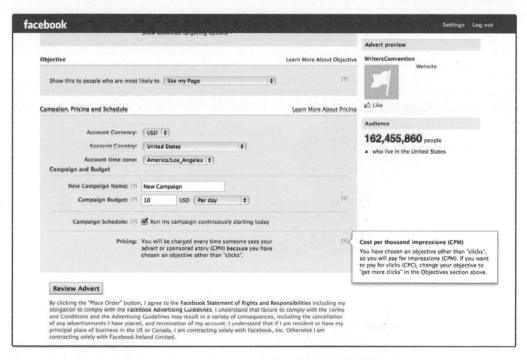

Above: The cost-per-click method is likely to bring better results as users have already shown their interest by clicking.

Video Ads

For those wanting to reach a larger audience, you can create video ads. These 15-second videos start playing as the page loads but with no sound. They stop if you scroll past. Click on the video ad and it will expand to a full-screen view and the sound will start.

SELLING WITH FACEBOOK

F-commerce, as it's known, can be done in several ways. You can show your products on your Facebook page and redirect users to your site when they're ready to buy. Local businesses can also run 'check-in' deals which are special offers for people who come to a store or restaurant. When people visit and 'check in' using Facebook, an update will say where they are, acting as a personal recommendation.

Above: Integrate your shopping cart system into Facebook so users can buy off the page, as shown here. Third-party apps can help simplify this.

TWITTER FOR BUSINESS

A single tweet can reach millions of people, making it as potent as TV advertising for promotion, and tweeting costs nothing, so if you have something to promote, whether a product or service, Twitter is the ideal tool.

FOLLOWERS

Once you have signed up for Twitter and created your profile, you can begin to send tweets. However, there is little point in tweeting until you have built up some followers.

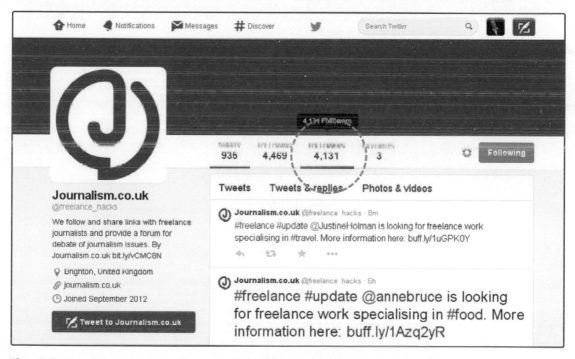

Above: Followers are the currency of Twitter. The more people that follow you, the more exposure your tweets will receive.

Follow the Leaders

You can follow people without them following you, so that's where to start. Use search to identify people who are tweeting about the sorts of products you sell, have similar interests, or are well known in your industry. Retweet them, ask questions or involve them in the conversation by including their @username in your tweets.

Hot Tip

Twitter's Advanced Search tab on the left-hand side of the search results page lets you use any combination of keywords to look for people with similar interests or people within a certain radius.

TWEETING CONTENT

The key to promotion on Twitter is to drive traffic to your website or sales page using a link. To get people to click your link, you will have to be creative.

○ **Benefits:** Rather than try to sell a product in a tweet, outline a main benefit.

Above: Advanced Search lets you fine-tune your search results.

- **Tease**: Tempt users to click a link by making them want to know more about your product.

- **Reward**: Offer discounts or freebies to make Twitter users feel privileged.

Composing Promotional Tweets

A promotional tweet has to centre on your link. Space is at a premium, so you need to compose your tweet as concisely as possible. Try to include powerful and evocative words, much the same way headline writers do. The more you can grab a reader's attention, the more likely it is they will click on your link.

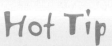

Hot Tip

Websites such as nearbytweets.co.uk and twellow.com can help you locate Twitter users nearby.

GOING LOCAL

If you're a local business, you may be looking for trade in your area. Add your location as the keyword in your search and you'll see tweets that mention it. Click Near you from the options on the left and you'll see all those that include the location in their profile. Click the follow button for any that interest you.

Above: Clicking Near you, brings up results for people close to your location.

GOT A COUPON?

Everyone loves a bargain and sites like TwtQpon (twtqpon.com) let you create a coupon for your followers on Twitter. The coupons can be for anything from money off to two products for the price of one. You can tweet them to your existing followers, offer them as an incentive for following you or promote them through other social media sites.

QUESTION TIME

Setting up a Twitter poll can be a good way to get feedback, whether it's on your product, brand or industry, while making it interesting for your followers. Sites like twtpoll (twtpoll.com) will help you create and organize Twitter polls.

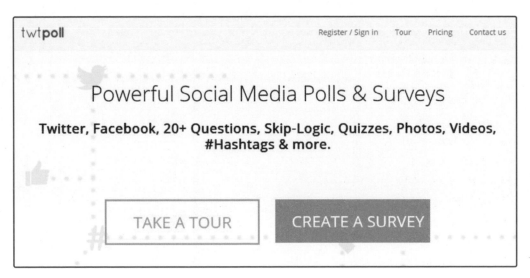

Above: It is easy to set up polls and surveys using twtpoll.

TWITTER PARTIES

If you're looking for a different way to reach your audience, consider throwing a Twitter party. This is an online event where you can meet customers, launch a product, debate some industry trend or simply have a get-together of people with similar business interests. Announce your event as widely as possible and offer a small incentive for people to attend.

Hashtags

A hashtag is a word or phrase following a # symbol. When you click on a hashtag, you'll see other tweets containing the same keyword or topic, so make sure you use a unique hashtag for your promotional tweets. Do a search for your hashtag to make sure it is not already in use.

Above: Hashtags help people find relevant tweets.

ADVERTISING ON TWITTER

If you really want to reach large numbers of people and tap into the huge audience potential of Twitter, you may consider Twitter advertising. Twitter offers businesses three types of Twitter advertisements:

○ **Promoted Accounts**: These appear in people's # Discover page as Twitter suggestions of accounts worth following. You can tailor the people you want to reach by their interests, location or even gender.

○ **Promoted Tweets**: These appear in users' timelines with their other tweets. You can target users by their interests, those that have tweeted specific keywords or those based in a specific location.

○ **Promoted Trends**: These appear in the list of trending topics and are useful for promoting projects or campaigns you are running.

Above: Promoted tweets, like this one for Intel, have an orange symbol attached to them.

How Twitter Advertising Works

Twitter's advertising prices are based on pay-per-action (PPA). This means you only pay when a person follows your account, replies, retweets, favorites or clicks a link. Like Facebook, their pricing system is based on bidding, which means you set the amount you are willing to spend per follow or click.

Setting up Twitter Advertisements

1. Visit https://biz.twitter.com/ad-products. Click on Let's go!

2. Select your business location from the drop-down menu, your estimated monthly digital advertising budget, and fill in details of your business and advertisement.

3. Choose the type of Twitter advertisement you would like and how you would like to target your tweets.

4. Set a daily budget for your campaign (Twitter will stop showing your ad once you hit your budget). Place a click-through bid and select a date for your promotion to begin.

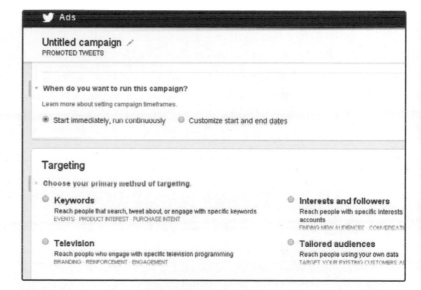

Above: Select how you want to target your tweets.

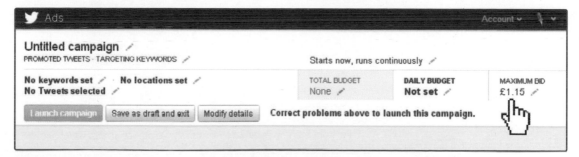

Above: You can set a maximum click-through bid to ensure you do not overspend.

LINKEDIN FOR BUSINESS

LinkedIn is a professional network for companies and individuals. Even if you have a personal account, you can set up a company page to interact with other businesses, spread the word, find partners and even recruit new staff.

SETTING UP A LINKEDIN COMPANY PAGE

In order to set up a business page, you need to vouch that you have the right to act on behalf of the company to create the page. You will also need to give your company email address, as free accounts at Gmail and Hotmail won't work.

Below: Creating a company page is quite simple.

1. Click Interests on the navigation bar, then Companies and click the Create button under the Create a Company Page section on the right. Enter your company name and email.

2. A verification email will be sent to the address you gave to check it does exist. Click the link in the email to continue setting up the profile. You can add other people with a company email address to administer the account with you.

3. Add two logos (or images) – the smaller one will appear next to all posts.

4. Complete the company description – the first thing people will see on your page. You should link this to your website or blog, if you have one, to increase traffic.

5. There are a few other details to include, such as company type, size, main industry and operating status. Click Publish to finish.

Below: Your logo and company description are the first things people will see on your page.

SHOWCASING YOUR PRODUCTS AND SERVICES

LinkedIn is a useful platform to show off what you do.

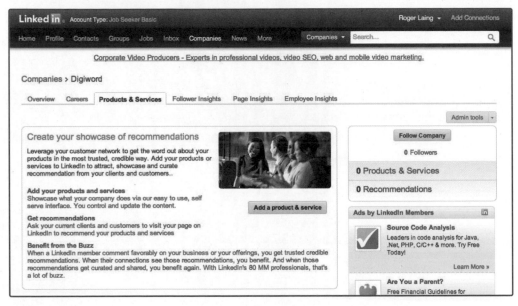

Above: LinkedIn Showcase Pages enable you to highlight your individual brands rather than the company itself.

○ **Setting up Showcase pages:** Click the Edit menu on your Company Page and select Create a Showcase Page. You can have a maximum of ten. Add a description, key points, images, sales contacts and display banners for each one.

○ **Enlist help:** Ask current clients and those in your network to visit your company page to follow your Showcase Page.

○ **For contacts outside LinkedIn:** Send them a link to your Showcase Page.

GROUPS

Groups are LinkedIn's discussion forums focused on specific topics, professions or industries. Find, join or start your own groups by going to Interests on the navigation bar and selecting Groups.

Connecting with People

LinkedIn is all about connections. These are like friends or followers on Facebook and Twitter. To connect with someone in a group click on the Members tab, move your cursor over a member's name and click the Invite to connect link on the right.

LINKEDIN ADS

Like most social media sites, LinkedIn allows you to advertise to a very precise audience, according to industry, location, job role, seniority, gender and so on. Ads are available on a cost-per-click (CPC) model or cost-per-thousand-impressions (CPM). You can set up an advertising campaign by clicking the Advertise link under Business Services.

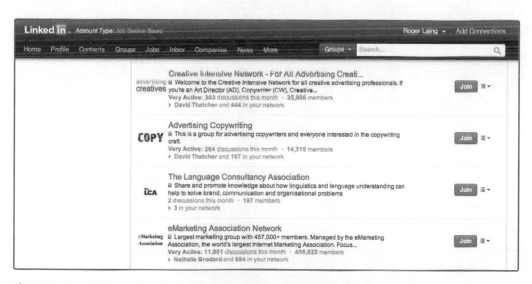

Above: Groups are LinkedIn's discussion forums focused on specific topics, professions or industries.

BUSINESS ON OTHER SOCIAL NETWORKS

While Facebook, Twitter and LinkedIn are the most popular social networks for business, they are not the only platforms that you can use to promote your products, services and brand.

GOOGLE+

Some people love Google+, others hate it. However, since it began, Google+ has grown faster than any other social network, making it a worthwhile platform for businesses.

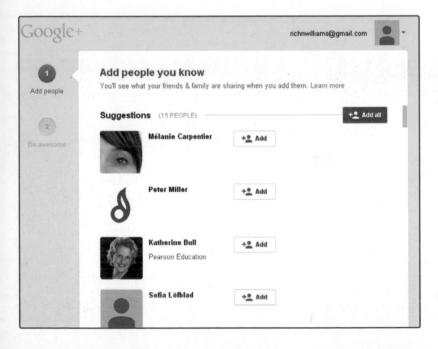

Business Page

To set up a business page, you do have to set up your individual profile first. Once you've done that you set up your business page by hovering over the **Home** button and selecting Pages from the drop-down menu.

Left: With Google+ you can assign your contacts into different circles, such as work colleagues, friends, business associates or customers.

PINTEREST

The pinboard social network works as well for businesses as it does for individuals. To get the best results you need to optimize your boards and pins so they appear high in the search results where they can go viral and spread. Ensure you include a description, with the right keywords, and ensure they are in the right category so they can be easily found.

Hot Tip

Many businesses especially like hangouts, the video chat service on Google+, which lets you set up conference calls or group chat among your circle of contacts.

YOUTUBE

Over six billion hours of video are watched each month on YouTube, so it is a community worth developing. You can set up a YouTube channel dedicated to your company or brand so you have one home for all your videos, which you can customize to match your company's visual identity.

Below: As with other social networks, Pinterest lets you sign up as a business user.

for Business   Getting Started   Tools   Success Stories   Blog   Join Pinterest

Get discovered by millions of people looking for things to plan, buy and do.

Join as a business

Already have an account?
Convert now

CREATING YOUR AUDIENCE

BUILDING A NETWORK

Building up a following on social media is as much dependent on what you say as where you say it. The emphasis has to be on providing customers with something interesting and informative that's of value, rather than just marketing spiel.

Above: Always remain professional, friendly and genuine. People can spot fakes, even on social media.

CONTENT IS KING

To keep your network happy, loyal and engaged, you need good content. Remember, social media marketing is about conversation, which means you need to be:

- **Responsive:** Remember, social media is about engagement. Respond to both positive and negative comments.

- **Professional**: Never get into arguments on social media or respond to negativity with snide or sarcastic comments.

- **Approachable and Genuine**: Try to be as friendly as possible when conversing with people and make sure you are being honest.

Focussing Content

Generating content that is both positive to a business and useful to followers can be difficult. Often it means trying to come up with tweets that cover several aspects:

- **Positivity**: Your content should always show your business in a positive light. If somebody says something negative about your business, try to address the concerns openly and honestly.

- **Benefits**: When promoting, target those aspects of your products or services that could benefit your customers, i.e. low price, quality, convenience, etc.

Below: Companies like BT use social media to address customer concerns and complaints.

○ **Engagement:** Make sure you are producing content that people will want to read.

○ **Useful:** Make sure you provide useful information or answer specific questions put to you by customers.

Authority

When you engage people about your business, make sure you do your research. You want to be seen as an authority on your subject matter so you need to provide good information that sparks debate and encourages interaction.

Responding to People

When you respond to comments and questions on social media, do so as positively as possible. Even if you do not hold with somebody's views and opinions, respond positively. Discuss what you agree and disagree with, but make sure you remain friendly, and whatever you do, never get into an argument.

Above: If customers feel your business is offering something of practical value rather than just products, they are more likely to be loyal to you.

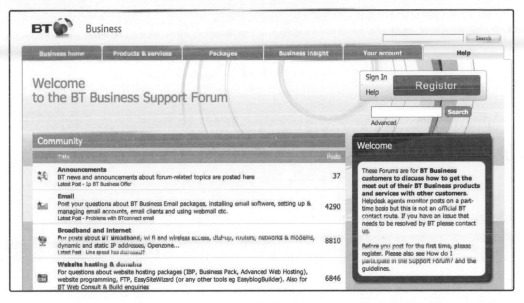

Above: Think about starting your own forum on your website to add value to your business and create a place for debate and opinions.

STARTING DISCUSSIONS

One of the best ways to engage with people on social media is to start discussions that get people interested and excited. Avoid being too controversial, as this can get people heated, but do not be afraid to express your views.

- ○ **Be opinionated**: Nobody is going to comment on your social media posts if you are just presenting straight information. Voice your opinions about the topic and be passionate.

- ○ **Be contrarian**: Nothing starts debate quicker than acting as the devil's advocate. Present your posts from contrarian viewpoints to provide a catalyst for discussion.

- ○ **Call to action**: Do not just leave it up to your audience to make a comment, prompt them with a question, such as 'What do you think?'

Keep the Conversation Going

When people ask questions or respond to your social media posts, try to keep the conversation going. Offer an open-ended response or pose an alternative question to allow the commenter to come back with a response. However, do not pressure people to respond.

Be Interested

One of the biggest turn-offs for people on social media is if people feel you are not interested in their views or anything they say. Always make sure people feel you appreciate that they have taken the time to comment and you value what they have to say.

> ### Hot Tip
>
> **Do not fall into the trap of making every post a promotional one. Social media is not about shamelessly promoting yourself. Try to strike a balance.**

Below: The supermarket Tesco has a separate Twitter account just for tweeting offers and promotions, which prevents their main account from coming across as too promotional.

FRIENDS AND FOLLOWERS

Building up Facebook friends, Twitter followers and LinkedIn connections can take time and effort, but you do not want just anybody in your network, which means finding the right social media community for your business.

EXPANDING YOUR AUDIENCE

Once you start building up a following, you may want to expand your followers by seeking people out. Social media is a web of connections, so see who is connected with your existing friends and followers and use your social network's suggestions facility for new people to connect with.

Finding Potential Customers

Social media can be a great tool for finding potential customers. If you rely on local people for your business, you can use your social network's advanced search functions to find users in your area.

Below: See who is following your followers on Twitter to help you find new people for your network.

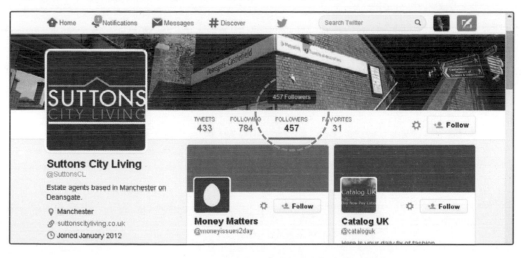

GROUPS

Joining groups on social networks is a great way to find new connections, especially those in the same industry or those that have an interest in your business area. If you cannot find a suitable group, start one, and then write posts and tweets to promote it.

Hot Tip

Make sure you include your Twitter handle and Facebook page on any traditional advertisements and correspondence. These days, people often prefer to visit social media pages than websites.

LINKING WITH INFLUENCERS

Identify the key figures and social media accounts of those who have the most authority and influence in your business area and connect with them. Their connections could be a valuable following for your own social media accounts.

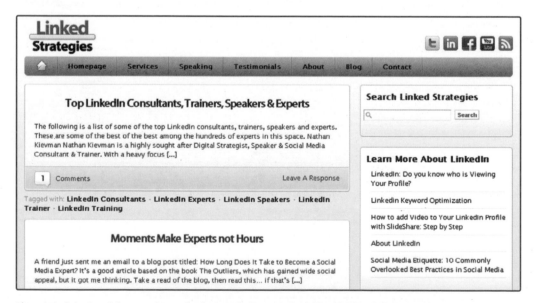

Above: LinkedIn has lists of all its most connected and respected experts in various fields at http://www.linkedstrategies.com/tag/linkedin-experts.

LIKES, RETWEETS AND FOLLOWS

Interactions are the goal for any social media marketing campaign. Likes, comments, reviews and retweets are the currency of social media and ensure your name is getting the maximum visibility, but it is not easy to get people to interact in this way.

MEASURES OF SUCCESS

In many ways, the number of Likes your Facebook page has and the number of retweets and follows you receive on Twitter can be an indication of the effectiveness of your social media marketing. The more Likes, reviews, followers, retweets and mentions you have, the more visibility you get. These interactions can snowball too as the more people get to see your

Above: Pop stars such as Rihanna manage to accumulate tens of millions of Likes on Facebook.

content the more Likes and retweets it receives. However, starting the ball rolling is not easy and many people find it difficult to get those first few interactions.

BUYING INTERACTIONS

Because of the visibility social media posts with high numbers of interactions receive they can be extremely valuable to businesses. All sorts of companies now offer services promising to get you a certain number of interactions for your Facebook and Twitter accounts for a fee. However, this is not only disingenuous, but also against the terms of service for most social networks and can lead to your accounts being closed.

Sockpuppets

Never pretend to be somebody else on social media. Creating fake accounts (known as sockpuppet accounts) to post fake Likes, reviews or comments can get you banned from social media and will do your reputation far more harm than good if you are found out.

Above: Buying Likes is not recommended. Having lots of likes will not increase your visibility if nobody is engaging with you.

ENCOURAGING INTERACTION

The best way to encourage Likes and other interactions is to start with something as simple as a starter message – news about your company, tips on a product, a training video or something that can be promoted across Facebook, Twitter and other social media. Promotional campaigns, such as money off, free offers and competitions are also a great way to get posts noticed and Liked.

Prompt your Friends and Followers

There is nothing wrong in asking people to Like your posts or fan pages, or retweet your tweets. Do not pressure people, but a gentle prompt can encourage those in your network to click the Like or retweet button or share your posts with their own friends and followers.

LEAD BY EXAMPLE

You cannot expect people to retweet your posts, give you Likes or share your content if you are not

Above: A little humour is a great way to encourage retweets.

doing the same. People often reciprocate these sorts of interactions, so if you see something you like on social media, comment on it, reply, retweet, Like or share it.

Make it Fun

Another way of increasing interactions is to turn it into a game, such as offering prizes or discounts if you reach a certain number of Likes within a timeframe.

Hot Tip

While buying Likes is not recommended, one of the types of advertisements Facebook offers is a 'Page Like Ad' that contains a call-to-action to 'Like Page', and can help you build up Likes without you falling foul of Facebook's terms of service.

Below: Facebook 'Page Like Ads' are a good way to accumulate Likes for a marketing campaign

Jasper's Market
We're now open downtown! Like our page for the latest news and invites to special events, weekly deals, and more.

Jasper's Market
Food & Grocery
541 people like this page

👍 **Like Page**

🌐 · Sponsored

ONLINE REVIEWS

As discussed earlier in this book, many ecommerce sites, such as Amazon, eBay and TripAdvisor, operate in a similar way to social media, by allowing users to post reviews, comments and ratings for products and services. These can be extremely valuable in encouraging others to make purchases. However, just as lots of positive reviews may encourage sales, negative reviews can put people off.

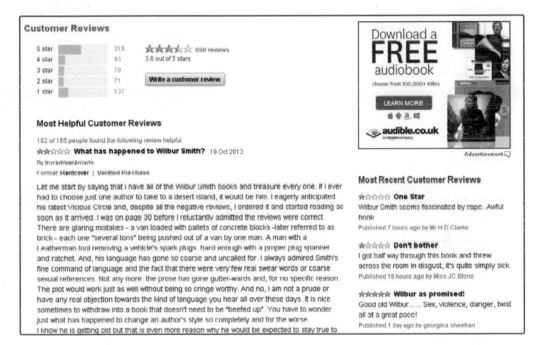

Above: Customers can leave an Amazon review for any of its products, from books and films, to lawnmowers and TVs.

Fake Reviews

As with other social media interactions, do not fall foul of the terms of service of these ecommerce sites by buying fake reviews and ratings. You may not get found out, but if you do, you could lose your sales privileges.

VirlVideo @virlvideo · Nov 5
#FREE COUPON - **Looking for honest REVIEWS for** my FIVE-STAR #Udemy
course, "Rank your video #1 on Google overnite." udemy.com/web-video-mean
... ...

 Udemy

Use YouTube to Rank #1 Google Overnite: YouTube for Business

Turn Simple YouTube Videos Into $5k+ Per Month Use YouTube Videos To Market Your Business and Grow Your Income Fast!

View on web

6:28 PM - 5 Nov 2014 · Details

            ···   Hide summary

Reply to @virlvideo

Above: You can use social networks to appeal for reviewers for your latest products or services.

Obtaining Reviews

Getting reviews can be difficult. In some cases, you may not make any sales until you have had reviews, but find you cannot get reviews until you have made sales. Think about offering free products to people in exchange for honest reviews. You can also ask customers directly, perhaps by including a note with the products you send out.

Hot Tip

Reviewers on websites like Amazon have their own profile. You can use these details to contact those people you think will make good reviewers for your products.

Don't Argue

Not everybody will like what you do. However, no matter how wrong you feel a reviewer is, avoid arguing with them. It is highly unlikely you will get them to change their mind, and you could end up coming across as unprofessional, as your comments will be visible to prospective customers and may show you in a bad light. At most, just thank somebody for taking the time to review the product and apologize for their lack of satisfaction.

Competitor Comments

It can also be very tempting for people to leave negative comments on competitors' fan pages or reviews on ecommerce sites. Never do this. Badmouthing your competitors will make you look far worse than they are. Even if your competitors are saying negative things about you, refrain from getting into an online argument.

Above: Responding to negative reviews is never a good idea as you may end up making matters worse.

GETTING THE MOST OUT OF SOCIAL MEDIA

PROMOTING ON SOCIAL MEDIA

Social media can be highly effective for promotion, but only if done right. Overdoing promotion can annoy people and any promotional campaign needs to be carefully thought out.

PROMOTIONAL CONTENT

Whether you are doing ongoing brand awareness or you have something specific you want to promote, you need to plan carefully how you are going to use social media and what you want to achieve.

Balance

Even if you are using social media to boost brand awareness, you have to be careful about overdoing promotion. People will soon get tired if you are constantly plugging your business. Try to get a good balance of promotion, information and entertainment.

Above: Combine entertainment and information with your promotional tweets to avoid boring your followers, and don't forget to use images.

PLANNING A CAMPAIGN

For specific promotional campaigns, such as for a new product release or a price offer, you need to establish the key aspects of your promotion.

- **When**: Ensure you have a firm date for when your promotion begins.

- **What**: Make sure you know exactly what you are promoting.

- **Why**: Do you want to increase sales, introduce a new product to market or push older goods?

Scheduling a Promotion

You should give yourself as much time as possible to begin publicizing your promotion, so you can get the word out before your promotion begins.

Hot Tip

If you are holding a price promotion or sale, you can tweet a countdown of the number of days until the promotion begins.

The Cumbers
@TheBatchBugle

⚙ +🧑 Follow

Three days to go... @ImitationGameUK @ImitationGame to hit theatres Nov 14 #countdown #BenedictCumberbatch

↩ ⇄ ★ •••

RETWEETS   FAVORITES
4   2

2:06 PM - 11 Nov 2014

Above: The hashtag #countdown is often used for promoting the releases date of a book, film or album, such as Benedict Cumberbatch here, promoting his new film.

Synchronization

The most effective way of running a promotional campaign is to ensure you are using all your social media platforms at once, to maximize exposure. Synchronize your campaign so you post promotional content on Facebook at the same time as sending out promotional tweets.

Landing Page

The idea of using social media as a promotional tool is not to convince people to make a purchase but to drive customers and prospects somewhere. That destination is typically the company website. However, you can set up a specific promotional landing page to which you can drive your promotional traffic. This helps you ensure people do not have to trawl through your website to find promotional items, and helps you monitor the success of your social media promotional campaign.

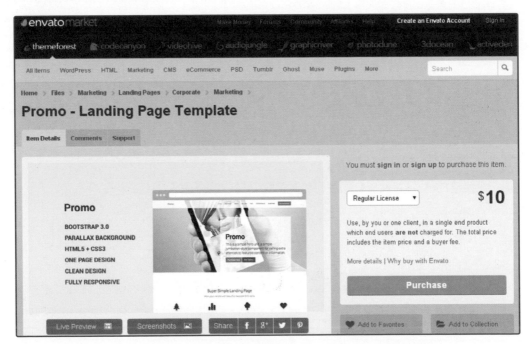

Above: You can download simple, template landing pages for your promotions from places such as http://themeforest.net/.

MANAGING YOUR CAMPAIGN

Posting on Facebook, Twitter and other social media can be time-consuming. For larger companies, you may want to designate a social media account manager to handle all your promotional messages. This also ensures all content is on message.

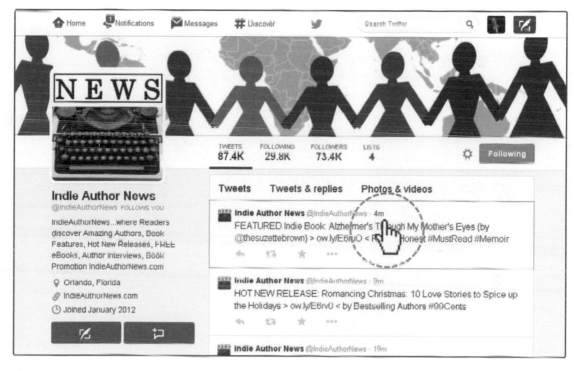

Above: You can see when people are active on Twitter by looking at the time when they are tweeting next to their Twitter handle.

Scheduling Content

Your followers and customers should govern when to send out your promotional tweets and posts. If most of your customers are active during the day then that is the best time to interact with them. However, if you find that your followers and friends are on social media mainly in the evening, you will want to send out your content at that time.

Social Media Tools

When running a promotional campaign, you do not have to spend all day and evening on social media. You can use various tools and social media clients to schedule your content.

- **Tweetdeck (https://tweetdeck.twitter.com/):** Twitter's own desktop client that has plenty of tools useful for promotion.

- **Hootsuite (https://hootsuite.com/):** Manage social networks, schedule messages, engage your audiences, and measure ROI right from the dashboard.

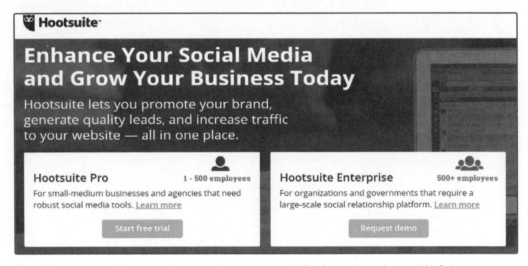

Above: Hootsuite is one of the most popular social media management tools. They have various packages available for businesses.

- **LikeAlyzer (http://www.likealyzer.com/):** Analyzes your Facebook pages and provides tips that highlight areas that can be improved so you can maximize your pages' potential.

- **Buffer (https://bufferapp.com/):** Lets you set up a specific scheduling pattern for LinkedIn, Twitter and Facebook. When you add an update to your Buffer, it will be sent out at the next available time slot.

BLOGGING

Blogs and bloggers are the new social commentators, often rivalling major media companies as a source of information. Blogs can be powerful marketing tools and can run in tandem with your social media efforts.

WHY BLOG?

Many people blog just for fun, and to share their interests and opinions with a wider world, but for businesses, blogs provide a valuable method of marketing.

Above: Millions of people read Virgin Atlantic's blog because they post useful travel information and destination guides, rather than just promoting their company.

- **Brand awareness:** A blog is a great way to boost your company's profile and demonstrate you are an authority in your field.

- **Improve visibility**: You can boost your internet presence with a business blog.

- **Promote new products**: While a blog is not a sales platform, blogging is a great way to let people know when you have a new product or service.

Advantage of Blogs

The great thing about a blog is that it is completely under your control. Your visitors see exactly what you want them to see. However, you have to ensure you are providing good content as it is as easy to lose your audience as it is to gain it.

MAKING YOUR BLOG SOCIAL MEDIA FRIENDLY

You need to make it easy for your audience to share your blog posts on social media and for this you will need to include social media buttons on your blog. When you write a new post, it

Rufus Wainwright

Mastertapes 2014

Rufus Wainwright speaks candidly to Mastertapes host John Wilson about his 2003 album Want One. The Maida Vale studio is transformed into a baroque boudoir where the stylish singer performs solo piano, and sings a cappella.

Mon 10 November, 9pm-4am
Tue 11 November, 9pm-4am
Wed 12 November, 9pm-9.26pm, 10.30pm-4am
Thu 13 November, 9pm-4am
Fri 14 November...
Read more

Above: Make sure your blog includes social media buttons to make sharing posts easier.

is also important to let your followers and friends know about it, so mention it on Facebook and Twitter and send links to your post.

BLOGGING PLATFORMS

To create a blog, you will need a blogging platform – the software needed to create and maintain a blog. Blogging platforms fall into two categories:

○ **Hosted**: Software that is hosted on a platform's server. You create and post your content online. These are easy to start and maintain, and many of them are free. However, you may be restricted in the type of content you can post.

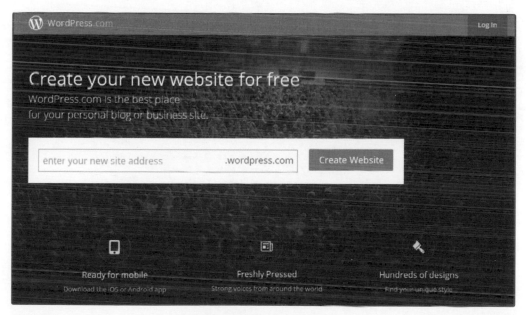

Above: Wordpress offers a free blogging platform at https://wordpress.com/ and free blogging software for self-hosted blogs at https://wordpress.org/.

- **Self-hosted**: Sometimes called non-hosted, where you have to provide your own server to host your blog. This may mean paying for third party hosting. Self-hosted blogs are more difficult for beginners, but they do offer more control over the blog and its layout.

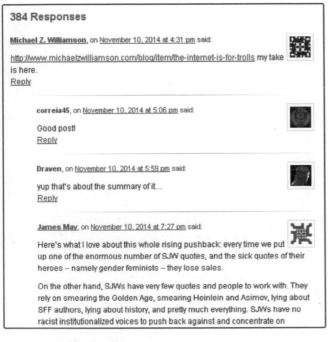

384 Responses

Michael Z. Williamson, on November 10, 2014 at 4:31 pm said:

http://www.michaelzwilliamson.com/blog/item/the-internet-is-for-trolls my take is here.
Reply

correia45, on November 10, 2014 at 5:06 pm said:

Good post!
Reply

Draven, on November 10, 2014 at 5:59 pm said:

yup that's about the summary of it...
Reply

James May, on November 10, 2014 at 7:27 pm said:

Here's what I love about this whole rising pushback: every time we put up one of the enormous number of SJW quotes, and the sick quotes of their heroes – namely gender feminists – they lose sales.

On the other hand, SJWs have very few quotes and people to work with. They rely on smearing the Golden Age, smearing Heinlein and Asimov, lying about SFF authors, lying about history, and pretty much everything. SJWs have no racist institutionalized voices to push back against and concentrate on

Above: Comments are crucial for the success of a blog. Having an active audience can turn your blog into a community.

BLOGGING DOS

- **Do be yourself**: What makes blogs different to every other medium is that it is your personality that's on show.

- **Do attribute content you use**: If you quote someone, or use content from their blog, give them a credit and a link. This not only avoids any problems of plagiarism, but also helps your blog's search engine rankings.

- **Do include images**: Perfect as your words are, visitors like pictures.

- **Do comment on comments**: When someone takes the trouble to comment it's good to reply and start a conversation. That won't happen if you simply thank them for the comment, as some recommend.

- **Do use social media**: Use Facebook, Twitter and LinkedIn to promote and push readers to your blog.

BLOGGING DON'TS

○ **Don't set music or videos to auto-play.** However much you like the tune, or laugh at the video of your cat falling off the windowsill.

○ **Don't write long posts:** Because you can't be bothered to edit your thoughts and create shorter ones.

○ **Don't forget to spellcheck:** You don't want anything, however trivial, to put readers off.

○ **Don't make it too difficult to add comments:** You have to balance precautions to stop spammers against killing feedback.

Hot Tip

Blogs have come a long way from their origins as personal online diaries. Now it's easy to add audio and video as well as photos, messages, illustrations, links and more.

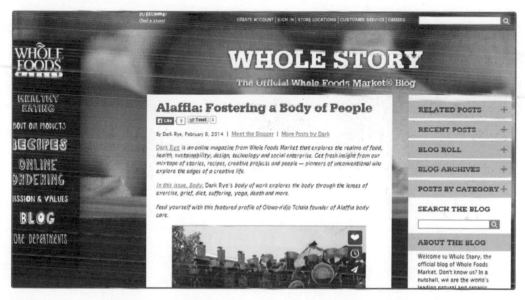

Above: To keep a blog interesting, you can embed videos, pictures, links to other websites and even your Twitter feed on your blog.

MEASURING YOUR INFLUENCE

If you are using social media as part of a marketing or promotional campaign, you need to know what is working and what is not, and that means being able to measure your influence.

FRIENDS, FOLLOWERS AND CONNECTIONS

Your influence on social media goes beyond just how many followers, friends and connections you have. The quality of your network is just as important, if not more so, than how many people you interact with. For instance, friends and followers with the most people in their own friend and followers list are going to be more valuable to you than people with just a handful of connections attached to their own accounts.

Above: Barack Obama has nearly 50 million Twitter followers – that's almost as many people who voted him into office.

Authoritative Connections

Another aspect to your influence is those people connected to you with the most authority. These people include industry experts, trade organizations and news outlets who not only have a large reach but are also trusted sources of information to people. Therefore, interactions with these account holders will give you more influence on social media than from less authoritative people.

Interactions

Another way of gauging your influence on social media is by how many interactions you are receiving. Likes, retweets, mentions, shares and comments are all a good gauge that what you are putting out is being well-received. You can use the number of interactions to help you decide what sort of content is the most effective.

Hot Tip

If you are posting links to your website, sales page or blog on social media, these can be tracked, allowing you to establish how effective you are at engaging people enough to drive them to your web pages.

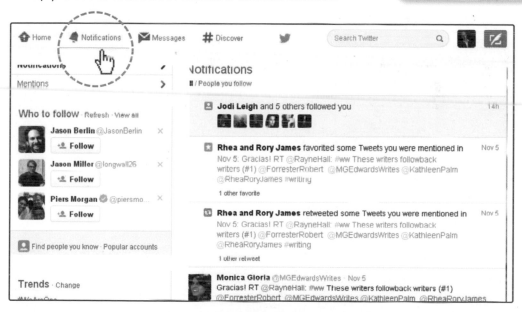

Above: You can see all your interactions on Twitter by using the Notifications link at the top.

Conversions

Simply sending users to your website is only half the battle when it comes to promotion. You need to keep them there too. If people are clicking a link in your social media posts, visiting your website, but then disappearing soon afterwards, your social media marketing is being effective but your content may be misguided and promising things to users that your products or sales page are not delivering on.

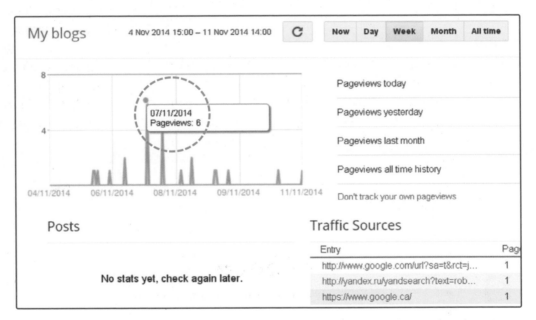

Above: Tracking your page views and where they come from can help you work out the effectiveness of social media marketing.

MEASUREMENT TOOLS

Just as there are all sorts of tools to help with the management of social media, you will find a lot of tools that can help you measure your influence on the social media platforms.

○   **Klout (http://klout.com)**: Uses analytics from social networks to rank you according to your online influence. You receive a 'Klout Score' out of 100 depending on how influential you are. The higher your score, the more social media influence you are wielding.

○ **Simply Measured (http://simplymeasured.com)**: Lets you gather all your social media metrics in one place, enabling you to analyze and compare your effectiveness across various different platforms.

○ **TweetReach (www.tweetreach.com)**: Provides metrics, statistics and analysis for tweets so you know how much exposure hashtags, URLs, usernames or phrases have had.

Above: A Klout score is a simple way of judging your influence on social media.

STAYING AHEAD

In addition to monitoring your own influence, you need to be aware of others', particularly your customers and competitors. By knowing what they are talking about and which platforms they use, you can stay ahead of the game.

WHAT ARE YOUR CUSTOMERS DOING?

Various tools are available that can help you find where your prospective clients are going on the internet and what interests them.

- **Google alerts (www.google.com/alerts):** Set these up to track mentions of you, your brands, your products and also your competitors.

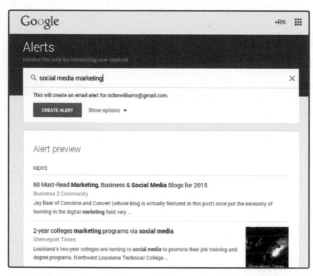

Above: Google alerts are easy to set up and highly effective at seeing what is being said about you, your products, your business topic and your competitors.

- **Blogs and posts:** Use www.blogsearchengine.org/ to find blogs associated with your interests.

- **Social network searches:** Search engines on Facebook, Twitter and LinkedIn can help you find pages and account holders interested in your business topic.

- **Forums:** OMGILI (Oh My God I Love IT) (omgili.com) will search discussions in forums and message boards.

WHAT ARE YOUR COMPETITORS DOING?

You can keep an eye on your competition in a number of ways.

- **Search**: Search Google for your niche. Click through to the sites with the highest rankings and see what keywords they are using to get noticed.

- **See**: See where they appear in ranking engines. This can provide the metrics and analysis to improve your own position. One ranking engine is Alexa (www.alexa.com).

- **Look**: Look for them on social media, see what they are saying, who their followers are and what has gained the most response.

- **Find out**: Find out what they are using social media for. Is it customer support, loyalty programmes, contests, polls or promotions? While you don't want to copy what they're doing, you should be aware of what seems to work for them.

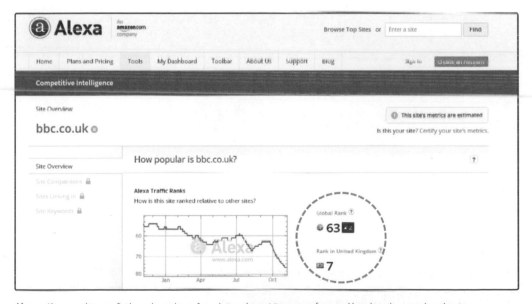

Above: Alexa.com lets you find out the ranking of a website, where visitors come from and how long they spend on the site.

SAFETY AND PRIVACY

Much is made of the dangers of social media sites but like everything else online, if you take a few sensible precautions it is extremely unlikely that you will experience any problems.

STAYING SAFE

The same rules apply to meeting people online as in the real world. Be very cautious about giving out any personal details – especially your phone number, address, full birth date or place of birth – as these can be useful for identity thieves. Certainly do not publish these in your profile. If you're using location-aware social networks, be particularly careful about saying where you live and never publicize family holiday dates or other times when your home is empty.

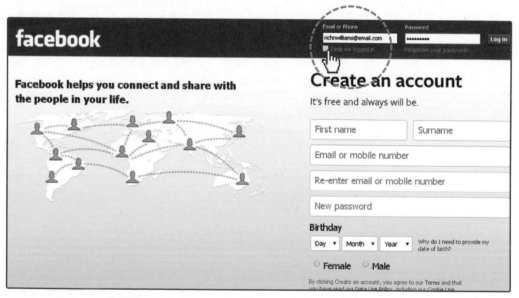

Above: If you use a shared computer, ensure the Remember me box remains unchecked otherwise the next user might be able to access your account.

Privacy

In the attempt to offer more personalized services, social media sites have sometimes tried to introduce policies that many users have felt invaded their privacy. Keep an eye on privacy settings to make sure that by default you are not being asked to share more than you are comfortable with.

Images

Never post compromising pictures in a tweet or photographs of people who may take exception to the whole world seeing them. On most social networks, you have little control over what happens to your images. If you post a photo on sites like Facebook and Twitter that you later remove, any copies that your friends have made will still exist and may be displayed.

> ### Hot Tip
>
> Even if you are only planning to connect with friends and family on the social networks you join, you should still regard any information you give as being publicly available and act accordingly.

Above: When you create a new post on Facebook you can choose to make it public or just share it with friends

PRIVACY AND SECURITY OPTIONS

Most sites have a series of privacy and security options that control who can see your personal information and view your photos or videos. For example, Facebook lets you set the default privacy level for your status updates and photos. However, these options are not always obvious. Make a point when you join a site of finding where they are and setting them to the most secure level. You can always relax them later when you know more about how the site works.

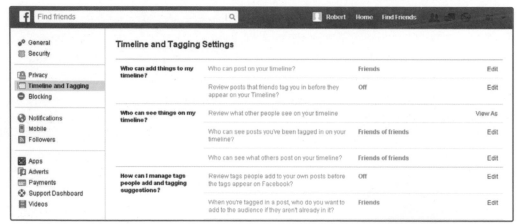

Above: You can adjust all sorts of privacy settings in Facebook.

Below: Privacy settings for Twitter.

VALUE OF PERSONAL INFORMATION

Your personal information is worth money. There are many companies willing to spend significant amounts to get to know more about your browsing habits, interests and lifestyle choices. They do so largely through cookies, small files sent to your PC, smartphone or tablet which store information that can be accessed if you revisit the site.

An EU law now makes it compulsory for sites to give users more information about cookies, so you can consent to them being used. Cookies are primarily used to personalize your experience on their site; however, some social network sites are sending data about you – without you knowing – to other companies. You can stop this.

Above: Cookies are used by organizations and retailers to personalize your internet experience, but beware: they sometimes pass on data without your knowledge.

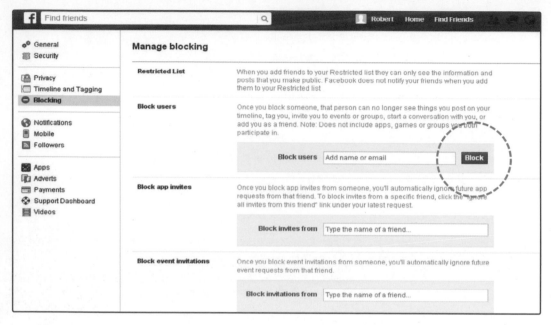

Above: Both Twitter and Facebook make it easy to block users. In Facebook go into your settings menu.

CYBER-STALKING

Everybody is entitled to a certain level of privacy and respect. While rare, some people have found users on social networks have harassed or bullied them online. This can involve:

- **Abuse**: Persistent abusive posts aimed at or about you.
- **Threats**: Somebody is making threats of violence towards you.
- **Privacy**: Somebody is revealing private information about you.

Handling Online Harassment

If you suffer problems because somebody is harassing you on social media, there are steps you can take. Both Twitter and Facebook enable you to block users, so you no longer see their content and they can no longer see yours. You can also report users for abusive behaviour.

THE LAW

Social networks such as Twitter have become almost as controversial as they have become popular. Many news stories have centred on libel and other legal issues, which all social media users need to be aware of.

INTELLECTUAL PROPERTY

Intellectual property law protects creative works, such as poetry, books, song lyrics and photos. You can easily fall foul of intellectual property law, especially with copyrighted works. Cutting and pasting text or images for use on your own blog or fan page could result in a breach, as you may need the permission of the copyright owner to use the material. The reverse is also true, and copyright law protects your text and images so others need your permission to use them.

Right: Always ensure that you are not infringing anyone's copyright before you share a photo or image.

Playing Poker," you're great and all, but "Dogs Playing Dungeons and

Using Other People's Work

Generally, creative content falls into four main groups:

- **Public domain:** Free for you to do what you want with it, whether that is to use it as is, change it or even sell it.

- **Copyleft/fair use content/Creative Commons License system:** Where content is generally available to use but some rights are reserved. This can cover a range of activities from personal to commercial use.

Above: Sites like Wikimedia Commons (http://commons.wikimedia.org) have lots of public domain and Creative Commons images you can use on social media.

○ **Copyright.** The traditional standard where the owner reserves all rights and you need the owner's express permission to use the content in any way.

○ **Fair-use:** Also known as free use or fair dealing, it allows you legally to use a small section of copyrighted material, such as a quote, comment or sentence from a news story.

CITIZEN JOURNALISM

Until social media, the average person had little chance to reach as many people with their views and opinions. In essence, blogs, Facebook and Twitter have turned everybody into a publisher. However, while journalists from traditional media undergo training so they understand what can be reported in newspapers and magazines, few people on social media have such a working knowledge of the law, but the same laws that govern traditional publications govern social networks.

Above: Even retweeting what somebody else has said can be libellous.

Libel

One of the most reported legal issues governing social media is libel. There have been some high profile incidents in recent times, especially on Twitter. If you say something about somebody else that is untrue and defamatory (could cause their reputation harm), you could be taken to court.

Contempt of Court

Unlike in countries such as the United States, the UK has strict rules about what can be said with regard to court cases. Social media users who make comments about court cases can end up in contempt of court, which can result in a prison sentence.

Above: When reporting on criminal cases, mainstream sites like the BBC or the Guardian block users from making comments to avoid issues of contempt.

NETIQUETTE

Like every community, the net has its own etiquette, or rules of engagement, which is referred to as netiquette.

ENGAGING WITH OTHERS

Generally, the way you treat people online is no different to the normal rules of polite behaviour in everyday life. Never engage in rude, aggressive and abusive behaviour, no matter how obtuse or abusive other users are being.

OPENNESS AND ANONYMITY

The ease by which you can join social networks means that you do not need to prove who you are and can quite easily be anonymous or pretend to be somebody you are not. However, your profile information should be about the real you, unless there's a good reason. There are some exceptions. People in certain jobs – the police, teachers and so on – may have a reason to be discreet about their true identity.

Above: Being aggressive or abusive on social media will just get you blocked by other users.

Hot Tip

If you do decide later to unfriend or unfollow someone, you can do it quietly, as most social networks do not notify people. However, there are web platforms such as www.justunfollow.com and http://who.deleted.me/ that can let people know.

Above: People are not notified when you unfollow them on Twitter.

FRIENDING AND FOLLOWING

It is not compulsory to accept friend requests or follow people who ask. You really don't have to say yes. Likewise, you can unfriend or unfollow anybody you like without having to give a reason. Do not feel obliged to follow back and do not be afraid to cull your list of friends or followers if you feel they are not adding anything to your interactions on social media.

Following Celebrities

Part of the attraction of social media is following celebrities who also have accounts. Just don't be surprised if you can't get Lady Gaga or Lord Sugar to follow you back.

COMMUNICATING ON SOCIAL MEDIA

Commenting on other people's blogs or timelines is a good way of interacting and will lead them to respond in kind. There is, of course, an etiquette to consider:

1. Make your comment about the point that is being made. Do not try to steer the conversation to your own agenda.

2. Do not get into an angry and aggressive exchange (flaming) or post deliberately inflammatory comments (trolling).

3. Racist remarks, comments likely to offend religious groups and pornographic posts are also unacceptable.

10:47 PM

Anonymous said...
Rick Chapman was banned by David Gaughran from posting on his blog because of the way he interacts. Thought I'd throw that out there.

12:55 AM

Leave your comment

You can use some HTML tags, such as <b>, <i>, <a>

Choose an identity

Above: When commenting on blogs and forums, keep to the topic and avoid 'flaming'.

LINKING

If your post is a reaction to a news story or what someone else has written on their blog, link to it. Also, disclose any commercial links you have with a product or person you are discussing, especially affiliate links (where you are paid a percentage of any purchase that follows from the customer following the link on your site).

SOCIAL NOT PROMOTIONAL

Do not overdo your promoting and marketing on social media. As a rough guide, think of the rule of thirds:

1. Promote your own business and ideas in your updates for a third of the time.

2. Push content from other sources about the topics that interest you a third of the time.

3. Communicate with people directly for a third of the time.

Below: Always link to your sources when you write blog posts.

THURSDAY, OCTOBER 30, 2014

Agents Behaving Badly

Joe sez: Super-agent Andrew Wylie, in what seems like a conscious effort to make sure he never gets another query addressed the Toronto Festival of Authors and taught them all about hyperbole.

"I believe with the restored health of the publishing industry and having some sense of where this sort of ISIS-like distribution channel, Amazon, is going to be buried and in which plot of sand they will be stuck, [publishers] will be raise the author's digital royalty to 40% or 50%," he said. "Writers will begin to make enough money to live."

I have a few contacts at Amazon, so I asked them for a response, but they were too busy beheading innocent people to

The amount of stupid that Wylie fit into that single sentence is commendable. I'll deconstruct.

1. The publishing industry's health will never be restored. They're middlemen whose value-added services cost too mu the majority of authors.

TAKING SOCIAL MEDIA FURTHER

Are you ready to take things further? You can maximize your social media marketing in all sorts of ways, and take your social media use beyond just Twitter, Facebook and LinkedIn.

SOCIAL MEDIA AND SEARCH ENGINES

Social media has come a long way in a short space of time. Before the advent of Facebook and Twitter, if you wanted to find something online you had to use a search engine such as Google. Now, not only do social media posts rank in search engine results, but also people are frequently turning to social media to search for things online. All this means you need to think about searches when you write your posts and tweets to maximize your visibility.

Below: Social media posts and profiles often appear high up in search engine rankings.

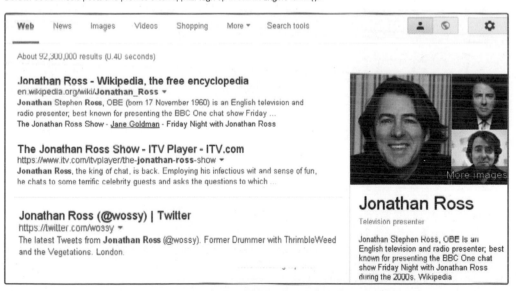

Search Engine Optimization (SEO)

Search Engine Optimization is key for bringing traffic to a website. People trust results the higher up they appear, especially those on the first page. Just as websites optimize their pages to ensure they appear high up in search rankings, you can do the same with your social media posts.

- **Keywords**: Keywords are the currency of search engines. Make sure you know the words and phrases people use to search for products in your industry, and include these terms in your Tweets and Facebook posts.

Hot Tip

Search engine traffic usually consists of people who are not connected to you on social media, so you can get new friends, followers and customers by having your posts rank highly in search results.

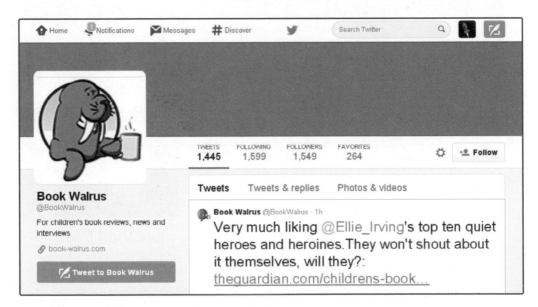

Above: Twitter and Facebook make it easy to insert links into your posts.

○ **Likes and Retweets**: The more popular a social media post, the more currency it will hold in search results.

○ **Links**: Search engines love links, but only authoritative ones. Increase the number of links in your posts but make sure they are good quality sources.

Expert Search

Advanced Search is also a useful tool for finding experts in a specific field. Many media professionals now use Twitter when they want some expert comment, as it is much easier to find people with specific knowledge than trawling through the phone book or calling specific organizations, such as universities. Because so many people access social media from their mobile, it is also a lot easier to find contactable people than by landline, especially if you need a query answering out of normal office hours.

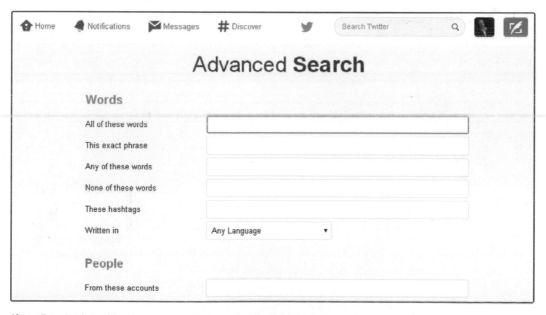

Above: Twitter's Advanced Search is a useful tool for finding people and organizations.

SOCIAL MEDIA AS A PORTFOLIO

Not only is social media useful for promoting your work and business, it can be used as a mini-portfolio. For writers, artists and designers, tweeting links to your work and associating a unique hashtag to it lets you store a complete portfolio in your Tweets section. You can also send a prospective employer or client a link to your Facebook page where you can store examples of your work.

Hot Tip

You can find plenty of sites that cater for special interests, whether that's music, travel or news. Platforms such as Digg (www.digg.com) and Reddit (www.reddit.com) cover a range of topics that focus on a specific areas such as politics or technology.

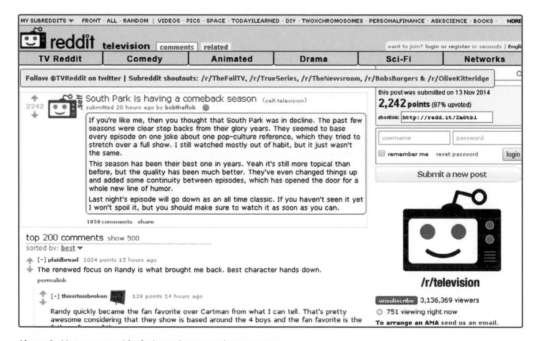

Above: Reddit is a great tool for finding niche or special interest news.

SOCIAL REVIEW SITES

Not only do websites such as Amazon include customer reviews on their products, but also various social review sites exist that allow people to share their opinions and experiences of products or services.

- **Epinions (www.epinions.com):** A site containing 'unbiased reviews by real people'. Reviewers can earn part of an Income Share Pool, based on how often other people use their reviews to make a decision on a purchase.

- **Ciao (www.ciao.co.uk):** Rewards reviewers. There's a very small cash payment (about 0.5p– 2p) for every time a member rates a review as helpful, very helpful or exceptional. There's also a premium fund (about £2–£15) that is awarded to particularly high-quality reviews.

- **Reseller Ratings (www.resellerratings.com):** Provides customer reviews of merchants selling other people's goods and offers sellers the opportunity to appear in their listings.

Above: Sites like Reseller Ratings help consumers make buying decisions and can be useful for promoting your business.

USEFUL WEBSITES AND FURTHER READING

WEBSITES

www.blogs.com
A service that helps you find blogs by category and topic or read daily roundups of some of the best blog content around the web.

www.brandwatch.com
Brandwatch is one of the world's leading tools for monitoring and analysing social media.

www.dailymotion.com
Watch anything from breaking news, lifestyle topics and sporting events on this video-sharing platform.

www.facebook.com
With over 1 billion active users worldwide, this is the big daddy of social networks, used more and more by business.

www.hubspot.com
Hubspot make an inbound marketing software that offers businesses an all-in-one marketing solution.

www.instagram.com
Share photos and video with family and friends.

www.linkedin.com
A networking site where alumni, business associates, recent graduates and other professionals connect online.

www.mashable.com
Online news site with big emphasis on social media.

pinterest.com
A content-sharing service that allows members to 'pin' images, videos and other objects to their pinboard.

www.reddit.com
A popular social news site with a large user base.

www.socialmediaexaminer.com
Online social media magazine helping businesses to best use social media tools.

www.tumblr.com
A free blog-hosting platform offering features such as templates and mobile apps.

twitter.com
Follow your friends, experts, favourite celebrities and breaking news.

www.youtube.com
Watch and share video content.

FURTHER READING

Brown, E., *Working the Crowd: Social Media Marketing for Business*, British Informatics Society Ltd., 2012

Carvill, M. and Taylor, D., *The Business of Being Social: A Practical Guide to Harnessing the Power of Facebook, Twitter, LinkedIn & YouTube for all businesses*, Crimson Publishing, 2013

Clapperton, G., *This is Social Media: Tweet, Blog, Link and Post Your Way to Business Success*, Capstone, 2009

Collins, T., *The Little Book of Twitter: Get Tweetwise!*, Michael O'Mara Boks Ltd., 2009

Kawasaki, G., and Fitzpatrick, P., *The Art of Social Media: Power Tips for Power Users*, Portfolio Penguin, 2014

Kerpen, D., *Likeable Social Media: How to Delight Your Customers, Create an Irresistible Brand, and Be Generally Amazing on Facebook (& Other Social Networks)*, McGraw-Hill Professional, 2011

Safko, L., *The Social Media Bible: Tactics, Tools, and Strategies for Business Success*, John Wiley & Sons, 2012

Schaefer, M. W., *Social Media Explained: Untangling the World's Most Misunderstood Business Trend*, Mark W. Schaefer, 2014

Vaynerchuk, G., *Jab, Jab, Jab, Right Hook, Left Hook: How to Tell Your Story in a Noisy Social World*, HarperBusiness, 2013

Zimmerman, J. and Ng, D., *Social Media Marketing All-in-One for Dummies*, John Wiley & Sons, 2015

INDEX

A

activating accounts 25
Adobe Acrobat forms 41
advanced searches 60, 123
advertising on Facebook 54–58
  inbound/outbound marketing 17
  targeted 33, 54, 56, 65, 75–76
  on Twitter 63–65
affiliate links 40, 119
Alexa ranking engine 105
Amazon 44–46, 47, 85, 86
analytics 52, 102–05
anonymity 116, 117
apps, ecommerce 46–47
arguments, avoiding 87, 119
aStore 45
auto-play content 99

B

Bigcommerce website 47
blocking users 112, 117
blogs
  commenting on other blog
    sites 11, 36, 118–19
  defined 11, 19
  dos and don'ts 98–99
  platforms 97–98
  reasons for blogging 95–96
  social media friendly tips 96–97
blogsearchengine.org 104
bookmarks 20
brands: creating and building 34–37, 39
Brandwatch website 31
budget fixing 57
Buffer software 94
businesses 30–47
  building interaction 36
  communication 32
  customers 34–37, 39, 41
  goal-setting 39
  humanizing interactions 37
  monitoring interaction 37
  nanotargeting 33
  promotion and marketing 16–17, 40
  reputation management 31
  research 40–41
  restricting connection categories 43
  social media strategies 38–43
  time-saving strategies 38
buying and selling 44–47
buying interactions 82

C

campaigns 40, 90–94
Ciao reviews website 125
citizen journalism 115–16
commenting on other blog sites 11, 36,
  118–19
communities for businesses 34–37
connections 56, 69, 80, 100–01
contempt of court 116
contents: guidelines 74–76, 90, 96–97, 120
cookies 111
copyright law 113, 115
cost per click (CPC) 33, 57, 69
cost-per-thousand-impressions (CPM) 33, 69
countdowns to campaigns 91
coupons 62
Creative Commons License system 114
cyber-stalking 112

D

Delicious bookmarking website 20
Digg social news site 124
Digg social news website 21, 124
discussions 77–78

E

eBay 44–45, 46, 47, 85
ecommerce 44–47
Ecwid ecommerce 47
email addresses 23
entertainment 14
Epinions reviews 125
events organization 14

F

F-commerce 58
Facebook
  advertising 54–58
  audience tools 53
  bidding 57
  budget fixing 57
  for businesses 50–58
  buying interactions 82
  friend requests 40, 79–80, 100, 118
  Insights analytics 52, 53
  Likes 52–53, 81–82, 123
  Page Like Ads 84
  portfolio storage 124
  privacy settings 56, 109–10, 112
  profiles 52
  selling (F-commerce) 58
  setting up a page 50
  storefronts 46, 47
  timelines 51
  targeting advertising 56
  unfriending 118

video ads 58
fair-use 115
fake accounts 82
Farmville online game 22
feedback
  forms 41
  online reviews 85–87, 125
Flickr 18, 21
forums 20, 36
Friends Reunited 12

G

games 22, 84
goal-setting for businesses 39
Google+ 70, 71
Google alerts 104

H

hangouts (Google+) 71
harassment, online 112
hashtags (#) 63
Hootsuite dashboard app 94
hosted blogging platforms 97
Hot Tips
  Amazon stores 45, 47
  bidding on Facebook 57
  blogs 97
  building interaction for businesses 36
  commenting on other blog sites 11
  copyright ownership 114
  countdowns to campaigns 91
  eBay sales 47
  Facebook 'Page Like Ads' 84
  finding reviewers 86
  Google+ hangouts 71
  interest groups 124
  libel issues 116
  Likes on Facebook 52–53
  LinkedIn Showcase pages 68
  links to own websites 80, 101
  locating nearby Twitter users 61
  market research 40
  monitoring services 31
  multi-media blog contents 99
  people search on Twitter 60
  privacy 25, 109
  profiles 26
  promotional messages 78
  reward schemes 53
  saving tweets 19
  search engine rankings 122
  TripAdvisor 15
  unfriending and unfollowing 118

I

inbound marketing 17
influence, measuring 100–05
intellectual property 113
interactive communication
  avoiding arguments 87, 119
  for businesses 37
  discussions 77–78
  encouraging 83–84
  as measure of influence 101
interest groups 13, 22, 69, 80, 124

J

justunfollow.com 118

K

keywords 122
Klout analytics 102–03

L

landing pages for campaigns 92
legal issues
  contempt of court 116
  cookies 111
  copyright law 113
  intellectual property 113
  libel 115–16
LikeAlyzer software 94
LinkedIn
  advertising 69
  connections 16, 69, 80
  groups 69
  setting up a page 66–67
  showcasing products and services 68
links 20, 60–61, 96–97, 119, 120, 123
location-based networking services 21

M

managers of social media accounts 93
market research 40–41, 62, 104–5
McDonald's 35
measuring influence 100–05
media sharing 21
microblogs 11, 19
monitoring services 31
multi-media blog contents 99
music auto-play 99

N

nanotargeting 33
nearbytweets.com 61
netiquette 116–20
network building 74–87
news networks 13, 21

O

OMGILI search engine 104
organization
  social life 14–15
  working life 16–17
outbound marketing 17

P

parties, Twitter 62–63
passwords 24
pay-per-action (PPA) on Twitter 64
pay-per-click advertisements 33, 69
photo sharing
  privacy 109
  websites 11, 18, 21, 71
Pinterest 71
polls 62
portfolio storage 124
privacy 25, 108–12
profiles
  creating 23–27
  ecommerce sites 45
  Facebook 52
  promoting 42
promotional campaigns 40, 90–94
public domain material 114

R

ranking engines 105
Reddit 21, 124
referral marketing 47
reputation management 31, 41
Reseller Ratings 125
reviews, online 85–87, 125
reward schemes 53, 60–61
Rotten Tomatoes 14

S

safety, online 108–12
search engine optimization (SEO) 122
search engines 26, 104–5, 121–23
Second Life virtual world 22
security 24–25, 110
self-hosted blogging platforms 98
self-promotion 16
Simply Measured analytics 103
social bookmarking 20
social life organization 14–15
social media: definition 10–11
social networks 11, 18, 22
social news sites 21
SocialAppsHQ's ecommerce apps 47
sockpuppet accounts 82
special interests 13, 22, 69, 80, 124
spelling 99
surveys 62
synchronizing campaigns 92

T

targeting advertising 33, 54, 56, 65, 75–76
Tesco 30, 42, 78
time-saving strategies 38, 93
timing of promotional messages 91, 93
tools 94
travel 15
TripAdvisor 15
Tweetdeck dashboard app 94
TweetReach 103
tweets, promotional 61, 64
twellow.com 61
Twitter
  advanced search 60, 120
  advertising 63–65
  budget fixing 65
  for businesses 59–65
  buying interactions 82
  coupons 62
  followers 37, 40, 59–60, 100, 118
  hashtags (#) 63
  locating nearby users 61
  microblogs 19
  notifications 101
  parties 62–63
  polls 62
  portfolio storage 124
  privacy settings 110, 112
  profile page 26
  retweeting 60, 83, 115, 123
  saving tweets 19
  unfollowing 118
twtpoll.com 62
TwtQpon 62

U

Unfriend Finder plugin 118
usernames 23, 24

V

video ads 58
video auto-play 99
video sharing 11, 21, 71
Virgin Atlantic 95
virtual gaming 22
virtual worlds 22
Volusion 47

W

Wordpress 97
working life, organizing 16–17
World of Warcraft online game 22

Y

YouTube 21, 71

INTERMEDIATE FOOD HYGIENE

A text for food hygiene courses and supervisors

Richard A. Sprenger
B.Sc.(Hons.), D.M.S., F.C.I.E.H., M.R.E.H.I.S., F.S.O.F.H.T.

Chief Executive, Highfield Publications

© Highfield Publications

ISBN 1 871912 64

'Vue Pointe', ... 7LY U.K.
Telephon ... 303

websites: www.highfield.co.uk www.foodsafetytrainers.co.uk

Printed by Guildhall Leisure Services Limited
Doncaster

LIBREX —

Contents

Preface   3

Chapter 1   An introduction to food safety   4

Chapter 2   Microbiology   8

Chapter 3   Food contamination and its prevention   14

Chapter 4   Food poisoning and foodborne diseases   24

Chapter 5   Personal hygiene   37

Chapter 6   The storage and temperature
               control of food   43

Chapter 7   Food spoilage and preservation   57

Chapter 8   The design and construction of food
               premises and equipment   66

Chapter 9   Cleaning and disinfection   78

Chapter 10   Pest control   85

Chapter 11   Supervisory management   96

Chapter 12   Food safety legislation   112

Glossary   125

Index   129

The prevention of most food poisoning outbreaks is relatively simple and well understood. Cook food thoroughly, protect it from contamination and keep it cold or hot.

But despite our knowledge of these simple controls and the millions of first-tier food handlers, who have attended food hygiene courses, the number of cases of food poisoning remains at an unacceptable level. Attendance on food hygiene courses alone, even when obtaining certificates, appears to have had little effect. It could be argued that on-the-job training to promote competency, and effective instruction, supervision and control are an even more important part of the overall strategy necessary to significantly reduce levels of foodborne illness and food complaints. In other words knowledgeable and competent supervisors and managers are the key to food safety.

I have written this book with the intention of providing supervisors and middle managers with the essential, practical information to enable them to manage staff to provide safe food. "Intermediate Food Hygiene" is based on the syllabuses of the Intermediate Food Safety Courses provided by the Chartered Institute of Environmental Health, the Royal Environmental Health Institute of Scotland, the Royal Institute of Public Health and Hygiene and the Royal Society for the Promotion of Health.

In addition to assisting candidates to successfully complete the above courses, "Intermediate Food Hygiene" should be used as a reference to help supervisors make correct decisions with regard to food safety. Emphasis has been placed on the measures necessary to control the most common reasons for food poisoning outbreaks, including temperature control, effective cooling, storage and thawing, preventing contamination and the destruction of food poisoning bacteria.

Many of the food scares relating to, for example, salmonella in eggs, E. coli O157, listeria and high levels of food poisoning would probably not have occurred if the highest standards of hygiene had been observed and the recommendations in this book had been followed.

If you rigorously apply the principles of food safety detailed throughout "Intermediate Food Hygiene", you should avoid your food business becoming one of the food poisoning statistics or, even worse, starting off the next food scare.

Safe food is food which is free of contaminants and will not cause illness or harm. Persons involved in food poisoning investigations often remark about the cleanliness of the premises responsible. If food hygiene is intended to prevent food poisoning then it follows that hygiene is more than cleanliness, it involves all measures necessary to ensure the safety and wholesomeness of food during preparation, processing, manufacture, storage, transportation, distribution, handling, sale and supply. This involves:

◆ protecting food from risk of contamination, including harmful bacteria, poisons and foreign bodies

◆ preventing any bacteria present multiplying to a level which would result in illness of consumers or the early spoilage of food

◆ destroying any harmful bacteria in the food by thorough cooking, processing or irradiation

◆ discarding unfit or contaminated food.

The cost of food poisoning and poor hygiene

Persons carrying on a food business have legal, commercial and moral obligations to provide safe food. The costs resulting from food poisoning can be very high, as are those from poor hygiene. These costs, both financial and social, fall on employers and employees as well as those persons who are ill. Costs for employers include:

◆ the loss of working days, and productivity, from illness caused by employees eating contaminated food. Even minor infections increase costs for employers through absence of employees

◆ the closure of food premises by local authority action

◆ a loss of business and reputation, either from bad publicity or from public reaction to poor standards, food poisoning outbreaks and even deaths

◆ fines and costs of legal action taken because of contraventions of hygiene legislation or because of the sale of unfit or unsatisfactory food

◆ civil action taken by food poisoning sufferers, or those aggrieved by injury or trauma from foreign bodies in food

◆ food losses due to premature spoilage or damage, because of poor stock rotation, incorrect storage temperature or pest infestations

◆ low staff morale, higher turnover with attendant costs and inefficiencies from staff unwilling or unable to tolerate poor standards

◆ food complaints and costs of internal investigation

◆ loss of production.

Bad hygiene - lower profits!

Food employees may suffer by:

◆ losing their jobs because of closure, loss of business or because they become long-term carriers of food poisoning organisms, especially salmonella

◆ losing overtime or bonuses.

All of these factors could contribute to a lowering of profit.

The benefits of high standards of hygiene

Good hygiene - higher profits!

◆ satisfied customers, a good reputation and increased business

◆ compliance with food safety legislation

◆ less food wastage and increased shelf-life

◆ good working conditions, higher staff morale and lower staff turnover, which promotes increased productivity

◆ reduced risk of food poisoning and food complaints.

These factors contribute to higher profits.

High-risk foods

High-risk foods are ready-to-eat foods which, under favourable conditions,

High-risk foods.

support the multiplication of pathogenic bacteria and are intended for consumption without treatment which would destroy such organisms. They are usually high in protein, requiring strict temperature control and protection from contamination and include:

◆ all cooked meat and poultry

◆ cooked meat products including liquid gravy, stock, pâté and meat pies

◆ milk, cream, artificial cream, custards and dairy produce

◆ cooked eggs/products, especially those products made with raw eggs and not thoroughly cooked, for example, mousse, mayonnaise and home made ice-cream

◆ shellfish and other seafoods, for example, cooked prawns and oysters

◆ cooked rice (not high in protein).

Low-risk foods

These foods are rarely implicated in food poisoning and may be stored at ambient temperatures. Examples include:

◆ preserved food such as jam

◆ dried foods or food with little available moisture, such as flour, bread, biscuits. On adding liquid to powder food, such as milk, the food becomes high-risk

Low-risk foods.

- acid foods, such as fruit, vinegar or products stored in vinegar

- fermented products, such as salami

- foods with high fat/sugar content, such as chocolate

- canned foods, whilst unopened.

Raw foods

Raw foods are often contaminated with large numbers of food poisoning bacteria, for example, raw meat, poultry, eggs and root vegetables contaminated with soil. If raw foods are perishable, they should be stored in a refrigerator separate from high-risk food.

Raw food may present a serious risk of food poisoning if not cooked thoroughly, especially poultry, products made with raw egg, bivalves, such as oysters, and raw milk.

Raw foods.

Food poisoning

Food poisoning is usually an acute illness resulting from eating contaminated or poisonous food. It excludes allergies to food or toxins. The symptoms normally include one or more of the following: abdominal pain, diarrhoea, vomiting and nausea.

Gastroenteritis

This term is used to refer to an inflammation of the stomach and intestinal tract that normally results in diarrhoea.

Carriers

Carriers are people who show no symptoms of illness but excrete food poisoning or foodborne pathogens which may contaminate food, for example, salmonellae or shigellae. Organisms may be excreted intermittently.

Convalescent carriers are people who have recovered from an illness but still harbour the organism. The convalescent state may be quite prolonged and salmonellae are sometimes excreted for several months.

Healthy carriers are people who have displayed no symptoms but harbour the causative organism. Healthy carriers may have become infected with pathogenic bacteria from contact with raw food with which they work, particularly poultry or meat.

Allergy

An identifiable immunological response to food or food additives may be described as an allergy. The allergen is usually a protein and several systems within the body may be affected, for example, the respiratory system, the gastrointestinal tract, the skin and the central nervous system. Symptoms vary considerably and may include bronchitis, vomiting, diarrhoea, a rash and migraine. Reactions may be mild or extremely severe and may occur immediately the food is consumed, or up to 48 hours later. An allergic response should not be confused with food poisoning. The first exposure to the specific food, for example, peanuts or sesame seeds, does not produce symptoms, however, subsequent exposure results in a typical allergic response, or even death. Around one in two hundred people may have a peanut allergy.

THE INCIDENCE OF FOOD POISONING IN ENGLAND & WALES

The annual incidence of food poisoning is unknown. Several million people in England and Wales suffer from gastroenteritis each year, many of these will have food poisoning and a few will die. Those most at risk include the young, the elderly, the immunocompromised and pregnant women.

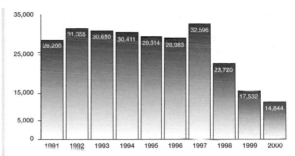

Salmonella Isolates from humans in England and Wales (1991-2000).

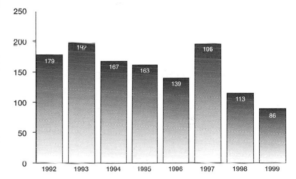

Outbreaks of Foodborne Infectious Intestinal Disease (excluding private residences) in England & Wales (1992-1999).

THE INCIDENCE OF FOODBORNE DISEASE IN SCOTLAND

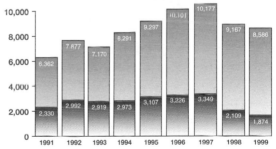

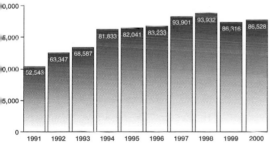

Annual corrected notifications of food poisoning in England and Wales (1991-2000). These include many cases of diarrhoea and vomiting which are probably non foodborne and therefore should not be used to indicate trends of actual food poisoning or food safety standards.
(Courtesy of the PHLS Communicable Disease Surveillance Centre.)

The annual number of notifications of foodborne disease and salmonella isolates in Scotland (1991-1999).
These include laboratory isolations of campylobacter.
The 1999 figures are provisional.
(Courtesy of the Scottish Centre for Infection and Environmental Health.)

Microbiology is the study of microscopic plants and animals and this includes bacteria, moulds and yeasts. The most important microorganisms of interest to the food industry are bacteria, and bacteriology is the study of bacteria. If food handlers are to understand food safety and how to prevent food poisoning, they must have some understanding of basic bacteriology.

Bacteria are single-celled microorganisms which are found everywhere; on raw food and people, in soil, air and water. A microorganism is an organism that is so small it can only be seen under a powerful microscope. Most bacteria are harmless and some are essential, for example, for breaking down decaying matter. Others are of benefit to the food industry, for example, in the manufacture of cheese and yoghurt. Unfortunately a small number of bacteria cause food spoilage and others, known as pathogens, cause illness including food poisoning.

Commensals are bacteria which live on or in the body without causing illness. Most bacteria on the body are commensals and are part of the normal flora. For example, some species of staphylococcus are found on the skin and in the mouth or nose. Other species are transient and may cause skin infections, such as boils. If harmful species of staphylococcus are transferred to high-risk food, they may cause illness.

The size, shape and structure of bacteria

Bacteria can only be observed under a microscope with a magnification of around 1000 times. Bacteria vary in size from around .001mm to .003mm. Although an individual bacterium cannot be seen, large numbers can be seen as small white or yellow spots on growth media in laboratories. These spots are known as colonies. Large numbers may also cause visible effects on food, for example, a slime layer on the surface of spoilt meat.

Bacteria vary considerably in shape:
Cocci are spherical.
Bacilli are rod-shaped.
Spirochaetes are spiral.
Vibrios are comma-shaped.

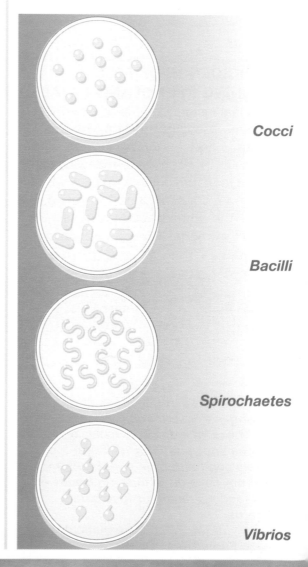

Cocci

Bacilli

Spirochaetes

Vibrios

Structure of a bacterium (simplified).

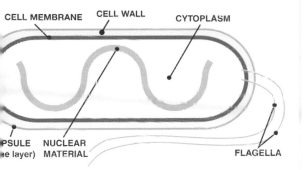

CELL MEMBRANE   CELL WALL   CYTOPLASM

PSULE   NUCLEAR
e layer)   MATERIAL   FLAGELLA

Cell wall – a rigid structure that gives the bacterium its shape.

Cell membane – controls passage of waste and nutrients into and out of the cell.

Cytoplasm – the 'body' of the bacterium.

Nuclear material – the 'brain' of the bacterium.

Flagella – attachments that allow bacteria to move in liquids.

Although some bacteria can use flagella to swim around in liquids, most bacteria rely on other objects to move them about, for example, moving from one food to another using a table top, a piece of equipment such as a knife or the hands of the food handler. Things which transfer bacteria from one place to another are known as vehicles.

As food poisoning bacteria are commonly found on raw food and people, it is impracticable to operate a food business without food poisoning bacteria being present at one time or another. It is therefore essential to deny them the conditions which would allow them to multiply to a level where they present a risk to customers. (Large numbers of bacteria usually need to be present in food to cause food poisoning.)

Bacterial multiplication

Bacteria reproduce by splitting into two. This process is known as binary fission and the time taken between each division (generation time) varies considerably depending on, among other things, temperature and the nutrients (food) available. In optimum (ideal) conditions some food poisoning bacteria can split in two every ten minutes, although at temperatures of around 10°C it may take up to ten hours or they may stop multiplying. The average generation time of the common food poisoning bacteria under optimum conditions is usually considered to be around 20 minutes. When bacteria are growing and multiplying this is described as the vegetative state.

If food is contaminated a common level of contamination may be around 1000 bacteria per gram of food. If this food provides optimum conditions then within one hour 40 minutes, these bacteria could double every ten minutes and become 1,000,000. This number of bacteria is likely to cause food poisoning.

Nutrients

Food poisoning bacteria obtain their essential basic nutrients from amino acids, fats, vitamins and minerals, which are usually provided by high protein food such as meat, fish and dairy produce. Foods with high sugar and salt content are usually unsuitable and therefore are unlikely to support bacterial multiplication.

Moisture

Bacteria require water to transport

nutrients into the cell and take away waste products. With the exception of dehydrated products such as milk powder, most foods contain sufficient moisture to enable bacteria to multiply. However, some bacteria can survive dehydration and when liquid is added to the dried food it once again becomes a high-risk food and must be stored under refrigeration.

Acidity and alkalinity (pH)

The pH of a food is measured on a scale of 0 to 14. Acid foods have pH values below 7, alkaline foods above 7 and a pH value of 7 is neutral. Most bacteria will not multiply in a pH below 4.5, i.e. an acid food such as fruit juice. However, if a large number of food poisoning bacteria are introduced into an acid food it may take some time for the bacteria to die. For this reason we must protect acid food from contamination at all times.

Temperature

Bacteria have a maximum and minimum temperature for multiplication as well as an optimum temperature when multiplication is the most rapid. Most food poisoning bacteria grow best at around 37°C (body temperature) although *Clostridium perfringens* prefers 46°C. The common food poisoning bacteria will not multiply below 5°C or above 50°C. However, many can survive outside this

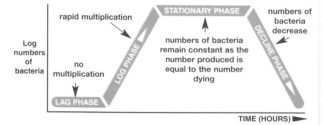

Bacterial growth curve which shows the four stages of bacterial growth when, for example, food is removed from a refrigerator.

temperature range and start multiplying again when temperatures are suitable. The range of temperature, which is likely to encourage the fastest multiplication, is between 20°C and 50°C. Some pathogens will grow between 0°C and 20°C but they multiply slower at the lower temperatures.

Some food spoilage bacteria multiply slowly under refrigeration, which is one of the reasons for food becoming unfit if stored longer than the recommended shelf-life.

Psychrophiles are bacteria which prefer temperatures below 20°C. Mesophiles prefer temperatures of 20°C to 50°C and this group includes the common food poisoning bacteria. Thermophiles multiply most rapidly above 45°C.

Presence of oxygen

Some bacteria can only multiply in the presence of oxygen and others can only multiply when there is no oxygen. The former bacteria are known as aerobes and the latter anaerobes. Many bacteria can multiply with or without the presence of oxygen and these are called facultative anaerobes, for example, salmonella.

Oxygen is normally present in food except in the case of liquids which have been thoroughly boiled. Cooking, for example, joints of meat, also drives off oxygen and the centre then provides ideal conditions for anaerobes.

Toxin production

Food poisoning bacteria produce toxins (poisons) and if they affect the gastrointestinal tract they are known as enterotoxins. Toxins may be either exotoxins or endotoxins.

Exotoxins are produced during multiplication of bacteria. Quite often exotoxins are released into the food and many are heat resistant, so that even if cooking destroys the bacteria, the toxin may remain and cause illness if the food is eaten. This results in a short onset time.

Endotoxins form part of the bacterial cell wall and are released on the death of the bacteria, usually in the intestines of persons consuming contaminated food. If the toxin is produced in the intestine, the onset period, for the first symptoms to appear, will usually be longer than if the toxin is in the food.

Spore formation

Some food poisoning bacteria, such as *Clostridium perfringens, Bacillus cereus* and *Clostridium botulinum* are able to form spores which are capable of surviving unfavourable conditions such as high temperatures, dehydration and the use of disinfectants. Spores are round protective bodies which form inside the bacterial cell

and allow survival for many years without food and water.

Temperatures in excess of 100°C are often required for long periods (as much as five hours) to destroy spores. When favourable conditions return, the spores split open and release the vegetative bacteria which then grow and multiply. The temperature used to ensure the safety of low-acid canned food is the equivalent of 121°C for three minutes.

Competition

When there are many different bacteria present, they will compete for the same food. Fortunately, most food poisoning bacteria are not as competitive as the normal flora found on food and, unless present in high numbers, will usually die.

Destruction of bacteria

Food poisoning bacteria can be destroyed by using high temperatures for sufficient time. The higher the temperature, the shorter the time required. However, the

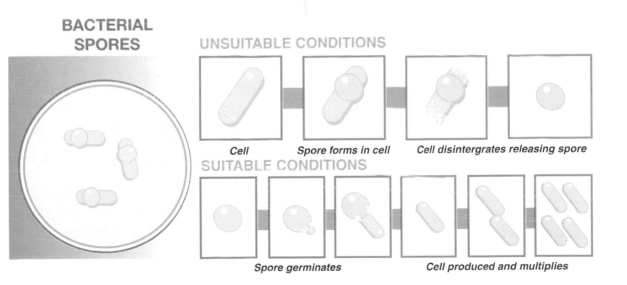

BACTERIAL SPORES

UNSUITABLE CONDITIONS

Cell   Spore forms in cell   Cell disintergrates releasing spore

SUITABLE CONDITIONS

Spore germinates   Cell produced and multiplies

type of bacteria (whether or not they produce spores), the number of bacteria present and the type of food also affect the time needed to kill bacteria and make the food safe. Bacteria will start to die at around 60°C. However, a core temperature of greater than 75°C is required when cooking food to be reasonably confident that most harmful bacteria will have been destroyed.

Unfortunately, much higher temperatures are required to destroy toxins and spores produced by some food poisoning bacteria. Spores are much more resistant to drying, boiling, disinfectants and other conditions, which usually destroy vegetative food poisoning bacteria.

Bacteria can also be destroyed by irradiation, steam or the use of disinfectants such as bleach. Freezing cannot be used to destroy bacteria as most will survive the freezing process and long periods of storage at freezing temperatures.

Moulds

Moulds are aerobic chlorophyll-free fungi which produce thread-like filaments (hyphae) and form a branched network of mycelium. Moulds, which may be black, white or of various colours, will grow on most foods, whether moist or dry, acid or alkaline and high in salt or sugar concentrations. The optimum growth temperature is usually 20°C to 30°C, although they will grow well over a wide range of temperatures and may cause

problems in refrigerators. Growth has been recorded as low as -10°C. High humidities and fluctuating temperatures accelerate mould growth.

Moulds commonly affect bread and other bakery products, and although spores are usually destroyed in baking, subsequent contamination is difficult to avoid. Mould inhibitors are usually added to bread.

Food must always be stored in accordance with the manufacturer's instructions and never sold outside its "use-by" date. Mishandling of vacuum packs of cheese may result in punctures and consequential mould growth. As the mycelium grows over the food, hyphae penetrate the substance and consequently mould soon returns if scraped off the surface. Regular checking of stock is

Mycotoxin producing mould (Courtesy of Anticimex).

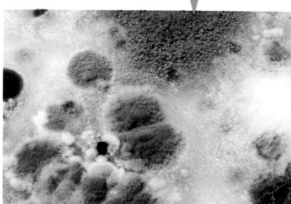

imperative to avoid customer complaints. The presence of mould on food is usually considered to render it unfit for human consumption. Cheeses produced with specific moulds are an exception.

Yeasts

Yeasts are microscopic fungi which reproduce by budding. Most yeasts grow best in the presence of oxygen, although fermentative types may grow slowly anaerobically. The majority of yeasts prefer acid foods (pH 4 to 4.5) with a reasonable level of available moisture. However, many yeasts will grow in high concentrations of sugar and salt. The optimum growth temperature for yeast is around 25°C to 30°C with a maximum of around 47°C. Some yeasts can grow slowly at 0°C and below.

Yeasts are used in the manufacture of foods such as bread, beer and vinegar. However, they cause spoilage of many foods including jam, fruit juice, honey, meats and wines.

Viruses

Viruses are even smaller than bacteria and can only be seen under a very powerful electron microscope. They multiply in living cells, not in food. Some viruses cause illness, including viral gastroenteritis and hepatitis A.

Protozoa

Protozoa are single-celled organisms which form the basis of the food chain. They live in most habitats such as oceans, soil and decaying matter. Some are pathogenic and usually result in waterborne outbreaks. They do not multiply in food but their cysts may remain infectious in foods for a long time. Furthermore, they have a low infective dose, i.e. only small numbers of cysts are required to cause illness. Two pathogenic protozoa causing illness in the U.K. are *Cryptosporidium parvum* and *Giardia lamblia*.

Key points

♦ bacteria are found everywhere but can only be seen under a microscope

♦ food businesses cannot operate without food poisoning bacteria being present at one time or another

♦ bacteria rely on food, people and equipment to move about in food premises

♦ bacteria require food, moisture, warmth and time to multiply

♦ the common food poisoning bacteria prefer a temperature range of 20°C to 50°C for rapid multiplication

♦ in optimum conditions, some food poisoning bacteria can multiply every ten minutes

♦ temperatures above 75°C are used to destroy bacteria but some exotoxins and spores may survive boiling for a considerable period

♦ most food poisoning bacteria will not multiply in refrigerators below 5°C, but they will survive freezing

♦ food poisoning bacteria do not multiply in high acid food, high salt or sugar concentrations or dried foods (until reconstituted).

Contamination of food is a major hazard and may be considered as the occurrence of any objectionable matter in or on the food. Therefore, carcasses may be contaminated with faecal material, high-risk food may be contaminated with spoilage or food poisoning bacteria and flour may be contaminated with rodent hairs. To prevent the consumption of food which is unacceptable or unsafe, contamination must be kept to a minimum.

There are three types of contamination:

◆ *Microbiological contamination by bacteria, moulds or viruses (microorganisms)*
Usually occurs in food premises because of ignorance, inadequate space, poor design or because of food handlers taking short cuts. In the early stages it will not be detectable. Contamination of this sort is the most serious and may result in food spoilage, food poisoning or even death

◆ *Physical contamination by foreign bodies including insects*
Physical contamination may render food unfit or unsafe but often involves pieces of paper, plastic, metal or string and is usually unpleasant or a nuisance

◆ *Chemical contamination*
Examples include pesticides on fruit and residues from cleaning chemicals.

CONTAMINATION BY MICROORGANISMS

Bacterial contamination is the most significant as it results in large amounts of spoilt food and unacceptable numbers of food poisoning cases. Food poisoning bacteria may be brought into food premises by the following sources:

◆ food handlers/visitors

◆ raw foods including poultry, meat, eggs, milk, fish and shellfish and water especially when polluted with sewage or animal faeces. Vegetables or fruit may become contaminated from manure or polluted irrigation water

◆ insects, rodents, animals and birds

◆ from the environment, including soil and dust.

Mould spores will be present in the atmosphere, on surfaces, especially damp surfaces, and on mouldy food. Food should always be covered and mouldy food must be segregated. Furthermore, mould must not be allowed to grow on walls, ceilings and window frames. Mould growth often occurs if food is stored at the wrong temperature, at high humidity and in excess of the recommended shelf-life. It may also affect cheese stored in vacuum packs which are pierced. Canned goods, which are removed from cases opened with unguarded craft knives, may become punctured, thus giving rise to mould growth inside the can.

Viruses are usually brought into food premises by food handlers who are carriers, or on raw food such as shellfish which have been grown in sewage-polluted water.

Vehicles and routes of bacterial contamination

Sometimes bacteria pass directly from the source to high-risk food, but as bacteria are largely static and as the sources are not always in direct contact with food, the bacteria have to rely on other things to transfer them to food. These things are known as vehicles and the main ones are:

◆ hands

◆ cloths and equipment

◆ hand-contact surfaces

◆ food-contact surfaces.

Cross-contamination is defined in the Catering Guide to Good Hygiene Practice as "the transfer of bacteria from contaminated foods (usually raw) to other foods." This includes direct contact, drip and indirect contamination by, for example, hands, equipment or work surfaces. The path along which bacteria are transferred from the source to the food is known as the route. Knowledge of sources, vehicles and routes is vital to food poisoning prevention, as different controls apply to each. It must be assumed that all sources are contaminated, i.e. every worker is a carrier and all raw meat, milk, animals, insects, used equipment

and the surrounding environment are contaminated.

SOURCES, VEHICLES AND ROUTES OF CONTAMINATION

Prevention of contamination depends on either removing the sources, or putting barriers between them and the vehicles or between them and food. Thus human access to food must be restricted, raw foods handled in separate areas, vermin excluded and work areas enclosed in suitably constructed and ventilated rooms.

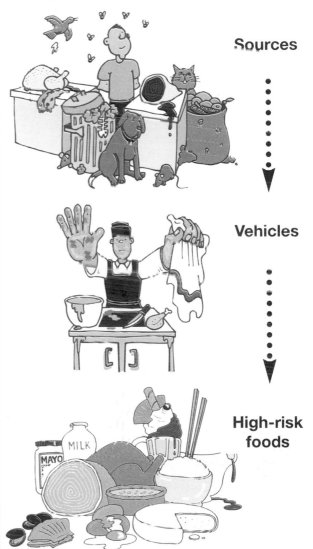

Sources

Vehicles

High-risk foods

Similarly, vehicles must, where possible, be excluded. Handling should be minimized, wiping cloths used sparingly or destroyed after each use, hand-contact surfaces, such as tap handles, replaced with knee or electronically operated taps, and the number of surfaces with which the food comes into contact limited.

In the nature of food preparation, however, routes between sources and vehicles survive, giving rise to contaminated vehicles. Consequently, routes must be disrupted by cleaning and disinfection. For example, should a work surface come into contact with a contaminated source, raw meat for instance, the surface must be cleaned and disinfected before it is used for cooked meat.

CHECK LIST FOR CONTAMINATION CONTROL

◆ purchase food and raw materials from known, reliable and hygienic suppliers. Test for quality and inspect suppliers' premises if appropriate

◆ accept deliveries only if transported in clean, properly equipped vehicles, with clean drivers wearing satisfactory protective clothing. Refrigerated vehicles may be necessary

Unsatisfactory deliveries must be rejected.

◆ inspect deliveries immediately on arrival. Reject or segregate any damaged, unfit or contaminated material. Where relevant, check temperature, codes and date markings and reject out-of-date food

◆ after checking, remove deliveries immediately to appropriate storage, refrigerator or cold store

◆ keep any unfit food, chemicals and refuse away from stored food. Use only food containers for storing food

◆ keep high-risk foods apart from raw foods at all times, in separate areas with separate utensils and equipment. Colour coding is useful. Separate food handlers are recommended

◆ maintain scrupulous personal hygiene at all times and handle food as little as possible. Exclude potential carriers

◆ keep food covered or otherwise protected unless it is actually being processed or prepared, in which case bring food out only when needed. Do not leave food lying around

◆ keep premises, equipment and utensils clean and in good condition and repair. Report or remedy defects with the minimum of delay. Disinfect food-contact surfaces, hand-contact surfaces and cleaning equipment

◆ ensure that all empty containers are clean and disinfected prior to filling with food

◆ control cleaning materials, particularly

wiping cloths. Keep cleaning materials away from food. Remove food and food containers before cleaning.

Care must be taken to ensure that all cleaning residues, including water, are drained from food equipment and pipes. Always clean from high-risk areas to low-risk areas.

◆ remove waste food and refuse from food areas as soon as practicable. Store in appropriate containers, away from food

◆ maintain an active pest control programme

◆ control visitors and maintenance workers in high-risk areas. Ensure hygiene disciplines apply to all personnel, including management

◆ inspect food areas and processes frequently, act on any defects or unhygienic practices. Train staff and monitor performance. Food handlers and engineers must be aware of the bacteriological and physical contamination they may introduce

◆ ensure adequate thawing of foods, separate from other foods

◆ make suitable provisions for cooling food prior to refrigeration.

PHYSICAL CONTAMINATION

Foreign bodies found in food may be brought into food premises with the raw materials or introduced during storage, preparation, service or display. It is essential that supervisors are aware of the types of foreign bodies commonly found in their particular sector of the food industry and that they take all reasonable precautions and exercise all due diligence to secure their removal or prevent their introduction. Product traceability systems must be introduced. A record should be kept of all customer complaints and steps should be taken to identify the source of the contaminant.

Contamination of food by extraneous matter will cause customer dissatisfaction and may result in bad publicity. If press and media coverage results, the impact on the business can be disastrous leading, in the worst possible case, to loss of product confidence and even company viability. It is therefore in the interests of the manufacturer to minimize the risk of foreign body contamination.

Foreign bodies, such as bones in chicken meat or stalks in vegetables, should be minimized by care in harvesting and processing, although foreign body detection and removal systems, such as the use of inspection belts, will also be necessary. The presence of foreign bodies in food, such as glass or rodent droppings, is usually of greater concern as this indicates a breakdown in hygiene and will not be tolerated by the consumer.

Common foreign bodies found in food.

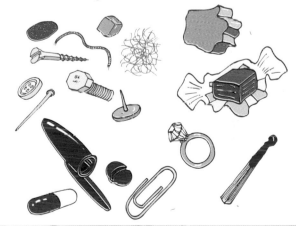

Although in the minority, some foreign bodies may be considered as a serious health hazard, such as glass, stones, wire or rodent droppings, which may result in cut mouths, dental damage, choking or illness.

However, all foreign bodies are, at the very least, a nuisance and manufacturers in particular must implement appropriate systems to prevent or remove such contamination. Their presence in food is likely to be an offence under The Food Safety Act, 1990. The hazard analysis and critical control point system (HACCP) provides the most effective preventive approach, especially for manufacturers, and will be extremely useful if the company wishes to avail itself of the due diligence defence in the event of a prosecution.

IDENTIFYING PHYSICAL HAZARDS AND CONTROL MEASURES
Raw ingredients

The variable nature of raw material quality may be a significant problem in food processing. Raw materials can be a major source of extraneous matter and food manufacturers use a range of cleaning, sorting and grading operations to separate out the offending material. In the manufacture of frozen peas for example, stones, metal screws, cigarette ends, stalks, sticks, caterpillars and dirt often accompany the vined peas as they arrive at the factory.

Control measures should include specifications to detail maximum permissible levels of contaminants in the incoming raw materials. By agreeing specifications with all suppliers and monitoring and evaluating the supplier performance in meeting the specifications, the company has an effective tool in minimizing the risk posed by extraneous matter.

Before using raw materials, cleaning or washing and inspection may need to be carried out. Most physical contamination has to be removed by food handlers as the vegetables pass along an illuminated inspection belt.

Liquids used in food production should be filtered and powders sieved. Filters, screens and sieves should be as fine as possible and must be cleaned and checked regularly. Worn equipment must be replaced. Wooden-framed sieves are usually unacceptable.

Packaging materials

Packaging may be a source of extraneous matter in the form of warehouse and transport dirt/dust, wood from the pallets, paper and polythene strips from over-wraps and a variety of insects and even rodents. Containers (cans, jars, bottles and plastic pots) may be used directly for filling with minimal cleaning and any rogue material in the container (metal splinters, glass, dirt, insects, etc.) may end up in the final product.

Staples, cardboard, string, fibres, cloth, rubber, plastic and polythene

Food may be delivered in various containers including paper sacks, cardboard boxes and polythene bags. Particular care is necessary when emptying containers to avoid contamination of food. As far as practicable, all unpacking and packing should be carried out in areas separate from food production or preparation, if open food is exposed to risk of contamination.

String removed from hessian sacks and ties removed from bags should immediately be placed in suitable containers provided specifically for the purpose. As an extra precaution, coloured string may be specified to aid detection should it end up in the product. Paper sacks should be cut open, although care must be exercised to ensure pieces of paper do not finish up in the food It is preferable for raw materials to be emptied into suitable lidded containers and not dispensed direct from paper sacks.

Particular care is needed to ensure that staples, which tend to fly considerable distances when boxes are prised open, do not contaminate food. Suppliers should be requested to use adhesive tape to fasten boxes, instead of staples. Many products are delivered in black polythene bags and small pieces of polythene often end up in the product.

Effective measures in terms of good manufacturing practice should be adopted within the HACCP scheme to minimize the risk of contamination. An example would be the use of secondary packaging which is removed prior to primary packaging material entering a high-risk area.

The building, installations and equipment

Wood splinters

As far as possible the use of wood should be eliminated from food production areas. Wooden containers used for transporting raw materials should be phased out. Pallets should not be double stacked over open food.

Hazards from wood splinters, rust and flaking paint.

Bolts, nuts and other pieces of metal

As far as practicable nuts should be self-locking. Bolts, nuts and screws should be non-corroding and positioned to ensure that, should they fall off equipment, they do not drop into the food.

Flaking paint or rust

Ceiling structure, pipes or equipment should be non-flaking and rust-free. This is especially important when such fixtures are positioned directly above open products. In some older factories this problem is very difficult to overcome and consequently additional protection is necessary, for example, enclosed systems for conveying food and empty containers such as cans. New factories should be designed so that fixtures, ducts and pipes are not suspended over working areas or food if the product is exposed to risk of contamination, for example, from condensation.

Grease and oil

Wherever necessary, food-grade grease and lubricants should be used. It is important that engineers use the minimum amount necessary to lubricate moving parts and that grease is not left on the machine. Careful control will ensure the absence of complaints relating to grease in food. It is preferable for motors not to be positioned above open food. When this occurs, suitable non-corroding, cleansable drip-trays should be fixed underneath to catch oil spillages.

Glass

The use of ordinary glass, porcelain and enamelware in food factories should be avoided. Perspex or wired glass windows should be used. Diffusers should be fitted to all fluorescent tubes. All beakers, funnels, etc. used by the quality control staff in production areas should be unbreakable. Glass containers, other than those used for the final product, drinking cups, glass mirrors and gauges must all be eliminated from food production areas. Scales coated in vitreous enamel should be replaced, preferably by stainless steel. Particular care is necessary with glass containers used for product as any line breakages may result in glass contaminating other products.

Hazards from broken glass dials and windows.

Notices

Notices used for warnings, advice or instructions should be properly fixed and permanent. Sheets of paper sellotaped to equipment or close to open food are unacceptable. Recipe instructions should be enclosed in sealed polythene bags. Notice boards should be kept out of areas where open food is handled and should be covered in perspex or similar sheeting.

Hazards from wood splinters, drawing pins, nails and pieces of paper.

Food handlers

Contaminants, which originate from personnel, include earrings, hair, fingernails, buttons, combs and pen tops. Protective clothing, including head covering, must be of a suitable type and worn correctly. The personal hygiene of food handlers must be beyond reproach, and earrings and jewellery, other than wedding rings, should not be worn. Pencils, pens and pieces of chalk must not be used in situations which expose food to risk of contamination, for example, near filling hoppers and mixing vessels.

Sweet papers, cigarette ends and matches are common contaminants and staff should not eat sweets, chew gum or smoke in food rooms. Regular training and reinforcement, such as posters, should be used together with strict supervision and enforcement of company rules.

Cleaning activities

Care must be taken during cleaning and all staff involved should be trained to ensure thoy do not expose product to risk of contamination by using worn equipment, especially brushes which are likely to lose their bristles, or by using inappropriate methods such as high pressure spraying during the production of open food. Particular care must be exercised when using paper towels or cloths to ensure small pieces of paper or cloth do not end up in the product.

Maintenance operatives

Engineers must be trained to take extra care when working with food equipment to ensure that they do not leave loose nuts, swarf and pieces of wire in food rooms on completion of maintenance. Temporary repairs with string should be avoided. It is good practice for managers to check areas where engineers or contractors have been working before food handling commences.

During production, areas which are being decorated or where repair or maintenance work is being carried out must be suitably segregated by screens, such as heavy-duty polythene, to avoid exposing product to risk of contamination. Maintenance workers should not wear grossly soiled overalls and should not stand on or climb over machinory or open food if there is the slightest risk of introducing contamination. If necessary, all food should be removed or protected with clean polythene sheeting. The use of ladders over open food or hoppers can result in dirt falling off shoes or rungs and ending up in the final product. After the work has been completed all tools, screws, swarf, grease, etc. must be removed and the area cleaned and, if necessary, disinfected before use. Whenever possible, equipment should be removed from food areas for repair.

Pests and pest control

Rodents, rodent hairs and droppings may be brought into food premises with the raw materials or introduced during the preparation or storage of food in infested premises. Food showing evidence of rodent contamination is unfit and should be rejected.

Insects, larvae and eggs may also be present in raw materials, although some may find their way into food rooms via openings. Several types of insect multiply rapidly and infestations can soon spread throughout food premises. Infested food should be discarded and appropriate control measures introduced. A reputable pest control contractor, experienced at working with food businesses, should be employed to lay rodent bait or traps and control pest infestations should they arise.

Bad pest control is likely to result in food contamination. For example, electronic fly killers positioned above open food, work surfaces or containers will probably result in dead insects in the food, as will the use of insecticides to destroy flying insects, for example, dichlorvos strips or sprays, in the presence of open food.

Electronic fly killer exposing clean food containers to risk of contamination.

Cleaners and other staff must be instructed not to touch bait trays, unless authorized to do so, and never to put bait trays on shelves above open products whilst cleaning is being undertaken.

Customer contamination

Customers may contaminate food which is not adequately protected especially when they serve themselves. Handling and sneezing over food is probable and inquisitive customers may break seals to examine the contents of jars and tubs. Furthermore, malicious tampering of products in supermarkets continues to pose a threat to manufacturers and retailers. Finally, contamination of the product may occur in the consumer's home and this should be considered when investigating a complaint.

All reasonable precautions and all due diligence

A food company facing a prosecution as a result of selling a contaminated product will need to demonstrate that they have installed and used an effective, documented detection and rejection system, which is checked regularly, if they are to successfully use the due diligence defence provided in the Food Safety Act, 1990. It will be up to the courts to decide what is "reasonable" having regard to good trade practice, Industry Hygiene Guides and the risk and consequences in relation to cost.

Foreign body detection and removal

No system can guarantee to remove every contaminant and the effectiveness of a particular machine or system will depend on the type of foreign body, the initial level of contamination and the maintenance of the equipment. The performance of most machines will deteriorate with age and use and constant testing is essential. There are many contaminant detection and removal systems available including:

◆ metal detection systems
◆ X-ray systems
◆ sieves and filtration
◆ optical systems, including colour sorters
◆ magnets
◆ air or liquid separation systems
◆ the use of operatives, for example, as spotters, on bottle lines or illuminated inspection belts.

CHEMICAL CONTAMINATION

Unwanted chemicals can enter foodstuffs during:

growth, for example, veterinary drugs, fertilizers, pesticides and environmental contaminants such as lead or dioxins;

processing or food preparation, for example, oil, cleaning chemicals or insecticides;

transport, as a result of spillage or leakage; and

sale, for example, cleaning chemicals, insecticides and leaking of such things as plasticizers from packaging. Chemicals may cause acute poisoning or cause long-term illnesses such as cancer.

Cleaning chemicals

To avoid taint, some cleaning chemicals, such as phenols and perfumed soap, must not be used in food premises, especially by those handling dairy/fatty foods. All cleaning materials must be kept in properly labelled containers and stored in

Chemicals must not be stored in food containers or bottles.

a manner which obviates any risk of contamination.

Key points

contamination is a major hazard and may be considered as any objectionable matter in or on food

there are three types of contamination: microbiological, foreign bodies and chemicals

sources of food poisoning bacteria include people, raw foods, pests and the environment

vehicles of contamination include hands, cloths and equipment, hand-contact surfaces and food-contact surfaces

routes are the path bacteria take when being transferred from sources to high-risk food

routes can be disrupted by good design, good practice and cleaning and disinfection

physical contamination results from packaging, the building and equipment, notices, food handlers, cleaning activities, pests and customer contamination

all reasonable precautions and all due diligence should be taken to avoid prosecution as a result of the sale of contaminated food

chemical contamination can occur during growth, processing/preparation, transport or sale.

Food poisoning is an acute illness which usually occurs within one to 36 hours of eating contaminated or poisonous food. Symptoms normally last from one to seven days and may include diarrhoea, vomiting, abdominal pain, nausea, fever and prostration.

Food poisoning may be caused by:

◆ bacteria or their toxins

◆ poisonous fish, including scombrotoxic fish poisoning.

◆ chemicals such as insecticides, excessive additives and fungicides

◆ metals such as lead, copper and mercury

◆ poisonous plants such as deadly nightshade and toadstools

◆ moulds (mycotoxins)

Bacteria are responsible for most food poisoning cases, with poisonous fish, plants, chemicals or metals occasionally causing problems. Mycotoxins rarely cause illness in the UK. Because it is impossible to operate a food business without food poisoning organisms being present, in either small or large numbers, good hygiene practices are essential to minimize risk of illness from consuming contaminated food.

Causative agent (organism)
The causative agent is the bacteria, virus, toxin or poison that contaminates the food and causes food poisoning when the food is consumed.

Onset or incubation period
The onset period is the time between consuming the contaminated food and the first signs of illness.

The food vehicle
The food vehicle is the food consumed that contains the causative agent.

The source
The source is the point from which the causative agent first entered the specific food chain. For example, a cow or a hen. It may also be considered to be the vehicle that brought the causative agent into the food premises responsible for the outbreak, for example, a person, raw milk or an egg.

IMPORTANT FOOD POISONING BACTERIA

Salmonella
Sources

The intestines of ill people and carriers, animals and animal food, raw meat, raw poultry, raw milk, raw eggs, pets, rodents, terrapins, faeces, flies, insects and sewage/water.

Common food vehicles

Undercooked or contaminated cooked meat and poultry, raw milk, raw eggs and uncooked foods using raw eggs in their preparation, for example, mayonnaise, mousses and tiramisu.

Onset period

Six to 72 hours, usually 12 to 36 hours. Endotoxin in intestine (infective food poisoning).

Symptoms and duration of illness

Abdominal pain, diarrhoea, vomiting and fever. The duration is usually one to seven days. Occasionally deaths are recorded usually involving the elderly, the very young and people who are already ill.

Specific characteristics

Usually requires millions of bacteria to cause illness. However, outbreaks involving low numbers have been recorded in food vehicles with high fat content, such as chocolate, milk and cheese. Salmonella multiplies from 5°C to 47°C under aerobic or anaerobic conditions.

Specific controls
- sterilize animal feed and avoid subsequent contamination
- segregate ill animals
- hygienic transport from farm to abattoir
- avoid overcrowding of vehicles
- hygienic slaughtering
- prevent cross-contamination between raw and high-risk food from storage through to serving
- complete thawing of frozen poultry
- thorough cooking to above 75°C. Use heat-treated milk
- high standards of personal hygiene, especially hand-washing after visiting the toilet and before handling high-risk food
- effective cleaning and disinfection
- chlorination of water
- safe sewage disposal
- exclude symptomatic food handlers
- exclude pests and animals from food premises or food contact.

Clostridium perfringens
Sources

Intestines of humans and animals, faeces and sewage, soil, dust, insects, raw meat and poultry.

Common food vehicles

Rolled joints, casseroles, stews, sauces and meat pies when cooking has removed oxygen.

Onset period

Eight to 22 hours usually 12 to 18 hours. Enterotoxin produced in the intestines. Infective food poisoning.

Symptoms and duration of illness

Abdominal pain and diarrhoea. Vomiting is rare. Symptoms usually last 12 to 48 hours.

Specific characteristics

Clostridium multiplies between 10°C and

50°C under anaerobic conditions. The optimum temperature is between 43°C and 47°C. At 46°C *Clostridium perfringens* can double every ten minutes. It produces spores which can survive high temperatures and dehydration. Illness usually results from consuming millions of organisms. Spores germinate as a result of normal cooking temperatures and long, slow cooling allows the vegetative bacteria to multiply rapidly.

Specific controls

- separate raw and high-risk foods, especially meat and vegetables
- use ready prepared and washed root vegetables to avoid bringing soil into the kitchen
- rapidly cool joints, sauces, pies, etc. especially between 60°C and 20°C and then refrigerate
- high standards of personal hygiene, especially handwashing after visiting the toilet and before handling high-risk food
- maximum joint sizes 2.5 kg
- exclude symptomatic food handlers
- effective cleaning and disinfection
- reheat the food to 82°C and then serve immediately.

Staphylococcus aureus

Sources

Human nose, mouth, skin, hands, boils, scratches, spots and cuts, especially if septic. Raw milk from cows or goats with mastitis, or products such as cheese made from raw milk. Up to 50% of the population may carry *Staphylococcus aureus* on their hands or in their mouth or nose.

Common food vehicles

Milk and dairy products, trifles and cream desserts, custard-type products, cold cooked meat and poultry and peeled cooked prawns.

Onset period

One to seven hours. Heat resistant exotoxin produced in food. Toxic food poisoning.

Symptoms and duration of illness

Abdominal pain, nausea, mainly vomiting, diarrhoea, prostration and occasionally subnormal temperatures. The duration is usually between six and 24 hours.

Specific characteristics

Sporadic cases may be common but are rarely notified and are not recorded. Staphylococcus multiplies in aerobic or anaerobic conditions between 7°C and 48°C. Can tolerate relatively high salt content. Usually requires millions of organisms to produce sufficient toxin to cause illness. Is usually harmless when not in food. Toxin may survive boiling for up to 30 minutes.

Specific controls

- high standards of personal hygiene, especially frequent handwashing before handling high-risk food and not touching the mouth, nose or hair during food preparation
- avoid handling high-risk food, where possible use utensils
- exclude food handlers with respiratory infections especially those involving coughing or sneezing; boils or septic cuts; or skin infections that encourage scratching or flaking
- avoid consuming raw milk or products made from raw milk
- prevent cross-contamination (it may be

present in chicken skin)

◆ cover cuts with waterproof dressings.

Bacillus cereus

Sources

Cereals, especially rice, cornflour, spices, dust and soil.

Common food vehicles

Reheated rice, cornflour products and foods containing spices.

Onset period

Usually one to five hours. Exotoxin in food, which can survive temperatures of 126°C for up to 1.5 hours. Toxic food poisoning.

Symptoms and duration of illness

Nausea, vomiting, abdominal pain and some diarrhoea. The duration is usually 12 to 24 hours.

Specific characteristics

Bacillus cereus is a spore former, which produces an exotoxin in food and multiplies under aerobic or anaerobic conditions. Both the spores and the exotoxin will survive normal cooking temperatures. Millions of organisms are usually required to cause illness and bacteria multiply between 7°C and 48°C with an optimum between 28°C and 35°C. There is a second type of Bacillus cereus, which resembles Clostridium perfringens in that it produces a toxin in the intestine. The onset period is eight to 16 hours and symptoms are primarily abdominal pain and diarrhoea with some vomiting.

Specific controls

◆ rapidly cool cooked food and store under refrigeration

◆ cooking must be thorough and, if unavoidable, reheating should be carried out at least to 82°C

◆ particular care with rice which should never be reheated more than once.

Clostridium botulinum

Sources

Fish intestine, soil and vegetables.

Common food vehicles

Low-acid processed food contaminated after canning or vacuum packing, smoked fish, bottled vegetables and products containing spices.

Onset period

Two hours to five days but usually 12 to 36 hours. A heat-sensitive neurotoxin produced in the food. (Affects the nervous system) Toxic food poisoning.

Symptoms and duration of illness

Difficulties in swallowing, talking and breathing. Double vision and muscular paralysis. Diarrhoea at first, followed by constipation. Fatalities are common and survivors may take several months to recover.

Specific characteristics

Clostridium botulinum multiplies between 3.3°C and 48°C under anaerobic conditions. Heat resistant spores are produced and the safety of canned food is based on the destruction of these spores, i.e. 121°C for a minimum of three minutes (botulinum cook).

Specific controls

◆ prevent post-process contamination of cans or vacuum packs of low-acid food

◆ ensure time/temperature combinations used in canning will destroy any spores ot *Clostridium botulinum* that may be present

◆ do not use blown cans or cans with badly damaged seams

◆ use of preservatives such as nitrite in vacuum packs of meat

◆ thorough cooking of food immediately prior to consumption will probably destroy any toxin that is in the food

◆ smoked fish should be produced in accordance with good manufacturing practices and preferably stored in a freezer to prevent multiplication and toxin production.

Generic controls for most food poisoning organisms

◆ high standards of personal hygiene, especially handwashing and exclusion of symptomatic food handlers

◆ keep raw food and high-risk food separate at all stages of production, from delivery through to service. Prevent cross-contamination

◆ store high-risk foods below 5°C or above 63°C. Cool food rapidly and keep it out of the danger zone

◆ ensure food is thoroughly cooked to core temperatures above 75°C

◆ ensure effective cleaning and disinfection

◆ ensure effective pest control

◆ avoid consuming raw foods likely to be contaminated with food poisoning organisms, especially bivalves, milk and eggs

◆ implementation of HACCP/hazard analysis

◆ the effective food safety training of all persons who can influence food safety, especially managers, supervisors and high-risk food handlers.

Food vehicles

The foods most commonly involved in food poisoning outbreaks are:

◆ poultry

◆ red meat and meat products

◆ desserts

◆ fish and shellfish

◆ salads, vegetables and fruit (usually low infective dose organisms)

◆ raw or undercooked egg products such as mayonnaise, mousse, and home made ice-cream

◆ milk and milk products.

CAUSAL FACTORS RELATING TO OUTBREAKS OF FOOD POISONING

◆ preparation too far in advance and storage at ambient temperature

◆ inadequate cooling

◆ inadequate reheating

◆ contaminated processed food including canned

◆ undercooking

◆ inadequate thawing

◆ cross-contamination

◆ raw food consumed

◆ improper warm holding

◆ infected food handlers

◆ use of leftovers

◆ extra large quantities prepared.

More recently, Dr Richard North has been investigating the "failure of management" as the most important reason for food poisoning, for example:

◆ failure to carry out a risk-assessment when there is a change of menu, ingredients or recipes

◆ lack of contingency planning, for example, when the oven or refrigerator breaks down

◆ communication – a failure of management, or head office, to provide the frontline staff with the correct information

◆ management disincentives, for example, bonus paid in relation to the amount of cleaning chemicals used

◆ commercially driven misuse of equipment or premises, for example, overloading refrigerators or catering for numbers beyond the capacity

◆ a failure to recognize potentially hazardous procedures of the operation, for example, colour-coded equipment all being washed in the same sink with no disinfection

◆ failure to implement recommendations, following an earlier outbreak

◆ failure to replace complex or time-consuming operations, for example, refrigerators positioned a considerable distance from workstations. This mitigates against small amounts of food being prepared, which results in temperature abuse

◆ unrealistic demands placed on junior management or untrained staff

◆ the absence of routine planning and consistent procedures.

FOOD POISONING OUTBREAKS DEMONSTRATING MANAGEMENT FAILURES

Staphylococcus aureus

Ten people developed symptoms after eating rolls filled with egg mayonnaise. Three people were admitted to hospital. The filling had been made from hard boiled eggs. After chopping, these eggs had been left in a refrigerator overnight which had been too warm, as a result of loss of refrigerant. The filled rolls had then been placed in a "refrigerated" display counter which was non-operative, the ambient temperature being 25˚C. The source of the outbreak was the food handler who had prepared the eggs and while suffering from a skin infection. Although a "classic" outbreak involving contamination from a food handler and inadequate temperature control, the underlying cause was the lack of equipment maintenance. This contributed significantly to the outbreak. Management also failed to recognize the hazards of inadequate temperature control and failed to realise that a food handler with a skin condition could present a serious hazard.

Salmonella

A hospital outbreak resulted in the death of three people and 119 cases of food poisoning. The vehicle of infection was roast lamb which had been cooked the day before it was served and had been left covered with cloths in a hospital corridor because of the "sultry evening". Conditions were considered "absolutely perfect for bacterial multiplication". The total consignment of 25 joints of lamb had been pre-cooked because the ovens were being repaired the following day. The hospital refrigerators were not used because they were full of jellies which

would not have set at room temperature. The coroner was "satisfied" this was an isolated incident, when some-one had not "gone by the book". At some stage the roast lamb had become contaminated and there had been a "classic" failure of temperature control. However, the underlying cause was clearly the failure of management to plan for the contingency of the oven repairs and to make satisfactory alternative arrangements.

Clostridium perfringens

In a hospital outbreak, patients in one of six wards who were served with roast meat and gravy succumbed to Clostridium perfringens food poisoning. Unaccountably, none of the patients in the other wards suffered, even though they had apparently been served the same meal. On investigation, however, it transpired that the chef had run out of gravy towards the end of serving and had quickly made up additional stock from the stock pot, without having had time to cook the mixture thoroughly. Further investigation showed that ingredient planning had been deficient in that there had been no specific quantities set out for a given number of meals. Quantities prepared were left to the judgement of the chef who estimated what was needed on an ad hoc basis. There were no established procedures, written or otherwise.

Clostridium botulinum

In June 1989 a botulism outbreak affected 27 people and one person died. The implicated product was hazelnut yoghurt. The contamination was traced to the manufacturer of canned hazelnut puree used in the yoghurt. The manufacturer was more used to producing high-acid fruit purees, in which the acidity from the fruit suppressed the growth of botulinum bacteria. However, he had employed the same process to make hazelnut puree. But this was a low-acid product, presenting a completely different order of risk. Changes to the ingredients were also made. Before the recipe had been changed, a full risk assessment should have been carried out

Chemical food poisoning

Some chemicals are extremely poisonous and if ingested may result in severe vomiting within a few minutes and in some cases fatalities. Chemicals can enter foodstuffs by leakage, spillage or other accidents during processing or preparation. Unacceptable levels of benzene migration from plastic packaging and inappropriate use of fungicides have resulted in poisoning. However, acute chemical poisoning from food premises is rare and is usually caused by negligence, for example, storing weedkiller, pesticide or cleaning chemicals in unlabelled food containers.

Chemical additives of food have to undergo rigorous tests before they are allowed and are usually harmless.

However, some may cause problems if ingested in large amounts, for example, three persons became ill after consuming sausages containing sodium nitrate and sodium nitrite at levels of 200 times that permitted for cured meats. Symptoms included drowsiness, dizziness and a greying colour of the skin.

Residues of drugs, pesticides and fertilizers may be present in deliveries of raw materials. Pesticides sprayed on to fruit and vegetables just prior to harvesting may result in cumulative toxic effects and should be strictly controlled Approximately 20,000 Spanish people became ill after using olive oil sold by street vendors, which allegedly contained industrial waste oil. At least 350 people died.

Metallic food poisoning

Several metals are toxic and if ingested in sufficient quantities can give rise to food poisoning. The symptoms, mainly vomiting and abdominal pain, usually develop within an hour. Diarrhoea may also occur. Metals may be absorbed by growing crops, or contaminate food during processing. Acid foods, such as fruit, should not be cooked or stored in equipment containing: antimony (enamel coatings); cadmium (refrigeration apparatus); copper (pans); lead (ceramics, earthenware and lead crystal) or zinc (galvanized metals). Soft water may absorb lead from old pipes.

Tin and Iron

Acid foods may also cause problems if stored in tin-plated iron cans for too long. The acid foods react with the tin-plate and hydrogen gas is produced. Iron and tin are absorbed by the food which may become unfit for human consumption.

Poisonous plants

Poisonous plants are rarely the cause of food poisoning in food premises. Plants responsible for causing acute poisoning include deadly nightshade, death cap (which may be mistaken for edible mushroom) daffodil bulbs and rhubarb leaves.

Red kidney beans or haricot beans, which are consumed raw or undercooked, occasionally result in food poisoning. Nausea, vomiting and abdominal pain are likely within one to six hours of consuming the beans. Temperatures of canning will destroy the toxin.

Poisonous fish

The gonads, liver and intestines of some fish are highly toxic. For example, the puffer fish. Several incidents of red whelk poisoning have been recorded in the UK, due to a poison present in the salivary

glands of these whelks. Symptoms include tingling of the fingers, disturbance of vision, paralysis, nausea, vomiting, diarrhoea and prostration.

Scombrotoxic fish poisoning

Scombrotoxic fish poisoning is caused by toxins which accumulate in the body of some fish, including tuna, mackerel, sardines, pilchards, herring, anchovies and salmon, during storage, especially above 4°C. The onset period is between ten minutes and three hours. Symptoms

last up to eight hours and include headache, nausea, vomiting, abdominal pain, a rash on the face and neck, a burning or peppery sensation in the mouth, sweating and diarrhoea. Problems arise in canning fish as, once formed, the toxin is very heat-resistant and will not be destroyed during processing. Refrigerated storage of fish should prevent toxin formation.

Paralytic shellfish poisoning (PSP) and diarrhetic shellfish poisoning (DSP)

PSP and DSP may result from the consumption of mussels and other bivalves which have fed on poisonous plankton. The aquatic biotoxins causing PSP and DSP may withstand cooking. Symptoms of PSP include a tingling or numbness of the mouth almost immediately and this spreads to the neck, arms and legs within four to six hours. Death, when it does occur, is usually caused by respiratory paralysis within two to twelve hours. DSP symptoms include nausea, vomiting, abdominal pain, diarrhoea and chills with an onset time of thirty minutes to twelve hours.

FOODBORNE DISEASES

Foodborne diseases may be considered to differ from food poisoning in that:

◆ a relatively small number of organisms is capable of causing the illness

◆ the food acts purely as a vehicle and the multiplication of the organism within the food is not an important feature of the illness

◆ vehicles other than food may transmit the organism via the faecal/oral route

◆ person-to-person spread and airborne transmission is more likely.

Viral gastroenteritis

Incidents of gastroenteritis are being increasingly attributed to viruses and undoubtedly contribute to a large number of notified cases of "food poisoning". However, viruses are predominantly infections of children and are rarely incriminated in foodborne transmission. Outbreaks in institutions and other "closed" communities are common.

Small round structured viruses (SRSVs), such as the Norwalk virus, are the major cause of viral foodborne cases and outbreaks in the UK. Symptoms include vomiting, the predominant symptom and usually projectile, some diarrhoea, abdominal pain, fever and nausea. Symptoms usually last around 24 to 36 hours and patients are infectious for a further two days. The onset period is around 15 to 60 hours and is dose dependent. The infective dose is very low, between ten and 100 organisms.

Viruses are around 3/100ths the size of bacteria and can only be seen through an electron microscope. They multiply in living cells not in food. Transmission depends on contamination of food by food handlers or sewage. Filter feeding bivalves, such as oysters harvested from sewage-polluted waters, are a major problem. Foods which are handled the most present the greatest risk, ice, desserts, cold meats, salads and some fruits are frequently involved, but the vehicle is rarely identified.

The virus is present in vomit and airborne infection and person-to-person spread often occurs. Re-infection is common. Viruses thrive in cold conditions and are destroyed at temperatures above 60°C. Relaying of shellfish in clean water is ineffective against viral contamination.

Control measures include staff training, the implementation of hazard analysis, effective cleaning and disinfection of surfaces and equipment, the detection and elimination of viruses from the food chain, the use of reputable suppliers and good quality raw materials.

Typhoid and paratyphoid fever

Sometimes known as enteric fever, typhoid is caused by the bacterium *Salmonella typhi* and paratyphoid by the bacterium *Salmonella paratyphi*. The incubation period is normally between one and three weeks. Symptoms include fever, malaise, slow pulse, spleen enlargement, rose spots on the trunk and constipation or severe diarrhoea. The fatality rate for typhoid is between 2% and 10%. Paratyphoid is generally much less severe and symptoms may be similar to salmonella food poisoning.

The organism is excreted in the faeces and urine of patients and carriers. Enteric fever may be waterborne, due to contamination by sewage, or foodborne, for example, milk or cooked meat contaminated by polluted water or by carriers who are food handlers. Laboratory confirmation is by bacteriological examination of blood, faeces or urine.

Control measures

◆ ensuring the safety of all water supplies. Water used for food preparation or drinking should be chlorinated

◆ ensuring the satisfactory disposal of sewage

◆ ensuring the heat treatment of milk and milk products, including ice cream

◆ preventing the sale of raw shellfish from sewage-polluted waters

◆ identifying carriers and ensuring that they are not employed within the food industry. Medical questionnaires should be used as an aid to recruitment

◆ maintaining high standards of personal hygiene amongst food handlers, especially with regard to thorough handwashing after visiting the toilet

◆ ensuring high standards of hygiene in food production and distribution.

Dysentery

In the UK, bacillary dysentery is usually caused by the bacterium *Shigella sonnei*. It is an acute disease of the intestine characterized by diarrhoea, fever, stomach cramps and often vomiting. Stools may contain blood, mucus and pus. Fatality is normally less than 1%. The incubation period is usually around four days, although it varies between one and seven days. Dysentery is spread through faecal-oral transmission from an infected person or by the consumption of contaminated foods, including water or milk. Control measures are similar to those used for typhoid, with the emphasis on personal hygiene.

Campylobacter enteritis

Campylobacter jejuni is now the most frequently reported reason for acute bacterial diarrhoea. In 2000, around 54,000 faecal specimens submitted to laboratories in England and Wales tested positive for campylobacter and 6,000 in Scotland. However, high-risk food was only proven to be a vehicle for a few of these. The main vehicle has yet to be identified.

Symptoms include headache, fever, diarrhoea (often bloodstained), persistent colicky abdominal pain (may mimic acute appendicitis) and nausea (vomiting is rare). The incubation period is usually between two and five days and the normal duration of illness is one to seven days.

Campylobacters disappear from the stools within a few weeks of illness and long-term carriers have not been detected. Animals and wild birds are the main source and as campylobacters can survive in water for several weeks, untreated water is a potential source. Campylobacters are commonly found on raw poultry, in raw milk and sewage and on carcase meat and offal.

Transmission is thought to be from raw and undercooked poultry and meat, raw milk, bottled milk pecked by birds, especially magpies, contaminated water (private supplies) and infected dogs and cats. Person-to-person spread and secondary cases are rare. Cross-contamination from raw poultry is extremely likely and hands can carry

campylobacters for up to an hour. Campylobacters multiply quickly between 37°C and 43°C but not below 28°C. The organisms may be destroyed by heating food to 60°C for 15 minutes and are sensitive to drying. Illness can be caused by less than 500 organisms.

Control measures include reducing the numbers of campylobacters in raw meat and the food chain, hygiene training of food handlers, especially on the dangers of cross-contamination and the importance of thorough cooking, and also raising the hygiene awareness of consumers.

Listeriosis

Although food is not the only means of transmission, and in the majority of cases a food vehicle is not identified, listeriosis is considered to be a foodborne illness. It is caused by *Listeria monocytogenes,* which is widely distributed in the environment. It is commonly found in effluents and sewage sludge and survives many weeks after spraying. In one outbreak involving coleslaw, the cabbage, stored for several months, had been grown in a field fertilized by sheep manure. The bacteria may be excreted by human or animal carriers, and many cases of cross-infection have been recorded. Symptoms include fever, diarrhoea, septicaemia, meningitis and abortion; neonates, pregnant women, immuno-suppressed persons and the elderly are most at risk. The incubation period is one to 70 days.

A death rate of up to 30% is possible but mainly involves persons with other serious illness. The Government has issued warnings to riskgroups to avoid soft cheeses, reheated meals and paté, although small numbers of listeria can be found in most foods from time to time.

Escherichia coli O157

Most *E. coli* that are found in the intestine are harmless. However, *E. coli O157* causes serious illness, which is sometimes fatal, particularly in young children and the elderly. Symptoms vary from a watery diarrhoea, nausea and abdominal pain to bright red bloody diarrhoea and severe abdominal cramps, usually without fever. Up to 30% of patients develop haemolytic uraemic syndrome (HUS). This generally involves young children and *E. coli O157* is the major cause of acute renal failure in children in the UK. Fatality rates range from 1% to 5%, but in some outbreaks, for example, involving the elderly, may be much higher. The onset period is one to 14 days, with a median of three to four days. The duration of illness is approximately two weeks, unless complications, such as HUS, develop. *E. coli O157* disappears from adult faeces within a few days.

Although *E. coli O157* can multiply in food, it has a very low infective dose involving less than 100 bacteria. Infection results from eating contaminated foods, person-to-person spread and direct contact with animals, especially farm animals and their faeces. The main food vehicles are undercooked meat products, especially burgers and mince, contaminated cooked meat, vegetables fertilized with manure and unwashed, contaminated fruit. Other foods implicated include raw milk, cheese made with unpasteurized milk and apple juice.

However, because of the low infective dose, cross-contamination of many ready-to-eat foods from raw meat is likely

to result in illness. The main reservoir of *E. coli O157* is the stomach and intestines of cattle and, possibly, sheep. It survives and multiplies in some foods at ambient temperatures, although numbers may decline at 4°C. It is destroyed by normal, effective cooking processes. Most outbreak investigations fail to identify a food vehicle.

Hepatitis A

Infectious hepatitis is a viral infection with an abrupt onset. Symptoms include fever, malaise, nausea, abdominal pain and later jaundice. The incubation period is 15 to 50 days and the duration one week to several months. Man is the reservoir and transmission is by the faecal-oral route. Faeces, blood and urine may be infected and can contaminate food, especially water, shellfish and milk.

Control measures are similar to those used for typhoid. A temperature of 90°C for 90 seconds will inactivate the virus.

Parasites

A parasite is a plant or animal which lives on or in another plant or animal known as the host. The parasite obtains its food from the host. They often have complicated life cycles which may involve different hosts. For example, tapeworms, such as *Taenia saginata* live in man, whereas the eggs are eaten by grazing cattle and develop in the muscle of cattle. If undercooked infected beef is eaten, the adult tapeworm develops in man. Parasites may be destroyed by cooking or by commercial freezing.

The Food Safety (General Food Hygiene) Regulations, 1995 require:

◆ every person working in a food handling area to maintain a high standard of personal cleanliness, including wearing suitable, clean and, where appropriate, protective clothing

◆ the supervision and instruction and/or training of food handlers in food hygiene matters commensurate with their work activity

◆ persons known or suspected to be suffering from, or carriers of, a disease likely to be transmitted through food, including infected wounds, skin infections or diarrhoea, must be excluded from food handling if there is a likelihood of contaminating food with pathogenic organisms.

Food handlers must, therefore, be in good health, have clean habits and be instructed or trained to ensure they do not contaminate food or allow food to become contaminated or maintained at ambient temperatures which are likely to promote the multiplication of food poisoning or spoilage bacteria.

Food handlers must have high standards of personal hygiene.

Training of food handlers

Training involves the provision of knowledge and its implementation (practice) to ensure proficiency. Food handlers need to understand the controls, monitoring and corrective actions to be taken at points critical to food safety for which they are responsible. Thus food handlers involved with high-risk food preparation require more training than those only handling packaged or low-risk foods.

Food businesses require a planned training programme which includes induction, awareness and refresher training. The knowledge provided will depend on the risks and responsibilities associated with each job, knowledge may be provided by instruction, attending in-house or formal courses or from computer programmes. However, to be successful it is essential that there is commitment and support from directors and managers, effective supervision and adequate resources. High standards of food safety result when the culture of the business ensures good hygiene pratices are implemented and rewarded.

Hazards from food handlers

Potential hazards arise from *Staphylococcus aureus* which is often present on the hands, in the nose or mouth and in spots and septic cuts. Cross-contamination is also probable if hands are not properly washed after touching raw meat, or other contaminated sources, before handling high-risk foods. A very serious hazard is presented if food handlers fail to wash their hands after using the toilet. The faecal-oral route is one of the main ways that low-dose pathogens (those organisms which only require a few to be present on food to make you ill), such as *E. coli O157*, *Shigella sonnei* or campylobacter result in illness. Persons with loose stools and carriers may be responsible for several serious outbreaks of foodborne illness because of poor personal hygiene.

Hands

Hands are the main vehicle for transferring food poisoning bacteria to high-risk food. For this reason, hands should be kept clean and washed frequently throughout the day and especially:

◆ after visiting the toilet

◆ on entering the food room, after a break, and before handling any food or equipment

◆ after dealing with an ill customer

◆ between handling raw food, such as poultry, red meat, eggs or shellfish, and handling high-risk food

◆ after changing or putting on a dressing

◆ after combing or touching the hair, nose, mouth or ears.

◆ after eating, smoking, coughing or blowing the nose

◆ after handling external packaging or flowers

◆ after handling waste food or refuse

◆ after cleaning, or handling dirty cloths, crockery etc

The correct handwashing procedure is essential.

Around 3 to 5ml of soap should be applied to wet hands. A good lather should be produced by rubbing the hands and fingertips together. Inbetween the fingers, around the thumbs, the forearms and wrists should be thoroughly lathered for around 20 seconds. The lather should be rinsed off in warm flowing water at around 43°C. Efficient drying of the hands with a clean disposable paper towel will reduce the number of bacteria even more. A paper towel may be used to turn off the tap. Sufficient lather, friction and warm running water are the essential features to removing transient bacteria from the hands.

A soft nailbrush must be used to remove bacteria from the fingertips and under the fingernails after using the toilet, cleaning up vomit or faecal material, changing a dressing or handling raw poultry or meat before handling high-risk food. Excessive use of a stiff nailbrush and bactericidal soap both increase the risk of dermatitis. Gloves are often defective or abused and not necessary in most food handling situations. If disposable gloves are used in very high-risk situations the hands should be washed before and after putting on the gloves. The gloves should be discarded frequently.

As fingernails may harbour dirt and bacteria, they must be kept short and clean. False nails should not be worn. Nail varnish may chip and contaminate food and should not be used. Persons who continually put their fingers in their mouth, for example, nail biters should not be employed as food handlers. Keeping the skin in good condition will reduce the likelihood of harbouring *Staphylococcus aureus* bacteria in cracks.

As far as practicable, the best policy is to avoid handling food by using hygienic utensils and equipment, such as serving tongs, trays and plates which are carried by the rim. Furthermore, the hands should not come into contact with the parts of the glasses, cups, spoons, etc. that will end up in a customer's mouth.

The nose, mouth and ears

Up to 40% of adults carry *Staphylococcus aureus* in their nose. Coughs and sneezes can carry droplet infection for considerable distances and contaminate food and/or work surfaces. Persons with bad colds should not handle open food. Hands should be washed after blowing the nose and single-use disposable paper handkerchiefs are preferred.

As the mouth is also likely to harbour *Staphylococcus aureus,* food handlers

Unwashed spoons must not be used for tasting food.

should not eat sweets, chew gum, taste food with fingers or a previously used spoon, or blow into glasses to polish them.

Spitting is obviously prohibited as is nose and teeth picking or poking fingers into the ears.

Discharges from the ears, eyes and nose may contaminate food and such ailments must be reported to the supervisor. Medical clearance will normally be required before resuming work.

Cuts, boils, septic spots and skin infections

Food handlers with boils and septic lesions should be excluded from high-risk food handling areas as they will be infected with *Staphylococcus aureus.* All wounds should be completely protected by a conspicuously-coloured waterproof dressing. Green or blue dressings are used to improve their visibility in food if they fall off. Loose dressings should be replaced immediately. Loss of dressings must be reported immediately to the supervisor.

Cuts on hands may need the extra protection of waterproof fingerstalls. Waterproof dressings are necessary to prevent blood and bacteria contaminating the food and to prevent bacteria from food, especially raw meat or fish, infecting the wound which may turn septic. Furthermore, waterproof dressings do not collect grease and dirt. Metal strips incorporated in dressings assist detection only where metal detectors are in use.

Staff who report for work wearing unacceptable dressings must have them changed before they enter a food room or commence food handling duties.

First aid

Food businesses must have a suitable and sufficient supply of first aid materials. One person should be given the responsibility of ensuring adequate provisions are always available. It is advisable to have at least one person trained in first aid and this may be a legal requirement.

The hair

Hair is constantly falling out and, along with dandruff, can result in contamination of food products by bacteria, especially *Staphylococcus aureus*. The hair should be shampooed regularly and completely enclosed by suitable head covering. Hairnets worn under hats and helmets are recommended. Combing of hair and adjustment of head covering should only take place in cloakrooms and should not be carried out whilst wearing protective clothing, as hairs may end up on the shoulders and then in the food. Hair grips and clips may also contaminate food and should never be worn outside the head covering. Scratching of the head should be avoided.

Jewellery and perfume

Food handlers should not wear earrings, watches, jewelled rings or brooches as they harbour dirt and bacteria. Furthermore, stones and small pieces of

metal are a potential physical hazard. They may end up in the food and result in a customer complaint.

Strong-smelling perfume, handcreams or aftershave are a potential chemical hazard and should not be worn by the food handlers as they may taint the food, especially food with a high fat content.

Smoking

Smoking and the use of tobacco is prohibited in food rooms or whilst handling open food because:

- of the danger of contaminating food from fingers which touch the lips and may transfer bacteria to food

- cigarette ends contaminated with saliva are placed on working surfaces

- cigarette ends and ash may contaminate the food

- it encourages coughing

- an unpleasant environment may be created for non-smokers.

Notices should not be ignored.

Legible notices should be displayed instructing food handlers who need to smoke to use specified locations and never to smoke in the food rooms.

Protective clothing

All food handlers should wear clean, washable, light-coloured protective clothing, preferably without external pockets. Press studs or Velcro fastening are preferable to buttons. Protective garments should be appropriate for the work being carried out and should completely cover ordinary clothing. Jumper and shirt sleeves must not protrude and, if short-sleeved overalls are worn, only clean forearms must be visible. Staff must be aware that protective clothing is primarily worn to protect the food from risk of contamination and not to keep their own clothes clean. Outdoor clothing and personal effects must not be brought into food rooms. Dust, pet hairs and woollen fibres are just a few of the contaminants carried on ordinary clothing. Lockers for outdoor clothing should be provided in non-food rooms.

The correct procedure must always be followed when putting on protective clothing. Head covering should always be put on first, followed by coats or boiler suits to avoid hairs getting on to the shoulders of protective clothing. Protective head covering should not be removed at breaks unless the protective overall or coat is removed first. The protective overall should always be removed before the head covering. Protective clothing should not be kept in toilets and, if practical, should be removed prior to using the toilet. Protective clothing should not be worn outside the food premises, not used to travel to and from work and not worn during lunch time sporting activities such as football or laying on the grass.

The use of different coloured protective clothing is recommended to distinguish between staff who handle only raw food and those who handle high-risk food. In addition, disposable protective clothing is becoming more widely available.

Aprons, if worn, should be suitable for the particular operation, light-coloured and capable of being thoroughly cleaned or disposable. Aprons which are torn or have badly-worn surfaces which create cleaning difficulties should be replaced. Facilities should be provided for cleaning waterproof aprons at various times during production and at the end of each working day. Cleanable hooks should be provided for hanging up aprons.

Suitable footwear should be worn to prevent slipping and to protect the feet. Boots may be provided for wearing in wet areas. They should be anti-slip, unlined and easy to clean. Suitable facilities should be provided for cleaning and storing cleaned boots.

Exclusion of food handlers

Supervisors must be aware that apparently healthy, symptom-free employees may be carriers of, and excrete, pathogenic bacteria. Laboratory testing cannot be relied on to detect small numbers of intermittently excreted pathogens. High standards of hygiene are

therefore the only way to prevent the contamination of food by an infected food handler. It is a legal requirement for food handlers to advise their supervisor if they are suffering from diarrhoea or vomiting and/or suspect they may be carrying a food poisoning organism.

Food handlers with food poisoning symptoms, such as diarrhoea or vomiting, or suspected of carrying foodborne organisms, e.g., because of close contact with a confirmed case of typhoid or consuming a meal known to have caused illness, must be excluded from any job which would expose food to risk of contamination. Where appropriate, the Environmental Health Department should be informed immediately so that an environmental health officer can carry out urgent investigations. The guidance from the Department of Health, "Food Handlers: Fitness to Work" states that any person who is excreting food poisoning organisms must not be allowed to engage in food handling until they have been free of symptoms for 48 hours, once any treatment has ceased, and have received medical clearance. However, it is critical that good hygiene, particularly handwashing, is observed.

If the supervisor has no confidence in the hygiene standards of a food handler who is a carrier of a food poisoning organism, even when symptom-free for 48 hours, they should not be allowed to handle high-risk food.

Food handlers returning from holidays abroad, particularly from countries with warm climates and suspect sanitation, should complete a short medical questionnaire. Even if they have fully recovered from symptoms of diarrhoea or vomiting experienced on holiday, they should be excluded from food handling until they have provided at least one negative specimen.

Food handlers with skin infections such as psoriasis, boils or septic cuts, respiratory tract infections, infection of the eyes or ears, dental sepsis or purulent gingivitis must also be excluded until medical clearance has been obtained.

Key points

◆ most food handlers will carry food poisoning organisms at one time or another

◆ high standards of personal hygiene are essential to avoid contamination of food

◆ hygiene training of food handlers will assist in the prevention of food poisoning

◆ frequent handwashing is essential

◆ cuts should be protected with brightly coloured waterproof dressings

◆ food should be handled as little as possible

◆ food handlers who are suffering from or are suspected of carrying infections, which may contaminate food, should be excluded until medical clearance has been received.

The storage of food is important to ensure adequate provision throughout the year and to overcome fluctuations in supply. However, failure to ensure satisfactory conditions of temperature, humidity, stock rotation and the integrity of packaging can result in problems of unfit or spoiled food and will, at the very least, result in a considerable reduction in shelf-life. Inadequate temperature control is the most common cause of food poisoning. Correct storage and good temperature control is therefore crucial to food safety.

Raw materials

Most raw food of animal origin, shellfish, vegetables, spices and some fruits may be contaminated with pathogenic microorganisms and should be considered as potentially hazardous. Inadequate cooking/processing or cooling, and contamination of high-risk foods from raw foods are common causes of food poisoning. Therefore, food premises must have adequate and suitable storage facilities to keep all raw materials satisfactorily. Furthermore, the quality and bacteriological condition of raw materials has a significant influence on the finished product. Unsatisfactory deliveries may introduce problems such as insects, rodents or mould into the production area.

To assist in demonstrating due diligence, should the need arise, and to ensure that deliveries meet the agreed specification, effective, documented checking systems are advisable. Systems required will depend on the type of product and the condition of other deliveries from the same source. Checks may include: quantity, temperature, date code and quality – with particular emphasis on damaged or discoloured packaging.

Perishable food must be checked quickly and removed to cold stores, freezers or refrigerators without delay. Unloading of vehicles should take place, as far as practicable, in covered bays screened from adverse weather. Raw food and high-risk food should be completely segregated to avoid risk of contamination. Non-food items and strong-smelling foods which may cause taint problems should normally be delivered separately. When unloading, batches of food should be clearly marked, if they do not already bear suitable markings, to ensure that they are used in strict rotation and to identify the date of delivery in the event of subsequent complaints.

Unsatisfactory deliveries should not be accepted.

Raw meat and poultry

Raw meat joints should be stored between -1°C and +1°C, with a relative humidity of around 90%. Joints should keep for up to a week, although processed raw meats and offals will have a shorter life. Products should not touch the wall surface. Only approved suppliers should be used.

Eggs

Eggs should be sourced from a reputable supplier and stored in a clean, dry place, at a constant temperature below 20°C (ideally between 10°C and 15°C) and used within three weeks of lay. Temperature fluctuations should be avoided. Stock rotation is essential and cracked or dirty eggs should be rejected.

Meat pies, pasties and sausage rolls

These products must be obtained from a reliable source and should preferably be stored under refrigeration. Temperatures of around 7°C, with good air movement, are recommended so that the pastry remains crisp. As these foods are cooked to temperatures as high as 90°C, very few bacteria survive. Consequently, they remain bacteriologically safe at higher refrigeration temperatures. However, stock rotation is important and such products should be sold on the day of production or the following day. Pies or pasties to which something has been added after baking should be stored at or below 5°C. Temperatures should be kept constant as fluctuations result in condensation and mould growth.

As these products may be consumed without further cooking they must never be stored with raw meat or vegetables. Strong-smelling foods, such as cheese, may introduce taint or mould problems. Price tickets must not be stuck into pies or any other food. If pies are to be sold hot from retail outlets they must be cooked thoroughly and, if stored, maintained above 63°C. Alternatively, pies may be microwaved as required. They must never be re-warmed.

Fruit and vegetables

Although each fruit and vegetable has its own optimal storage conditions, a general guide is to keep them in a cool room or a refrigerator. However, tropical fruits such as pineapples and bananas should be stored at 10°C to 13°C to avoid "chill injury". Care must be taken to prevent warm moist conditions and condensation which will encourage bacterial spoilage and mould growth. Low humidities and excessive ventilation result in dehydration and must also be avoided. Fruit should be examined regularly and mouldy items removed to avoid rapid mould spread. Transit wrappings, especially "non-breathing" plastic films, may need to be removed to avoid condensation.

Ice-cream

Ice-cream should be kept in clean, dedicated freezers. Ice-cream must not be stored with raw products. It should always be kept frozen and discarded if defrosted. Tubs should be used completely before fresh tubs are started and nothing should be placed on top of open tubs. Lids should normally be kept on. The texture of ice-cream is more temperature sensitive than other frozen foods and it may be held at -12°C before use.

Milk and cream

Milk and cream should be stored under refrigeration (below 5°C) and should be placed in the refrigerator or cold store as soon as received. Imitation cream should also be refrigerated. Crates of milk should not be stored below raw meat.

Flour and cereals

Large quantities of flour and cereals should preferably be stored in bulk containers. Lids must be tight-fitting. Large stocks of flour kept in original sacks must be stored clear of the ground and free from damp. Condensation may result in mould growth on wet flour and must be prevented. Regular cleaning of containers used for flour storage must not be overlooked. Frequent inspections, at least weekly, should be carried out for rodents or insects.

Canned foods

Canned goods should be examined regularly and blown or leaking cans must be rejected. They should be kept in cool, dry conditions. Acid foods should not be stored in opened cans within refrigerators, because of the acid attack, in the presence of oxygen, on the internal surface of the can. This can lead to metallic taint.

The shelf-life of canned foods

High-acid cans of fruit, such as prunes, rhubarb, tomatoes and strawberries, may blow if kept longer than recommended by the manufacturer. The acid juice attacks the tin and iron of the can, especially at the seams. Some large cans of meat, especially ham, may only have been pasteurized and therefore need to be refrigerated. If this is the case, the can will be clearly labelled.

On opening, can contents should be placed in a suitable plastic or stainless steel container, if not intended for immediate use. If the food is discoloured or has an unusual smell or texture, or the interior of the can is rusty or discoloured, the food must be rejected.

Wrapping and packaging

Packaging and wrapping materials must be stored in clean, dry areas where they are not exposed to risk of contamination.

Cling film

Cling film is useful for stopping food drying out and protecting it against contamination (special breathing films are available for raw meats). Under certain conditions, however, it can speed up spoilage and mould growth by trapping moisture. It is important therefore that:

- raw meat or wet food is unwrapped when removed from the refrigerator

- food wrapped in cling film is not left in bright light or sunlight.

Because of the risk of chemical migration, cling films should not be used where they could melt into food during heating, or for wrapping foods with a high fat content, unless manufacturer's advice indicates their suitability for this purpose.

Vacuum packing

Vacuum-packed food, and modified atmosphere packs, should be refrigerated, unless the labelling indicates otherwise. Immediately after opening a vacuum pack, the contents should be removed completely. Slightly darker colours of meat and the acid odour will disappear shortly after being removed.

Care must be taken to avoid puncturing packs, for example, with sharp bones or rough handling. Defective seams commonly result in the loss of pack integrity. However, air-tight vacuum packaging may blow if the contents ferment. It is advisable to purchase branded vacuum packs from reputable suppliers to avoid receiving low-grade meat of dubious origin. Unmarked packs without "use-by" dates should always be regarded with suspicion.

Damaged stock

All damaged stock should be segregated and thoroughly examined before use. If there is any doubt regarding the fitness of food it should be discarded, or the local Environmental Health Department may be asked for advice.

The greenhouse effect

Food, especially high-risk food, should not be stored in windows or in glass display cabinets which are exposed to direct sunlight. The heat within the cabinet will build up in the same way that it does in a greenhouse, providing conditions ideal for bacterial multiplication. The greenhouse effect may even occur in chill cabinets without proper chilled air circulation, and fluorescent tubes may exaggerate the problem.

Stock rotation

Satisfactory rotation of stock, to ensure that older food is used first, is essential to avoid spoilage and unnecessary wastage. Stock rotation applies to all types of food. Daily checks should be made on short-life perishable food stored in refrigerators whereas weekly examination of other foods may suffice. Stock which is undisturbed for long periods will encourage pest infestations. The rule is: "First in, first out". Written stock control records are recommended and are useful to assist a "due diligence" defence.

Codes

Stock rotation has been much easier since the advent of open-date coding but some products do not require a "use-by" or "best-before" date. In these cases, retailers should adopt their own code to identify the date of delivery. A colour code system is one of the easiest to use: a blue line for Monday; a red line for Tuesday; etc. A double coloured line should be used the following week. "Use-by" dates are placed on perishable, short-life products, whereas "best-before" dates are used on longer life products. Products with an expired "use-by" date should be considered as unfit, whereas those products with an expired "best-before" date are more likely to be of an unacceptable quality. The practice of selling old stock cheaply is not recommended. It is an offence to sell any food which is unfit or foods bearing an expired "use-by" date or to change this date.

Dry-goods stores

Rooms used for the storage of fruit and vegetables, dried, canned and bottled foods should be kept dry, cool (preferably between 10°C and 15°C), well lit, and well ventilated. They must be kept clean and tidy and spillages should be cleared away promptly. Rodent and bird-proofing should be maintained and any gaps in the fabric should be sealed. As far as possible food should be kept in rodent-proof containers. All goods should be stored clear of walls and floors to allow cleaning and pest control.

Non-food items, including cleaning equipment and chemicals, and strong smelling foods should not be stored in dry-goods stores. Packs of food should be handled carefully to avoid damage. Part-used packs should be resealed to prevent contamination. Alternatively, food may be transferred to clean containers with pest-proof lids.

REFRIGERATORS

Refrigerators should be readily accessible, and sited clear of heat sources unless they are designed for high-temperature environments. Ideally they should be in well-ventilated areas away from the direct rays of the sun. Multi-deck, open display cabinets should be sited clear of drafts from doorways, and ventilation and heating grills fitted in ceilings, which may result in significant increase in temperatures. High humidities should be avoided, as these will cause condensation on stored foods. The siting of all units should permit the cleaning of surrounding areas as well as the cooling coils. Regular maintenance and defrosting (where not automatic) should be carried out and door seals checked.

Cleaning should be frequent, taking in both exteriors, especially door handles, and interiors. Internal surfaces and fans should also be disinfected. Base plates and baffle plates should be removed to check for debris such as price tickets and packaging which can obstruct air flow and block drains in multi-deck units. Drip trays, if present, should be emptied and cleaned. Dust on evaporator coils and air ducts must be removed to maintain performance.

Defective refrigerator door seals should be replaced.

After cleaning and disinfection, units should be completely dried and brought to correct operating temperatures before being reloaded. Stock should be kept in back-up chill stores during cleaning operations. Food which experiences a significant increase in temperature, above 10°C for excessive time, due to breakdown or power cut should be destroyed.

Operating temperatures

The optimum temperature for multi-use refrigerators, in which high-risk foods are stored, is between 1°C and 4°C. Cook-chill foods with a maximum shelf-life of five days must be kept between 0°C and 3°C.

Hot food

Hot food, not intended for immediate consumption, should be cooled rapidly. It should not be placed directly into a refrigerator as this may raise the temperature of food already stored, as well as increasing the ice build-up on the cooling unit. Condensation may also occur on some foods, resulting in an unacceptable drip on to food stored below. However, depending on the amount of food and the capacity of the refrigerator, it

Ice build up on the cooling unit.

may be preferable to place a small amount of food which has cooled to around 50°C into a large capacity unit instead of leaving it in a warm environment for prolonged periods or overnight.

Contamination

It is essential that precautions are taken to avoid contamination. Raw food must always be kept apart from high-risk food. It is recommended that separate, clearly labelled units be used. If only one refrigerator is available, high-risk food must be stored above raw food. Shelves previously used for raw foods must not be used for high-risk foods without cleaning and disinfection. All foods should be adequately covered to prevent drying out, cross-contamination and the absorption of odour.

Packing and rotation of food

Refrigerators should not be overloaded and they need packing in a manner which allows good air circulation. A gap of at least 3cm should always be allowed between trays stored on slatted shelves. Food should not be placed directly in front of the cooling unit as this reduces efficiency. Non-perishables should not be stored in a refrigerator if this takes up valuable space. Good stock rotation is essential, and daily checks should be made for out-of-date stock.

Staff responsibilities

Staff should be given clear instructions on how to use refrigerators. They should be instructed to open doors as little, and for as short a time, as possible. The temperature of the refrigerator should be checked at least three times per day and records of readings should be kept. Spillages should be cleared up immediately.

The storage life of perishable food under refrigeration

Shelf-life varies according to the operating temperature of the refrigerator and the specific perishable food. For example, at 1°C, most vegetables will keep for at least two weeks, butter for two months and fresh beef up to a week.

Chilled display cabinets

Cabinets should be loaded correctly so that cold air inlets are not obstructed and load-lines are not exceeded. Only chilled products should be placed in display cabinets.

Radiant heat can have a significant effect on food stored in chilled cabinets, particularly on the upper shelves. Cabinets, therefore, should be sited away from heating units and high-intensity lights and out of direct sunlight.

Monitoring temperatures

Cabinet thermometer readings should be checked using an accurate digital or infrared thermometer. Indicating or recording thermometers are essential and premises with a large number of units will need automatic monitoring equipment and alarms to warn of unacceptable temperatures. If records indicate temperatures above prescribed limits, between-pack temperatures should be taken. If concern remains then probing of the food should be undertaken.

Infrared thermometers

Infrared thermometers, which work by measuring the amount of radiant energy, can be used to scan foods very rapidly. Any identified problems can be checked immediately with a digital thermometer. Additional advantages include the fact that it is non-destructive testing and there is no risk of cross-contamination. It is particularly useful for scanning retail cabinets, frozen food, deliveries and despatch as large consignments can be checked for hot spots.

Temperature/data loggers

Data loggers and printers will provide a variety of useful information about refrigerated storage including current temperature, maximum, minimum and trends of temperature over a specified period. Should temperatures rise above a predetermined level they can also trigger an alarm.

Cooking

Cooking is used to make food palatable and safe for immediate consumption. Core temperatures of 75°C are usually adequate to destroy food poisoning bacteria although some performed toxins and spores will not be destroyed. Lower temperatures for longer times may be equally effective. A disinfected digital probe thermometer should be used to check correct core temperatures have been achieved, especially for poultry and rolled joints.

Cooling of hot food

Rapid cooling of cooked foods to be chilled or frozen is extremely important. Bacteria may survive cooking as spores or even in the vegetative state and there is always a risk of contamination after cooking. By

Food must be cooled quickly.

◆ Air flow from a fan about 10cm from the food will increase heat transfer by a factor of 3 (food should be covered)

Although there is a potential hazard if food is cooled too slowly, the risk may be smaller than that from post-cooking contamination.

Blast chillers

This is equipment designed specifically for the rapid chilling of food. Usually, chilled air at 2°C to 7°C is circulated in a cabinet around the product. Some blast chillers use the vapour from liquid nitrogen and solid carbon dioxide. Some equipment can be set to hold foods after chilling, acting as a normal refrigerator. Alternatively, if suitable blast-chilling equipment is not available, hot food can be cooled rapidly in an otherwise empty freezer and taken out when safe temperatures have been reached, for storage in a refrigerator.

For cooling liquids, ice-cream freezers can be used and, for very large quantities, vacuum chillers are available.

whatever route bacteria enter the food, it is essential that their multiplication during cooling is minimized. It is usually recommended that food is cooled below 10°C in less than 1.5 hours. Practically, only blast chillers can achieve this. A more pragmatic standard adopted by the Food and Drugs Authority in America is to cool joints from 60°C to 21°C in two hours and from 21°C to 7°C within a further four hours. Ice water baths cool faster than cold air.

When cooling food, the following basic rules should be applied:

◆ minimize bulk – the smaller the size of the food, the faster it will cool

◆ maximize surface area – square or rectangular containers present greater surface areas than round containers. Shallow containers should be used instead of deep containers

◆ maximize differential – the greater the difference in temperatures between the product and its surroundings, the faster it will cool.

Distribution of high-risk food

Vehicles used for the distribution of high-risk food must always be insulated and preferably refrigerated, even for short journeys. Insulation of the roof and floor is just as important as the insulation of the walls. Properly-located thermometers should be fitted to all vehicles.

Vehicles must be maintained in a clean and tidy condition. Raw food should never be transported with high-risk food unless they are completely segregated to avoid any risk of contamination. Stacking of vehicles should facilitate sufficient air circulation around the food.

Deliveries of high-risk food

The temperature of food should be checked on arrival. Food requiring refrigerated storage should be rejected if above 8°C and frozen food rejected if above 12°C. Deliveries must be placed in cold storage as quickly as possible to avoid temperatures exceeding the above rejection temperatures.

THE STORAGE OF FROZEN FOOD

At temperatures of around -40°C, most frozen food should keep for several years without noticeable deterioration. However, most domestic and retail freezers operate at -18°C. At this temperature a gradual loss of flavour and a toughening of texture occurs. Above -10°C spoilage organisms commence growth and, together with enzymes, can cause serious problems including souring, putrefaction and rancidity.

All frozen food should be coded to enable the recall of suspect batches which have escaped manufacturing controls.

The storage of frozen food at retail premises

To ensure that customers receive the highest quality of frozen food, managers must:

◆ only use reputable suppliers

◆ reject deliveries above -12°C or which show signs of thawing or having been refrozen, for example, packs of peas which have welded solid

◆ not allow frozen food to remain at ambient temperatures for longer than 15 minutes. Food will, of necessity, be at ambient temperatures during unloading of deliveries and stocking display units from back-up stores

◆ not use display freezers for freezing fresh food, as they are only capable of maintaining the temperature of food which is already frozen

◆ ensure that display units are not filled above the load line

◆ carry out regular inspections of freezers and check temperatures at least daily but preferably more frequently. Electronic probe thermometers should be used to ensure the accuracy of the indicating thermometers which should be fitted to all units in an easily readable position

◆ ensure that back-up stores are fitted with strip-curtains or air blowers and the doors are opened as little as possible to avoid unacceptable fluctuations of temperature. Ice build-up on the walls or floor of units must not be allowed

◆ implement effective systems of stock control and stock rotation. It is advisable to code food on delivery to assist rotation

◆ ensure that food is not mishandled. Damage to packaging may result in loss of product, contamination and freezer burn. For similar reasons packaging, designed to protect frozen food, must not be removed.

Storage times

All food should be used within the time recommended by the manufacturer.

However, a general guide for food kept at -18°C is:

◆ vegetables, fruit and most meat up to 12 months

◆ pork sausages, offal, fatty fish, butter and soft cheeses upto 6 months.

Salad vegetables, non-homogenized milk, single cream, eggs and bananas should not be frozen. Cream can be whipped and stabilized to overcome the separation in desserts. The star marking system is used to indicate the temperature and storage times of food in a frozen storage compartment.

Freezing and refreezing

Freezing of food will not improve its quality. The slow freezing of food in domestic freezers results in the formation of large ice crystals which rupture cells, leading to a slight deterioration in quality, due to changes in the composition of proteins in the presence of enzymes. This deterioration is much more noticeable if food is thawed and refrozen, apart from the obvious dangers if the thawed food is maintained above 10°C for a considerable time. Large ice crystals are particularly noticeable in ice-cream which has been refrozen. However, food which has been frozen, thawed and thoroughly cooked may be refrozen quite safely, although flavour and texture will be altered and nutritional value lowered.

Effect of fluctuating temperatures

Clear plastic packaging of food may act as a greenhouse and the radiant heat from fluorescent tubes and air conditioning may increase the temperature of frozen food significantly. Fluctuations from 3°C to 18°C

have been observed with the lower temperatures only being achieved during the night when heat sources have been switched off.

Freezer breakdown

If the freezer breaks down or food becomes thawed, for example, due to a power failure, the food may occasionally be treated as fresh. In certain circumstances the food may be cooked and refrozen. If the food has a solid core of ice it may be safe to refreeze without cooking. If in doubt advice should be obtained from the local Environmental Health Department.

In the event of breakdown, the lid of the freezer should be left closed and the unit covered in newspapers and blankets until repaired. Food may remain frozen for at least two days in a well-stocked, well-insulated freezer.

Thawing of frozen food

Many foods taken from the freezer can be cooked immediately but poultry, joints of meat and other large items must be completely thawed before cooking. The manufacturer's instructions should always be followed. If food is not completely thawed, ice is likely to be present at the centre and the heat from subsequent cooking will be used to melt the ice and not to raise the internal temperature above that required to destroy pathogens.

Thawing at room temperatures (25°C to 30°C) may result in the multiplication of bacteria on the warm surface of food, whilst the centre remains frozen. Thawing in a small refrigerator, operating at 1°C to 4°C, can be even more hazardous, if the food does not thaw completely. A 10kg turkey will take several days to thaw and the surfaces of the refrigerator, and high-risk food, may become contaminated with thawed liquid containing pathogenic bacteria. Thawing of frozen poultry is best carried out in a thawing cabinet or at 10°C to 15°C in a well-ventilated area entirely separate from other foods or in cold running water. Thawed food which is stored under refrigeration, as it is not required for immediate use, should be marked with a new date code.

Rules for handling frozen poultry
◆ segregate from high-risk food

◆ thaw completely in a cool room at less than 15°C or in a thawing cabinet. Clean, cold running water is preferable to thawing in warm kitchen temperatures or in refrigerators with limited space. Poultry will be ready for cooking when the body is pliable, the legs are flexible and the body cavity is free from ice crystals

◆ remove giblets

◆ once thawed keep in the refrigerator and cook within 24 hours

◆ cook thoroughly and cook the stuffing separately

◆ all utensils and surfaces used for the preparation of raw meat and poultry should be thoroughly cleaned and disinfected before being used for high risk food. It is preferable to use separate work surfaces

◆ eat straight after cooking or maintain above 63°C or, if the bird is carved cold, cool it quickly and store in the refrigerator. As with all meats refrigerated storage is essential within 1.5 hours

◆ avoid handling the cooked bird unnecessarily.

COOK-CHILL
Cook-chill is the name given to a catering system in which food is thoroughly cooked and then chilled rapidly in a blast chiller to a temperature of 3°C or below within 1.5 hours. The food is stored between 0°C and 3°C until required for reheating. The food is usually produced in a central production unit (CPU) and transported to satellite kitchens for regeneration (reheating).

There are usually eight stages in a cook-chill system:
◆ bulk storage

◆ preparation

- cooking to at least 75°C

- portioning, packaging and labelling

- blast chilling

- storage at or below 3°C

- distribution at or below 3°C

- regeneration to at least 75°C and serving.

The following benefits are claimed for the cook-chill system

- cost-effectiveness – fewer staff, reduction in overtime, shift and weekend working, central purchasing, better utilisation of equipment and reduced floor space

- better staff conditions and less work in unsociable hours. Staff turnover is usually reduced

- flexibility – orders for meals can be accepted at much shorter notice

- more accurate portioning and less wastage

- improved consistency, quality and palatability compared with meals kept hot, above 63°C, for long periods. Complaints of dried-up and overcooked food should not occur.

Cook-chill demands considerable management and supervisory skills and considerable forward planning. In order to ensure the safety of cook-chill the following rules should be observed:

- good quality raw materials
- good design to ensure continuous workflow from raw material to finished product. Cross-contamination must be avoided
- controlled thawing of frozen ingredients
- the implementation of HACCP or hazard analysis
- high standards of hygiene, especially personal hygiene
- food cooked, without delay, to a minimum temperature of 75°C
- food portioned and chilled to below 3°C within two hours of cooking
- hygienic food containers utilized and date marked
- the refrigerated store should maintain food at between 0°C to 3°C and should be fitted with indicating thermometers and alarms
- the maximum life of the food is five days, including the day of production and the day of consumption
- should the temperature of the food exceed 5°C it should be eaten within 12 hours, if the temperature exceeds 10°C during storage or distribution it should be destroyed
- refrigerated vehicles are preferred for distribution but pre-chilled insulated containers may suffice for short journeys
- food must be regenerated as soon as possible when removed from storage
- a centre temperature of at least 75°C should be achieved using effective heating units. Service should commence within 15 minutes and temperatures should not drop below 63°C.

COOK-FREEZE

The first four stages of cook-freeze are the same as cook-chill, namely bulk storage, preparation, cooking and portioning, packaging and labelling. The fifth stage is blast-freezing. Pre-cooked, lidded packs are loaded on to trolleys which are wheeled into tunnel-type blast-freezers which reduce the temperature to -20°C in less than 90 minutes. Rapid freezing is essential to avoid the formation of large ice crystals which result in poor texture and loss of nutritional value on regeneration. The frozen containers are kept at -20°C and may be stored for up to 12 months. The exact number of meals required can

be removed from storage on demand and regenerated to a temperature of at least 75°C in serving kitchens using, for example, forced-air convection ovens.

REHEATING AND HOT HOLDING

Reheating food presents a major potential

Thorough reheating of food is essential.

hazard in that bacterial growth may occur during the heating-up phase and during any subsequent storage, if sufficiently high temperatures are not reached and then maintained. Generally, food should be reheated as rapidly as possible, to a temperature of 82°C and then held at 63°C or above, until served.

To ensure adequate reheating, bulk should be minimized and, to ensure rapid penetration of heat, "surround" systems may be used, such as specialist regeneration ovens. Microwave ovens are a successful and efficient means of reheating, providing the food has a high water content. However, domestic models should not be used in commercial practice. Commercial convector-microwave ovens are particularly useful.

Liquid products, such as soups, should be brought to the boil and kept boiling for several minutes before use, to ensure destruction of toxins. The hot liquids may then need cooling before they can be served, to avoid scalding

Hot holding

A variety of equipment is available for keeping food hot, pending service. Liquids, semi-liquids and particulate products, such as vegetables and ready-to-eat portions of meat, may be kept in bains marie. These should always be brought up to operating temperature before use, and should not on any account be used for reheating foods. In water baths, checks should be made to ensure that the water levels are kept high. Topping-up should be with hot or boiling water. Container sizes should be matched to the water depth, limiting the amount of product which is above the water level.

Hot cupboards and hot plates may be used for storing reheated products. The latter are particularly valuable when used in conjunction with heating light arrays, but care should be taken to ensure that foods are kept fully in the lit areas, which corresponds with the areas exposed to the radiant heat.

On no account should any food, which has been cooled and then reheated, be then cooled again for further use. If a food, which has been through the full cycle of cooking, cooling and reheating, with or without subsequent hot-holding, remains unsold, it should be disposed of.

Key points

◆ raw food is likely to be contaminated with pathogenic microorganisms and should be considered as potentially hazardous

◆ raw food should always be stored and prepared separate from high-risk food

◆ vacuum packs should be stored under refrigeration

◆ satisfactory stock rotation is essential to avoid spoilage and waste food. Food must not be sold after its "use-by" date

◆ refrigerators should usually operate between 1°C and 4°C

◆ a core temperature of 75°C is recommended for cooking most foods

◆ hot food must be cooled rapidly. Although joints may take up to eight hours to cool to 3°C

◆ freezers should operate at -18°C

◆ frozen poultry and large joints must be completely thawed prior to cooking

◆ if food is stored hot it should be kept above 63°C

◆ if food is reheated a temperature of 82°C is recommended.

Immediately vegetables and fruit are harvested, fish taken from the sea or animals slaughtered, they start decomposing (spoiling). There are two ways in which this can occur:

◆ by the action of natural chemicals (enzymes) already in the food. These are known as autolytic (or self-splitting) enzymes

◆ by the action of enzymes from bacteria, moulds and yeasts. These are released by the organisms to break down the food so that it can be absorbed by them.

Spoilage usually starts with aerobic and facultative anaerobes. Then, as the oxygen is used up, obligate anaerobes take over. Moulds and yeasts tend to cause spoilage when the conditions do not favour bacterial growth. Signs of spoilage include discolouration, off odours and taste, slime and changes to the texture.

How fast food spoils depends on the condition of the food, the pH, water availability, temperature, oxygen, the presence of inhibitory substances (preservatives) and the type and number of spoilage organisms present.

Insects or vermin, and parasites, can also spoil food. So can some chemicals which,

even at very low levels, can cause unacceptable taint. Contamination, and the action of oxygen (oxidation), can cause deterioration. Even excessive cold can cause damage by extracting water from the food, a fault known as freezer burn.

Foods which are most prone to spoilage are known as "perishable". These include meat, poultry, fish, dairy products, fruit and vegetables. Foods, such as sugar, flour and dried fruit, are unlikely to be affected by spoilage unless they are handled badly, for example, by storing under damp conditions. These are often described as stable or "non-perishable".

The presence of mould usually results in food having a musty odour and flavour and, although usually considered harmless, increasing concern is being expressed about fungal toxins known as mycotoxins.

The acidity of fruit ensures that most primary spoilage is caused by moulds and yeasts which are able to multiply at higher acidity than bacteria. Thus, vegetables stored in vinegar, such as beetroot, may be attacked by yeasts. Yeast spoilage of food can often be detected by the alcoholic taste and smell and the presence of bubbles in liquid.

Moulds are responsible for most of the spoilage of baked products, especially bread and pies. As mould spores are destroyed by normal cooking temperatures, the spoilage usually arises from airborne spores and contact with contaminated surfaces after cooking.

Rope in bread and other bakery products is caused by a spore-forming bacterium in the flour. Affected bread becomes yellow or brown and develops a fruity, sickly smell and a soft sticky texture. Chemical preservatives are used to prevent rope.

Staleness of bread usually develops with prolonged holding, due to physical changes in the carbohydrates. Refrigeration increases the rate of staling, however, staling does not occur during frozen storage at -18°C.

Rancidity

Rancidity is the term used to describe the breakdown of fats or fatty substances. It occurs when the fats are broken down into free fatty acids by naturally occurring enzymes, known as lipases. These can also be produced by microorganisms. Heating may destroy lipase-producing bacteria but not any lipase already formed and rancidity may still occur.

Rancidity may also occur as a result of the interaction between fats and oxygen, often in the presence of copper or iron contamination. The prolonged cold storage of fatty fish, bacon and pork results in rancidity unless vacuum packed.

FOOD PRESERVATION

Preservation is the treatment of food to prevent or delay spoilage and inhibit growth of pathogenic organisms which would render the food unfit. Preservation may involve:

◆ the use of low temperatures or high temperatures

◆ moisture reduction

◆ the use of chemicals

◆ acid fermentation

◆ controlled atmospheres and the restriction of oxygen(vacuum packing)

◆ smoking

◆ irradiation.

Food preservation.

FOOD PRESERVATION BY THE USE OF LOW TEMPERATURES

This form of preservation is primarily to prevent spoilage by microorganisms, the enzyme-producing activity of which is slowed down or arrested by low temperatures. Temperatures used may be:

◆ above freezing (refrigerator)

◆ at freezing (commercially used with chilled beef)

◆ below freezing (freezer).

Temperatures above freezing

Refrigerators, operating at between 1°C and 4°C, are suitable for the short-term storage of most perishable foods. Most common pathogenic organisms stop growing below 5°C. Some can continue to grow down to about -2°C, although the growth rate is slow. Certain spoilage bacteria, and moulds, can also cause spoilage at refrigeration temperatures.

Temperatures below freezing

As well as stopping enzymes working, freezing reduces the moisture available for bacterial growth. It also destroys some bacteria, including pathogens, and a gradual reduction occurs during storage. Some parasites can also be destroyed by freezing. However, bacterial spores and toxins are generally unaffected.

Moulds and yeasts are more likely to grow on frozen food than bacteria as they are better able to withstand the reduced water availability and the low temperatures. In practice very few organisms grow below -10°C. On thawing, however, surviving bacteria can grow rapidly, compensating for those destroyed, especially if food reaches temperatures of 20°C or higher.

Before vegetables are frozen they must be blanched by dipping in hot water for a short period, approximately one minute. Blanching destroys enzymes which produce off-odours and flavours, and reduces the bacterial load. It also fixes colour, removes trapped air and softens some vegetables, which helps packing. Overblanching will result in excessive loss of vitamin C.

During the freezing process, ice crystals are formed. The slower the rate of freezing, the larger are the ice crystals formed, which can damage certain foods. To avoid this, quick freezing techniques are used.

Most foods will keep for prolonged periods in a freezer, although a recommended shelf-life is given because of loss of texture, flavour, tenderness, colour and overall nutritional quality.

Foods must be properly wrapped to avoid loss of moisture from the surface, i.e. freezer burn. The oxidation of food is slower at -18°C and this also assists in preservation. However, vacuum packing is essential to extend the shelf-life of frozen food susceptible to oxidative rancidity, for example, bacon.

Freezing systems

There are several commercial systems used to freeze food. Air-blast freezing is the commonest. It uses static tunnels where trolleys of boxed product, such as beef and cakes, are passed through. Solid continuous-belt freezers are used for fish fillets, patties and pizzas. Air circulates around the food at temperatures of -30°C to -40°C. Plate freezing is used for food packed in flat cartons, for example, fish blocks and ready-meals The cartons are placed between narrow metal shelves in which a very cold refrigerant circulates, so ensuring freezing. For products like peas, a process called fluidized-bed freezing can be used. The food is moved along a tunnel on a perforated tray, borne along by a cushion of freezing air forced up from below. Each item is individually quick frozen. In cryogenic freezing, food is sprayed with, or dipped into, a refrigerant such as liquid nitrogen. This is very quick, although more expensive than conventional techniques.

FOOD PRESERVATION BY THE USE OF HIGH TEMPERATURES

Heat treatment is used to destroy both

spoilage and pathogenic organisms and so preserve food. However, heat-resistant bacteria, some toxins and spores may survive. Furthermore, unless very high time/temperature combinations are used, some normal bacteria will survive. The number depends on the initial loading, the strain of organism, the acidity and the presence of protective substances such as proteins and fats.

To prevent recontamination of food after processing, suitable packaging is used, for example, bottles or cans, which can also prevent the multiplication of surviving bacteria. Alternatively, or additionally, products are kept refrigerated.

Pasteurization

Pasteurization involves heating food at a relatively low temperature for a short time, sufficient to kill target pathogens while keeping changes to the food at a minimum. A slight reduction in vitamins and nutritional value will occur. The process is commonly applied to milk, which may be heated at 72°C for 15 seconds and immediately cooled to below 10°C. The actual time and temperature combination chosen depends on the type of food and must be sufficient to destroy vegetative pathogens and most spoilage organisms, although *Lacto bacillus* can survive. Liquid egg can be pasteurized at 64.4°C for at least 2.5 minutes. Following pasteurization, the treated egg must satisfy the alpha-amylase test. Toxins and spores generally survive pasteurization.

Sterilization

Sterilization involves the destruction of all microorganisms. This is sometimes difficult to achieve, so processes are often designed only to destroy viable organisms,

i.e. not spores. In this case food is considered "commercially sterile". This means that organisms surviving treatment will be of no significance under normal methods of storage. Low-acid canned food is given such a treatment. Sterilization temperatures normally exceed 100°C and are usually achieved by means of steam under pressure.

The main advantage of sterilization is prolonged shelf-life. The main objections are a lowering of nutritional value, including loss of vitamins, and a marked difference in texture and flavour.

Ultra heat treatment (UHT)

The ultra heat treatment of milk is a technique used to extend its shelf-life without the changes caused by sterilization. Nutritional value is similar to that of pasteurised milk. Milk is heated to a temperature of not less than 135°C for one second before filling aseptically into sterile containers. This reduces the amount of caramelization and also enhances keeping quality. UHT milk will keep for several months without refrigeration.

Cooking

Cooking is a form of preservation but is essentially used to make food more palatable and safe for immediate consumption. Temperatures achieved during cooking are usually sufficient to ensure an effective reduction, or the elimination, of vegetative pathogens, although some pre-formed toxins and spores may be unaffected. In some cases, cooking activates spores and a significant multiplication of vegetative bacteria may occur during subsequent cooling. Internal temperatures of at least 75°C should be achieved to ensure bacteriological safety, although heating food to a lower temperature for longer periods of time may be equally as effective.

Cooked products, such as vegetables, will deteriorate more rapidly than raw products, and other methods of preservation must be used to prolong shelf-life if stored, for example, refrigeration, freezing or canning.

Canning

Unlike most other forms of preservation the food inside the can remains an ideal medium for bacterial growth. It is therefore imperative that:

◆ the heat process destroys all anaerobic pathogenic and spoilage microorganisms

◆ the closure of the can precludes the entry of microorganisms; and

◆ the post-process handling of the can prevents damage and subsequent contamination.

The most heat-resistant pathogenic organism is *Clostridium botulinum* and this bacterium will not grow below a pH of 4.5. Consequently, when determining the heat process, regard must be had for the pH of the can contents. All foods with a pH of less than 4.5 are known as acid foods and those with a pH of more than 4.5 are termed low-acid foods.

Fruits have a pH of less than 4.5 and consequently only receive a relatively low pasteurizing heat process. Vegetables and meats have pHs much higher than 4.5 and they are given a process known as a "botulinum cook" to render them

commercially sterile.

Before canned food is heat processed it is normally prepared in some way. The actual process of preparation will vary depending on the food type but the following flow chart shows the usual processes involved.

A schematic diagram of canning operations

Raw materials
Fruit & Vegetables – washing, peeling, grading and blanching.
Meats – cleaning, honing, cutting and curing.
Fish – washing, gutting and brining.
Milk products – filtering, standardizing and homogenizing.

Inspection (including metal detection and magnets)
Cans inverted and washed

Filling (normally hot)
Mixed packs

Brine/syrup

Exhausting to remove all residual air

Sealing to create vacuum
Double seam to hermetically seal the can

Processing: The "BOTULINUM COOK"
Using retorts, hydrostatic pressure vessels or horizontal cookers

Cooling
Chlorinated water

Drying

Labelling, casing and coding

Storage/Sale

The minimum safe thermal process for a low-acid canned food is one which would reduce the chance of survival of one spore of *Clostridium botulinum* to less than one in 10^{12}. This is achieved by ensuring the core of the food reaches a minimum of 121°C for three minutes, or an equivalent time and temperature combination. After the heating process the cans must be cooled with chlorinated water. The greatest care must be taken after heat treatment, especially whilst the can is still warm and wet, and before the sealing compound has hardened. Bacteria are capable of being sucked into visually satisfactory cans through microscopic holes in the seams. If these bacteria are spoilage or pathogenic organisms, problems will occur. Warm, wet cans must not be handled.

Pasteurized canned foods

As discussed earlier, most low-acid canned foods are processed to a minimum standard of the "botulinum cook". However, some foods if fully processed would be inedible. One example of this is canned cured ham. This product only receives a pasteurization process (a centre temperature of about 70°C). This means that chilled storage is essential to ensure its safety.

MOISTURE REDUCTION AS A MEANS OF PRESERVATION

All microorganisms need moisture to multiply. Dehydration reduces the amount of available water and thus prevents growth. However, some bacterial spores will germinate on the reconstitution of the dried product. Although yeasts and moulds usually grow at lower moisture levels than do bacteria, mould spoilage is also prevented, as is enzyme activity.

Provided dried foods are stored in suitable air-tight packs, and kept dry, they will keep for a considerable period of time.

Sun drying was the earliest method of dehydration and is still practised in hot climates, for example, for drying currants, raisins and figs. Artificial drying is quicker and normally more effective than natural means. Unfortunately, food undergoes irreversible changes to the tissue structure during drying, which affects both texture and flavour.

Artificial drying techniques include the use of hot air, for example in tunnel drying, fluidized-bed drying, roller drying and spray drying. Changes in protein structure and flavour can be reduced by using warm air, as in accelerated freeze drying. The choice of technique often depends on the type of foodstuff and the degree of dehydration required. Blanching of vegetables must be carried out before drying to obviate enzyme activity during storage.

In spray drying, a solution, paste or slurry is dispersed as small droplets into a stream of hot air. The small droplets result in a rapid loss of moisture and a large proportion of the colour, flavour and nutritive value of the food is maintained. However, because the evaporative cooling effect keeps the temperature of the droplets low, a pasteurization process is usually required prior to spray drying.

In roller drying, the food is turned into a paste which is dried on a heated drum and scraped off. Generally, product quality is inferior to spray-dried product. For fruits and vegetables, a tunnel drier, 10 to 15 metres long is used. Trays of product are passed through it while hot air is blown across the trays. This continuous process leads to a gradual loss of moisture.Total removal of moisture may not be necessary. The remaining water forms a strong solution with salts and soluble proteins This water remaining is not available to microorganisms.

Accelerated freeze drying
Food is frozen quickly and then lightly heated under vacuum. Ice in the food is then extracted as water vapour, a process known as sublimation. The processes minimizes the effects of drying and the product reconstitutes better.

CHEMICAL METHODS OF PRESERVATION
A wide range of chemical additives is available for food preservation and may he used to prevent microbial spoilage, chemical deterioration and mould growth. As high concentration of some chemicals, such as sulphur dioxide and sodium nitrate are poisonous, the use of additives is strictly controlled by legislation and maximum permitted levels are usually specified. Preservatives used include:

(1) Salt
Salt has been used as a preservative since ancient times. Its effectiveness depends on the concentration, contamination levels, pH, temperature, protein content and the presence of other inhibitory substances. In use, it may be rubbed into meat or, as brine, injected into the muscular tissue. It can also be an ingredient in the manufacture of sausages and used to preserve fish.

Some microorganisms are salt-tolerant but this tolerance is usually decreased by lowering the temperature or the pH.

Moulds are less affected by salt. Staphylococci will grow in relatively high salt concentrations and are often associated with food poisoning from semi-preserved salted meats.

In preservation the use of salt, with the addition of other chemicals such as sodium nitrate, is termed curing Its use for flavour or colouring is termed brining.

(2) Nitrates and nitrites
Sodium nitrate and sodium nitrite salts are used in curing meat. They help retain colour and reduce spoilage. They are also essential in such products as pasteurized ham to stop the production of botulinum toxin, by preventing the germination of spores.

Traditionally, salt and nitrate solutions were injected into meat, which was then immersed in brine to enable salt tolerant bacteria to convert nitrate to nitrite. Currently, nitrites tend to be used direct as they are much more effective than nitrates. The effectiveness of curing salts depends on various factors, including the pH of the meat, the number and types of microorganisms present and the curing temperature.

(3) Sugar
Sugar acts in a similar manner to salt but concentrations need to be about six times higher. It is commonly used for jam and other preserves, candied fruit and condensed milk. Certain types of cake have increased shelf-life due to the effect of sugar.

(4) Sulphur dioxide/sulphite
Sulphur dioxide may be used in gaseous or liquid form or as a salt. It is an

antioxidant and also inhibits growth of bacteria and moulds. It is used in some foods to prevent enzymatic browning. Sulphur dioxide is also used in wine, beers, fruit juice and comminuted meat products, including sausages, where it is allowed up to 450µg/g. Apart from reducing the growth of spoilage organisms, sulphur dioxide also limits the growth of salmonellae.

(5) Pickling/acidification
This process involves using an acid such as acetic acid, i.e. vinegar, to acidify the food to create an environment in which microorganisms will not multiply. The acidification process is controlled so that the pH of each part of the product drops below 4.5.

(6) Sodium and calcium propionate
Propionates are active in low-acid foods and very useful to prohibit mould growth. They are used in bread, cakes, cheese, grain and jellies.

(7) Antibiotics
These chemicals have a preservative role in addition to their normal function. Their use is strictly controlled by regulations to avoid the build-up of resistance by pathogenic organisms. An example of an antibiotic used for preservation is nisin, added to some cheeses and canned foods. Nisin is heat-resistant but is destroyed during digestion and should not cause problems of pathogen drug resistance.

FERMENTATION
Fermented foods are produced by the activtities of bacteria, yeasts or moulds and include cheese, yoghurt, salami, sauerkraut, pepperoni, bread and soy sauce. The fermentation process involves the use of starter cultures, for example lactic acid bacteria added to milk to produce yoghurt. Lactic acid bacteria ferment carbohydrates such as glucose to produce lactic acid which lowers the ph to preserve the food. Yeast fermentation produces carbon dioxide and ethanol.

CONTROLLED ATMOSPHERES
One of the simplest food preservation methods is to change the atmosphere around the food. This is termed modified atmosphere packaging (MAP). The proportion of the gases normally present around a product is modified to contain, for example, lower levels of oxygen and higher levels of nitrogen and carbon dioxide. This slows down the growth of many spoilage organisms and extends shelf-life. MAP should also be combined with correct chilled temperature control in order to guarantee the control of microbial proliferation.

The restriction of oxygen
The development of oxidative rancidity and the growth of strict aerobes such as moulds can be prevented by vacuum packing, although sufficient oxygen normally remains in vacuum packs of meat to facilitate the growth of some aerobes. Complete removal of oxygen allows the growth of anaerobes such as *Clostridium perfringens*. Vacuum packs of cooked meat must be stored under refrigeration to achieve a reasonable shelf-life.

SMOKING
Smoking is applied primarily to meat and fish, after brining or pickling, by suspending the food over smouldering hardwoods such as oak and ash. It is often used only to enhance flavour. Smoking

also has some dehydrating effect and there may be some preserving action due to the presence of bactericidal chemicals in smoke. Most non-sporing bacteria will be destroyed but moulds and *Cl. botulinum* type E may survive, especially in low salt concentrations Smoked products should, therefore, be refrigerated at 3°C or below.

Cold smoked food should be treated as raw and hot smoked food should be considered as high-risk food.

Another way of adding a smoke flavour to the food is to spray a liquid, produced by trapping smoke in water, onto the food. The preserving effect is limited and the food is not dehydrated.

FOOD IRRADIATION

This form of preservation involves subjecting the food to a dose of ionizing radiation. It is an effective and safe method of extending shelf-life. It destroys parasites, insects including eggs, bacteria, moulds and yeasts. However, microbial spores and toxins remain unaffected at the levels used. Foods most commonly irradiated outside the U.K. include chicken, fish, prawns, onions, potatoes, spices and strawberries. Irradiation may be used as part of a continuous or batch process.(In the UK only spices may be subject to irradation)

Preservation using irradiation has the same limitations as many other preservation techniques. Vitamins may be destroyed and enzymes are not deactivated. Other disadvantages include the encouragement of oxidative rancidity in fatty foods, the possible production of free radicals in food that stimulate a range of chemical reactions, and the softening of some fruit.

Key points

◆ spoilage of food commences when vegetables and fruit are harvested, animals are slaughtered and fish are removed from the sea

◆ spoilage occurs because of the action of enzymes, bacteria, moulds, yeasts and pests

◆ refrigeration of perishable foods slows down spoilage

◆ food preservation prevents or delays spoilage and inhibits the growth of pathogenic organisms

◆ preservation may involve: the use of low or high temperatures; dehydration; chemicals; controlled atmospheres and physical methods

◆ foods should be cooked to a centre temperature of at least 75°C.

A well-planned layout and the use of satisfactory building materials is essential to achieve high standards of hygiene. The size of the premises must facilitate efficient operation and the site must be large enough to accommodate possible future expansion.

Selection of a suitable site

The site must have sufficient services, i.e. electricity and gas, water supply and effluent disposal, and be accessible for delivery and waste disposal. It should not be liable to flooding or unacceptable contamination from chemicals, dust, odour or pests. Potential for noise generation should be considered if there are nearby residential premises.

General principles of design

To achieve a satisfactory design, the following principles should be considered:

◆ clean and dirty processes must be separated to minimize the risk of contamination. Where possible:
   a. work areas should be segregated into pre-cook and post-cook;
   b. a separate area should be provided for de-boxing and unwrapping raw materials;

◆ workflow should be continuous and progress in a uniform direction from raw material to finished product. Distances travelled by raw materials, utensils, food containers, waste food, packaging materials and staff should be minimized

◆ facilities for personal hygiene and disinfection of small items of equipment should relate to working areas and process risks

◆ where appropriate, suitable facilities must be provided for temperature, humidity and other controls

◆ the premises must be capable of being thoroughly cleaned and, if necessary, disinfected at the end of production

◆ insects, rodents and birds must be denied access and harbourage

◆ yard surfaces and roads within the boundary of the premises must have a suitable impervious surface with adequate drainage, and provision made for refuse storage

◆ suitable provision must be made for staff welfare, including cloakroom and, if necessary, canteen and first aid facilities.

THE CONSTRUCTION OF FOOD PREMISES

It is essential that the correct materials are chosen for all internal finishes and that they are properly fixed or applied. Materials should be non-toxic, durable and easy to maintain and clean.

Ceilings

Suspended ceilings are advantageous as horizontal pipework and services can be concealed in the ceiling void. They are normally constructed from a metal lattice incorporating cleansable panels. Aluminium backed and faced fibre-board has proved successful in many food factories. Flush-fitting ventilation grilles and lighting will often be provided.

Solid ceilings should be well insulated, smooth, fire resistant, light-coloured, and coved at wall joints. Finishes should be washable. A non-flaking emulsion may be suitable. Special attention must be paid to ceiling finishes above heat and/or steam-producing appliances such as ovens, sinks and retorts. Canopies and separate extraction units may be fitted in these areas.

Ceiling height will vary depending on the type of operations being carried out but should be high enough to provide satisfactory working conditions and allow the installation of equipment.

Walls

Smooth, impervious, non-flaking, durable, light-coloured wall surfaces are required which must be capable of being thoroughly cleaned and, if necessary, disinfected. Internal solid walls are preferable to those with cavities.

When constructing factories, it can be advantageous to use modular buildings, of standard dimensions, with the actual production areas built inside the external structure, leaving clear walkways outside these areas, but within the overall structure. The "building within the building" can be fabricated from modular panels of the type used for cold-store construction.

Wall surfaces in use include resin-bonded fibre glass, ceramic-faced blocks, plastic panelling, epoxy resin, glazed tiles with water-resistant grouting and rubberized paint on hard plaster or sealed brickwork. Some paints incorporate a fungicidal additive. Galvanized steel, aluminium and stainless steel are also used, and plastic sheeting is popular.

Wall or floor stops are needed to prevent doors damaging wall surfaces, and wall corners should be protected. Crash rails should be used if trolleys are likely to damage wall surfaces, although large, angled fillets to the wall-floor junctions can also prevent trolley impact.

Pipework and ducting should be bracketed at least 150mm from walls to facilitate cleaning. All lagging to pipes must be smooth and impervious. Pipes passing through external walls must be effectively sealed to prevent the ingress of pests.

Windows and doors

Any windows should either be fixed on north-facing walls to reduce glare and solar heat gains, or treated with solar film to counteract heat gain. Cleansable, well-fitting fly-screens must, where necessary, be fitted to opening windows. Windows should be constructed to facilitate cleaning and any internal window sills should be sloped to prevent their use as shelves.

Doors should have smooth, non-absorbent surfaces capable of being thoroughly cleaned. They should be tight-fitting and self-closing. Door handles and finger-plates should be capable of disinfection. Swing doors with kick-plates are preferable to handles. External doorways should, where necessary, be proofed against the entry of insects, and metal kick-plates should be provided to prevent gnawing by rodents. Clear plastic strips can be used to protect openings.

Floors

Regard must be had to initial cost, durability, performance and safety. In food premises, floors should be durable, non-absorbent, anti-slip, without crevices and capable of being effectively cleaned. Where appropriate they must be resistant to acids, grease and salts and should slope sufficiently for liquids to drain to trapped gullies or channels; a slope (or "fall") of 1 in 60 is the minimum recommended. The junctions between walls and floors should be coved.

Suitable flooring includes epoxy resin, granolithic (concrete incorporating granite chippings), welded anti-slip, vinyl sheet and slip-resistant ceramic or quarry tiles.

Services

These include gas, electricity, water supplies, drainage, lighting and ventilation.

Gas supplies

Supply pipes should always be mounted clear of the floor and never so close to other pipes as to restrict access for cleaning. Flexible connections, to facilitate removal of equipment for cleaning purposes, are recommended.

Electrical supplies

Adequate numbers of power points should be available for all electrical equipment. Cut-out switches for power circuits should be accessible and separate from lighting and ventilation supplies, so that cleaning can take place in safety. Separate cut-out switches should be provided for refrigeration equipment.

Controls should be fixed clear of equipment to avoid becoming dirty or wet during cleaning. Removable electrical components assist cleaning and are advantageous. Surface-mounted electrical wiring should be protected by waterproof conduits. All switches should be flush-fitting and waterproof (especially in production areas).

Water supplies

Cold water supplies for use with food, for cleaning equipment or surfaces or for personal hygiene must be potable. (Of drinking water standard). They should not be fed via an intermediate tank unless chlorinated; mains supplies are preferable.

Water heating provisions should be able to supply hot water at a target discharge temperature of 60°C, although higher system temperatures may be required to avoid legionnaires disease. In this case, mixer taps will be needed to avoid scalding. In hard-water areas, provision for softening should be made.

Non-potable water must be conveyed in identifiable systems which have no connection with, nor any possible reflux into, the potable water system. An external water supply should always be available.

Drainage

Premises should have an efficient, smooth-bore drainage system. Drains and sewers should be adequate to remove peak loads quickly without flooding. Sufficient drains should be installed to facilitate effective cleaning of rooms by pressure jet cleaners or other means. Channels or trapped gullies may be used. Grease traps, if fitted, should be large enough to allow adequate time for fat to separate and should be emptied regularly.

The direction of flow should be from clean areas to dirty areas. Toilets should feed into the system after food rooms. Inspection chambers should be placed outside food rooms but if interior location is unavoidable they must be airtight, i.e. triple seal, bolt down. All drainage systems must be provided with sufficient access points to allow rodding in the event of blockages. Petrol interceptors may be required for yard drains.

Drains should be constructed to inhibit the harbourage and movement of vermin. All external rainwater fall-pipes should be fitted with balloon guards to prevent rodent access. Circumference guards should be fitted around all vertical pipes fastened to walls, to prevent rodents climbing up them.

Ventilation

Sufficient ventilation must be provided to produce a satisfactory, safe working environment and to reduce humidities and temperatures which would encourage the rapid multiplication of bacteria. Normally, ambient temperatures should be below 25°C. Natural ventilation often needs supplementing by mechanical ventilation to ensure effective air circulation and adequate air changes. Extract ventilation should always flow from a clean to a dirty area. Its function is to prevent excessive heat build-up, condensation, dust, steam, and to remove odours and contaminated air. The source of input air must always be checked to ensure contaminants are not brought in to food rooms.

Steam-producing equipment, such as cookers, boilers and blanchers, should be provided with adequately-sized canopies. Provision of lower heat-emitting equipment such as pressure vessels and microwave ovens, and upgrading insulation on ovens will reduce heat production.

Lighting

Suitable and sufficient lighting must be provided throughout food premises, including store rooms, passageways and stairways, so that employees can identify hazards and carry out tasks correctly.

Artificial lighting is often preferred to natural lighting because of problems of solar heat gain, glare, shadows and flying insects entering open windows. Recommended illumination levels are as follows: 150 lux in storerooms and 500 lux in preparation areas. Fluorescent tubes, fitted with diffusers to prevent glare and product contamination in the event of breakage, are recommended.

Handwashing facilities

Adequate facilities for handwashing and drying should be provided wherever the process demands. In particular, a suitable number of basins or troughs should be sited at the entrance of food rooms to ensure all persons entering wash their hands. Wash-hand basins must be easily accessible, should only be used for washing hands and should not be obstructed. All basins and troughs,

Inaccessible wash-hand basins.

preferably made of stainless steel, should be connected to drains by properly trapped waste pipes.

Cleaning and disinfection facilities

Where appropriate, adequate facilities for the cleaning and disinfection of utensils, crockery, cutlery, glasses and equipment should be provided. These facilities will normally be constructed from stainless steel. Twin sinks are preferable to facilitate washing and disinfecting/rinsing. Sinks should be freestanding so that they can be removed easily after unscrewing the lower trap joint, freeing the waste pipe. "Sterilizing" sinks and units should be capable of operating at 82°C.

Separate sinks must be provided for food preparation and equipment washing if the volume demands it. In small operations the same sink may be used if there is no risk to food safety. Exclusive food sinks may be provided with cold water only.

Sanitary conveniences and washing facilities

All new premises should be provided with adequate staff sanitary accommodation, adequately ventilated and lit. Rooms containing sanitary conveniences must not communicate directly with a room where food is processed, prepared or eaten. Internal wall and floor surfaces should permit wet cleaning.

Foot-operated flushing devices are recommended. Doors to intervening spaces and sanitary accommodation should be self-closing and clearly illustrate the sex of the user. Suitable and sufficient washing facilities must be provided at readily accessible places. In particular, facilities must be provided in the immediate vicinity of every sanitary convenience and supplied with clean hot and cold or warm water, liquid soap and appropriate drying facilities.

Cloakrooms and lockers

Adequate accommodation for outdoor clothing and footwear, not worn by the staff during normal working hours, must be available. Such articles must not be stored in a food room unless in suitable cupboards or lockers provided only for this purpose. Adequate facilities for drying wet clothing should also be provided.

The storage and disposal of waste

Waste disposal systems must be planned, along with other services, when food premises are designed. Refuse collectors should not have to enter food rooms or dining areas.

Waste food should be kept separate from paper and cardboard packaging. In some instances, waste may be stored under refrigeration pending collection, for example, bones in butchers' shops. It is preferable for all waste food to be removed from food premises at least daily and general refuse to be removed at least twice a week.

Suitable facilities must be provided for the storage of waste externally, prior to removal from the establishment. Dustbins or bulk containers are commonly used, although skips and compactors are more appropriate for food factories. Compactors vary from units similar to a large dustbin to refuse-sack compactors and skip rams.

Dustbins should be stored clear of the ground, for example, on tubular steel racks, to facilitate cleaning and removal of spillages. All receptacles should be capable of being cleaned and provided with suitable tight-fitting lids or covers to prevent insects, birds and rodents gaining access.

Dustbins must be kept clean.

The refuse area must have a well-drained, impervious surface which is capable of being kept clean. Stand-pipes, hoses and, possibly, high-pressure sprayers should be provided for cleaning purposes. Covered areas to protect refuse from the sun and rain are recommended. Satisfactory provision should be made for the disposal of liquid food waste such as oil.

Refuse areas should not be too far from food rooms to discourage their use but they should not be too close to encourage flies to enter the food rooms. They should not be sited next to the main food delivery entrance. Covered ways between refuse areas and food rooms are useful to protect staff against inclement weather.

Perimeter areas

It is recommended that a concrete path, at least 675mm wide, abutting the external walls should be provided around all food buildings. This removes cover for rodents and enables early signs of pests to be discovered, for example, rodent droppings. Paths should be kept clean, free of vegetation and inspected regularly. A smooth band of rendering, around 450mm, at the base of external walls will discourage rodents from climbing.

Whenever possible, a perimeter fence should be constructed around food premises to deter unauthorized entry. Areas within perimeter fences must be kept clean and tidy. Rubbish, old equipment and weeds must not be allowed to accumulate or provide harbourage for insects or rodents.

Kitchen design

The layout of a well-designed, commercial kitchen has three main characteristics:

- clearly identified and separated flows

- defined accommodation, specific to the purposes allocated

- economy of space provision (commensurate with good hygiene practice).

The unit should also afford management personnel easy access to the areas under their control and good visibility in the areas which have to be supervised. Space is needed for management function and for equipment such as telephones and computers.

Flows
Four separate flows need to be considered: the food being produced; personnel; containers, utensils and equipment; and waste/refuse. Product flows should be subdivided into high-risk and contaminated (raw food) sections. Clear segregation should be maintained between the two. As far as practicable, flows should be unidirectional, without backtracking or crossover.

Accommodation
Accommodation should be sized according to operational need when at maximum production. Essentially, the working areas, stores, the equipment and its relative spacing should all be determined and laid out to suit the operation.

Areas should be allocated according to environmental compatibility; hot functions with hot, dirty with dirty, wet with wet, dry with dry, defined overall by segregation between high-risk and contaminated food handling.

Equipment required for specific functions should be grouped and accessible, in order to avoid excessive walking and the temptation to take shortcuts. Wash-hand basins should be strategically located to ensure that operatives entering food preparation areas wash their hands.

Size
There should be a minimum of circulation and dead space, commensurate with the efficient functioning of the unit. Size should be neither too small nor too large; there are penalties in the over-provision of space as much as there are problems with too small a provision.

The size of the kitchen can only be determined when its exact purpose and function have been defined. Items to take into consideration include:
- the state of raw materials, for example, ready prepared or not

- the extent of the menu and number of sittings

- the equipment used, for example, microwave ovens

- the amount of dishwashing. Disposable plates, etc. may be used.

THE DESIGN AND CONSTRUCTION OF EQUIPMENT
The hygienic design of equipment is necessary to comply with legislative requirements, avoid product contamination and to facilitate cost-effective cleaning and, if necessary, disinfection.

Poorly-designed equipment, which cannot be dismantled, may be uncleanable, incapable of being chemically disinfected

Plan of a well designed kitchen incorporating principles of continuous workflow and segregation of clean and dirty processes (not to scale).*

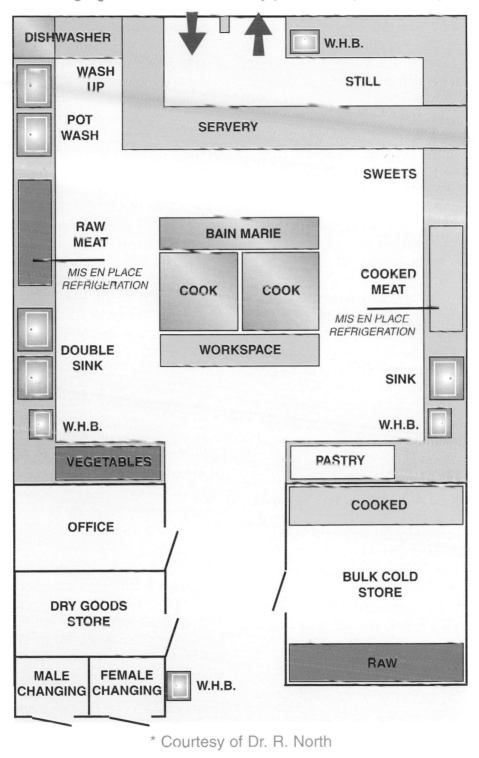

* Courtesy of Dr. R. North

and may result in product contamination by pathogenic bacteria. Even if equipment can be dismantled, unhygienic design may make cleaning and disinfection prohibitively expensive.

The legal requirements

The Food Safety (General Food Hygiene) Regulations, 1995 require all articles, fittings and equipment with which food comes into contact:

◆ to be kept clean

◆ be so constructed, of such materials and maintained in such condition and repair as to minimize risk of contamination

◆ enable thorough cleaning and, where necessary, disinfection.

Furthermore, equipment must be installed in a way which allows the surrounding area to be cleaned.

The Supply of Machinery (Safety) Regulations, 1992 (as amended in 1994)

The Regulations require that new machinery used for preparing and processing foodstuffs carries a CE marking and must be designed and constructed to avoid health risks and in particular:

◆ contact materials of foodstuffs must satisfy the conditions set down in the relevant directives. Machinery must be designed and constructed to facilitate cleaning

◆ all surfaces and joints must be smooth, without ridges or crevices which could harbour organic materials

◆ projections, edges and recesses should be minimal. Continuous welding is preferable. Screws and rivets should not be used unless technically unavoidable

◆ contact surfaces must be easily cleaned and disinfected. The design of internal surfaces, angles, etc. must allow thorough cleaning

◆ cleaning residues must drain from equipment surfaces, pipework, etc., there must be no retention in voids

◆ the design should prevent organic accumulations or insect infestation in uncleanable areas, e.g. by the use of castors or alternatively, sealed bases

◆ lubricants must not come into contact with any product.

In addition, equipment manufacturers must provide accurate information on recommended products and methods of cleaning, disinfecting and rinsing.

Construction materials

Materials in contact with food must be non-toxic, non-tainting and constituents from their surfaces must not migrate into the food or be absorbed by the food in quantities which could endanger health. Materials must have adequate strength over a wide temperature range, a reasonable life, be corrosion and abrasion resistant and be easily cleaned and disinfected. In most meat plants, the use of wood is forbidden except in rooms used for the storage of hygienically packed fresh meat.

The most widely used material is food-grade stainless steel. Some plastics may be suitable, but must be approved for food use. Aluminium should be avoided, as should copper and zinc. Handles of knives, brushes and other equipment should all be made from cleansable materials such as polypropylene or high-density stainless steel.

Surfaces should be non-porous, continuous, non-flaking and free from cracks, crevices and pits. Surfaces will need to retain a satisfactory finish throughout their life including anticipated abuse and normal wear and tear. Joints should be made by welding or continuous bonding to reduce projections, edges and recesses to a minimum.

Equipment exterior

The external surfaces of equipment must avoid ledges and dust traps, for example, round legs are preferred to rectangular. It is important to avoid recessed corners, sharp edges, unfilled seams, uneven surfaces and hollows and projecting bolt heads, threads, screws or rivets that cannot be cleaned. Inaccessible spaces, pockets and crevices where product may accumulate must be absent.

Fixing and siting of equipment

Equipment must be sited so that there is sufficient space to facilitate access to all external and internal surfaces and, where required, to allow for rapid dismantling and reassembly. Machinery may be mounted on coved, raised platforms of concrete to facilitate cleaning. Where necessary,

additional space may need to be provided. The bases and lower parts of machines, including motors and gears, may be difficult to clean and consequently collect dust and spillages which make ideal breeding sites for insects. Skirting or cover plates tend to trap dust.

Where practicable, and with due regard for safety, equipment can be mobile to facilitate its removal for cleaning.

Mobile equipment.

Drainage

All pipelines, vessels and equipment should be self-draining, not only to enable liquid deriving from foodstuffs to be discharged but also for cleaning and rinsing fluids.

Preparation surfaces

Preparation surfaces should be jointless, durable, impervious, the correct height and provide a firm base on which to work. If materials other than stainless steel are used, for example, food-grade plastic, care should be taken to seal the edges and gaps which may harbour food scraps. They must be able to withstand frequent and repeated cleaning and disinfection without any premature deterioration, pitting or corrosion.

Cutting boards

A variety of non-absorbent materials for cutting boards is now available, including good quality polypropylene. However, some are unsatisfactory.

A good board should not split or warp and it is advantageous if it can be passed through a dishwasher.

Dishwashers should be used for cleaning and disinfecting cutting boards.

As yet no ideal replacement has been found for hardwood chopping blocks. However, these should be maintained in good condition and used solely for chopping or sawing raw meat. A common colour-coding system for cutting boards involves using:

red: for raw meat **blue: for fish**

green: for salad **yellow: for high-risk food**

white: for dairy produce **brown: for raw vegetables**

Contamination

To avoid cross-contamination, it is important that the same equipment is not used for handling raw and high-risk products without being disinfected. To prevent the inadvertent use of equipment for high-risk and raw food the use of different colours and/or shapes is advantageous. Colour coding may be extended from knives and cutting boards to include washing facilities, trolleys, protective clothing, cloths and packaging material.

The cleaning of equipment

All operating instructions and procedures must be clearly communicated to the equipment users and cleaners. The equipment should be capable of being cleaned and, if necessary, disinfected safely, thoroughly and rapidly without the need for skilled fitters and specialized tools. If dismantling is necessary this must be achieved relatively easily, as should reassembly.

Sharp edges are a serious hazard for cleaners. A reluctance to clean equipment because of poor design will result in a lowering of hygienic standards. Hinges should be capable of being taken apart for cleaning. Angle iron is difficult to clean and tubular construction is preferred, open ends to tubular legs must be sealed.

Key points

- good design and the use of satisfactory building materials are essential to achieve high standards of hygiene
- clean and dirty (raw and high-risk) processes must be separated to minimize risk of contamination

- workflow must be continuous in a uniform direction from raw material to finished product

- surfaces and finishes must be non-toxic, non-flaking, durable and easy to maintain and clean

- all food premises must have potable cold water supplies

- premises must be well lit and ventilated with satisfactory provision for drainage and waste management

- adequate facilities for handwashing, cleaning and disinfection must be provided

- equipment must be kept clean and in good condition to minimize risk of contamination

- colour coding of equipment assists in minimizing the risk of contamination.

In any food business, soiling of both surfaces and equipment is unavoidable. The type and extent of soiling will vary considerably but, whatever the operation, it is essential that residues are not allowed to accumulate to levels which expose food to the risk of contamination.

The benefits of cleaning

Cleaning is an essential and integral part of a profitable food business. In addition to satisfying legal requirements, cleanliness will:

◆ ensure a pleasant, safe and attractive working environment which will encourage effective working and reduce the risk of accidents to both staff and customers

◆ promote a favourable image to the customer and assist in marketing the business

◆ remove matter conducive to the growth of microorganisms so facilitating effective disinfection and reducing the risk of food poisoning and spoilage

◆ remove materials that would provide food or harbourage for pests and prevent early discovery of infestations

◆ reduce the risk of foreign matter contamination and thereby obviate customer complaints

◆ prevent damage to, or a reduction in, the efficiency of equipment and services, and reduce maintenance costs.

Problems caused by ineffective or negligent cleaning

Negligent cleaning may achieve a satisfactory physical appearance but can also result in hazardous bacterial contamination, for example, cleaning from raw to high-risk areas. Selection of the appropriate cleaning chemicals often requires expert technical advice as the use of the wrong chemicals, or the right chemicals at the incorrect strength, temperature or contact time, may have serious financial consequences. This not only applies to direct costs relating to product, equipment and premises but also, the cost of effluent treatment. It is also important that all cleaning chemicals are stored separate from food in a locked chemical store. Ineffective or negligent cleaning may result in:

◆ microbiological hazards, contamination and a poor quality product which may lead to a reduction in shelf-life, customer complaints, loss of reputation, court proceedings, food poisoning, redress from suppliers and loss of sales

◆ wastage of food and production re-runs

◆ chemical hazards, including taint and other forms of food contamination

◆ corrosion and premature replacement of equipment

◆ production breakdowns, for example, following the incorrect use of caustic soda which has removed grease from bearings

◆ unacceptable deterioration of floor surfaces and drainage systems

◆ physical contamination hazards from worn and defective cleaning equipment.

Energy in cleaning

Cleaning is defined as "the systematic application of energy to a surface or substance, with the intention of removing dirt". Energy is available for cleaning in three distinct forms:

kinetic energy: physical – manual labour; mechanical – machines; turbulence – liquids (cleaning in place);

thermal energy: hot water; and

chemical energy: detergents.

Normally, a combination of two or more energy forms is used. Manual labour is the most expensive and chemical energy the most economic, although adequate contact time is also important. The correct energy balance is essential for cost-effective cleaning.

Detergents

Detergents are chemicals, or mixtures of chemicals, made of soap or synthetic substitutes, which are used to remove grease or other soiling and promote cleanliness. They are available as powders, liquids, foams or gels. Detergents should be harmless to operatives and equipment, non-toxic, odourless and tasteless, i.e. non-tainting.

The reduction of surface tension enables detergent solutions to penetrate dirt and grease and lift them from the surface to form a suspension which can then be rinsed away.

Cost-effectiveness of the cleaning operation depends on the correct mix of the following:

◆ choosing the correct chemical

◆ applying it at the optimum temperature and concentration

◆ allowing it time to function

◆ using it with the correct equipment.

Cleaning equipment

Consistent, high standards of cleanliness will only be achieved if the cleaning tools have been specifically manufactured for the stringent demands of the food industry. Correct choice is essential if operatives are to avoid recontamination of a cleaned surface with dirt or bacteria or, in the case of brushes, the contamination of product with bristles. The quality and cleanliness of tools which touch surfaces in direct contact with food is particularly important.

The use of colour coding for cleaning equipment, for example, handles of brushes, bristles and cloths used in high-risk situations, with different colours being used in raw and high-risk food areas, assists in reducing the risk of cross-contamination and reinforces hygiene training relating to the need to separate raw and high-risk food.

Brushes

Brushes constructed from materials such as high-density polypropylene for stocks with bristles of polyester or rilsan give improved performance and resistance to wear. They are capable of withstanding boiling water and the normal cleaning chemicals used throughout the food industry. Wood and natural bristles must be avoided and worn out brushes must be replaced. As brushes become worn they become less effective, they discolour and bristles are more likely to drop out. Blue coloured bristles are often preferred as they are more easily detected if they become loose. Nylon filaments are porous and quickly lose their stiffness in wet conditions, and inferior materials may even distort in hot water.

Mechanical equipment

These include floor scrubbers, rotating washers, power washers, air lines, steam cleaners, vacuum pick-ups, dishwashing and tray-cleaning machinery. Judicious use of mechanical equipment can significantly reduce labour requirements, but considerable care should be taken in selection to ensure that it is suitable for the use intended.

Gel or foam cleaning can improve performance.

DISINFECTION

Although cleaning may remove large numbers of microorganisms, it does not kill them. The process which is used to destroy microorganisms is known as disinfection. Normally, disinfection is carried out after cleaning, although sometimes the two processes are combined, when a sanitizer is used.

Disinfection is "the destruction of microorganisms, but not usually bacterial spores; it may not kill all microorganisms but reduces them to a level which is neither harmful to health nor the quality of perishable foods". Disinfection may be achieved by using heat, chemicals, irradiation or UV radiation. The term sterilization relates to the destruction of all microorganisms and spores and is normally unnecessary and impracticable to achieve within the food industry.

Heat disinfection

The application of heat is the most reliable and effective means of destroying microorganisms, although it may not be the most practical, especially for surfaces. It is used in machines, such as dish-washing machines, with a water temperature of 88°C and a contact time varying from 15 to 90 seconds. It is also used in sterilizing units where articles may be fully immersed for a period of 30 seconds at 82°C.

Steam disinfection

Lances producing steam jets may be used to disinfect machinery or surfaces which are difficult to reach. Steam-cleaned equipment is self-drying.

Steam disinfection of a can opener.

Chemical disinfection

Disinfectants suitable for use in the food industry are limited to those which, when used correctly, will not, at the concentrations used, have a deleterious effect on equipment, personnel or food. Types of chemical disinfectants available include: chlorine release agents, such as bleach; quaternary ammonium compounds; and alcohols.

Where to disinfect

Disinfection is usually only necessary for those surfaces where the presence of microorganisms, at the levels found, will have an adverse effect on the safety or quality of the food handled. Disinfection should normally be restricted to:

◆ food-contact surfaces

◆ hand-contact surfaces

◆ cleaning materials and equipment.

As microorganisms are rarely mobile and need to be physically carried onto food, the disinfection of non-food contact surfaces, such as floors and walls, is rarely necessary. Surfaces not directly coming into contact with food, but which are frequently touched by food handlers, need disinfecting to avoid the build-up of microorganisms on hands.

Hand disinfection

Hand disinfection increases the risk of dermatitis and is only necessary in aseptic conditions or to protect food handlers such as fish filleters from developing septic cuts. In the majority of food handling situations frequently washing the hands properly in warm water, using a liquid soap, is quite satisfactory. If hand disinfection is considered necessary it should be carried out after normal hand washing. Hand disinfectants should be fast-acting, dry rapidly and contain ingredients to protect the skin.

Disinfection of cleaning materials and equipment

Cleaning equipment is often an important vehicle of contamination and should be disinfected frequently. Normal machine laundering at 65°C or above, in the case of cloths and towels, will achieve this.

Disinfection frequency

In most operations, contamination by microorganisms takes time to build up to a significant level unless extraneous contamination is introduced by poor operational practice. Under normal circumstances, therefore, disinfection can correspond with cleaning intervals dictated by visual soiling or with work cycles. However, intermediate disinfection may be needed to counter the effects of inherent bad practice, such as the use of the same surface or equipment for cooked and raw meats.

PROCEDURES AND METHODS OF CLEANING

Whatever the location, industry, soiling type or circumstances, cleaning and disinfection comprises six basic stages:

◆ pre-clean: sweeping, wiping or scraping off loose debris, pre-rinsing and/or pre-soaking

◆ main clean: applying detergent and loosening of the main body of dirt

◆ intermediate rinse: removal of loosened dirt, chemical neutralization of cleaning agent residues

◆ disinfection: destruction of residual microorganisms

◆ final rinse: removal of disinfectant residues

◆ drying: removal of final rinse water.

In light-soil conditions, the pre-clean may be combined with the main clean and disinfection can take place in combination with the main clean using specific chemicals known as sanitizers. (This becomes a three stage process, i.e. main clean/sanitize, rinse and dry. Where there is no risk of taint the rinse may be unnecessary.) Drying can either be natural, as in air drying, or physical, using disposable paper towels, hot air or a clean dry cloth.

Manual dish washing

Manual dish washing is only recommended for washing-up in catering premises, public houses and retail outlets selling high-risk foods, when suitable dishwashing machines are not available. It also applies to food-processing, packing and distribution plants where small items are handwashed. Thermal disinfection is most effective if double sinks are used but a suitable chemical disinfectant, such as hypochlorite in a tablet form may be used, to minimize condensation problems and health and safety risks. However, the rinse water should still be hot enough to allow air drying. The full, six-stage procedure should always be followed:

◆ remove any heavy or loose soil by scraping and rinsing in cold water

◆ place articles in the first sink in detergent solution at 53°C to 55°C, scrub with a nylon brush and/or wipe with a clean cloth to loosen dirt residues

◆ re-immerse in the first sink to wash off loosened dirt

◆ place articles in the second sink to rinse off detergent

◆ leave for sufficient time at a high enough temperature to ensure rapid air drying. Baskets for disinfecting purposes should be maintained in good condition and inspected regularly. They should be loaded so that all surfaces of crockery and equipment are fully exposed to the rinse water. Hollow items such as cups should be placed on their side

◆ remove articles, allow to drain and evaporate dry on a clean, disinfected surface.

A rinse aid may be added to the rinse water to promote smear-free drying. Items should then be removed and stacked in a clean, protected area ready for re-use. Containers and pans should be stored inverted to minimize the risk of contamination.

Mechanical dish washing

Mechanical dish washing is preferable to, and often more economic than, manual washing, provided the machine is used according to the manufacturer's instructions. Machines, in addition to cleaning, are also a highly efficient means of disinfecting small items of equipment and should be used for articles such as the removable parts of slicing machines, polypropylene cutting boards and other items which come into contact with high-risk foods, provided that no damage to the item will result. The sequence is as follows:

- remove excess food into suitable waste bins; if necessary pre-soak or spray, unless the machine is fitted with a pre-wash cycle

- pack articles in a neat, orderly fashion so that items do not overlap, place in the machine and operate the wash cycle of hot detergent solution (49°C to 60°C), unless automatic

- operate the rinse cycle (82°C to 88°C), with injection of rinse aid

- remove racks, allow cleaned items to drain and evaporate dry.

As a rule of thumb guide to the efficiency of a machine, if items coming out are too hot to handle and dry rapidly to a clean, smear-free finish, then the machine is operating correctly.

Cleaning a cooked meat slicing machine

Pre-clean:

- switch off power socket and remove the plug

- set the slice thickness control to zero

- dismantle the machine, pre-clean and pass removed parts through the dish-washing machine. Alternatively, thoroughly clean removed parts in a sink using detergent and hot water at 55°C and then disinfect in second sink or using a chemical disinfectant

Where the machine is of a type that has a removable blade, a blade guard must be fitted before the blade is removed. Cleaning may then commence, with the proviso that no person may clean a slicer or other dangerous machine unless they have reached their eighteenth birthday and have been properly trained

- clean and disinfect the machine carriage using clean cloths, taking particular care with the electrical parts.

Post-clean:

- Reassemble the machine very carefully to avoid possible accidents

- Disinfect parts handled or otherwise contaminated

- Check the guards are properly fitted, reconnect the power and switch on the machine. Test run to check safe working. This procedure is vital because accidents have been caused by guards having been improperly fitted after cleaning. If any adjustments have to be made, the machine should be switched off and disconnected and the test run repeated

- Switch off the machine, disconnect the plug and cover with a freshly laundered tea towel or other suitable covering

- Supervisor to check.

Cleaning schedules

Cleaning schedules must be clearly and concisely written, without ambiguity, to ensure that instructions to staff are easy to follow and result in the objective of the schedule being achieved.

Written schedules should specify:

◆ what is to be cleaned

◆ who is to clean it

◆ when it is to be cleaned (frequency)

◆ how it is to be cleaned

◆ the time necessary to clean it

◆ the chemicals, materials and equipment to be used

◆ the cleaning standard required

◆ the safety precautions to be taken

◆ the protective clothing to be worn

◆ who is responsible for monitoring and recording that it has been cleaned.

Supervisors should ensure that, after each cleaning session, all items specified in the schedule have been cleaned satisfactorily and any equipment that has been dismantled is safe to use.

Key points

◆ effective cleaning and disinfection of food premises and equipment is essential to secure food safety

◆ negligent cleaning results in cross-contamination and may be a contributory factor in food poisoning outbreaks

◆ detergents are used to remove dirt and grease

◆ disinfectants are used to reduce microorganisms to a safe level

◆ staff involved in cleaning must be trained

◆ disinfection of food and hand-contact surfaces is essential

◆ cleaning equipment must be cleaned and disinfected after use

◆ cleaning schedules are essential to ensure effective cleaning and will assist a due diligence defence.

Cleaning schedules should prevent dirt and dust build-up and other cleaning problems.

Pest control is essential to prevent the spread of disease, although there are many other reasons for controlling pest infestations of food premises, including:

◆ to prevent the contamination of food by rodents or birds which may result in food poisoning. Rodents are scavengers and will feed on refuse, waste and unfit food. Rats often live in sewers and in close association with animals. They often carry food poisoning bacteria, such as salmonellae, both inside and outside their bodies and on their feet and in their mouths. When entering food premises, they can easily transfer food poisoning bacteria to food and food-contact surfaces from their fur, feet, mouths, urine and droppings

◆ to prevent contact with rat urine which may result in Weil's disease

◆ to prevent the wastage of food by contamination, and losses due to pest damage of packaging

◆ to avoid the costs associated with loss of production, recall of contaminated food or defending criminal or civil action as a result of selling contaminated products

◆ to prevent damage caused by gnawing. Electrical fires, burst pipes and subsidence, caused by burrowing, may all result from rodent infestation

◆ to comply with the law and avoid possible closure of the food business

◆ to avoid losing customers who object to pest infested premises or the sale of contaminated food

◆ to avoid losing staff who will not want to work in infested premises.

The common pests found in the food industry include:
◆ rodents: rats and mice

◆ insects: flies, wasps, cockroaches, psocids, silverfish, stored product insects and ants

◆ birds: mainly feral pigeons and sparrows

◆ mites.

Rodents
The two most common rodents encountered in food premises are the brown rat and the house mouse. The black rat is rarely encountered.

The brown rat
This is the predominant rat in the United Kingdom. It usually lives in burrows in the soil, especially beneath buildings, but may also be found in sewers, food stores, on farms and rubbish dumps. The brown rat is omnivorous but prefers cereals. One pair of adult rats can produce hundreds of offspring within a year but fortunately

many do not survive. It is essential to destroy lone invaders of food premises as a pair of established rats can soon become a major infestation.

The house mouse

The house mouse is normally found living in buildings which provide it with harbourage, warmth, food and nesting materials. The house mouse is omnivorous and a pair of adult mice can produce 2,000 young within a year, with the help of their offspring.

Signs of infestation

Certain members of staff should be specifically trained to identify evidence of pests. Cleaners are ideally suited for this purpose and should look for signs both inside and externally. Signs of infestation include:

◆ droppings : if very recent they are shiny and soft

◆ the animals themselves, either dead or alive

◆ gnawing marks and damage, for example, holes in sacks

◆ holes and nesting sites

◆ rat runs in undergrowth or smears around pipes

◆ smear marks from the animals coat

◆ the loss of small amounts of food

◆ footprints in dust.

Insects

Insect pests can attack and destroy large amounts of food which becomes contaminated with bodies, webbing and excreta. Furthermore, cockroaches and flies may transmit food poisoning organisms to high-risk food. No food is completely safe from insect attack, however, beans, cereals, flour and dried fruits are among the most susceptible to infestation.

Flies

Many types of fly can cause problems in the food industry including the housefly, the bluebottle and the fruit fly. Many pathogens have been isolated from flies, including salmonella, *E. coli O157*, campylobacter, listeria and rotavirus. Flies infect our food in four ways:

◆ to feed they vomit partly digested food from the previous meal

◆ they continually defecate

◆ they carry bacteria on the hairs on their body and legs

◆ pupal cases, eggs, maggots and dead bodies end up in our food.

Typical breeding sites for houseflies are refuse and decaying organic matter. The female housefly lays around 600 eggs and it takes less than two weeks to go from egg to maggot to pupa to adult in warm weather.

Blowflies usually breed on decaying matter of animal origin, especially meat.

Fruit flies generally occur in bakeries or fruit canning factories and beer cellars, and some lay their eggs in unwashed milk bottles. Control usually involves removal of the breeding material.

Wasps

Wasps may contaminate food by transferring bacteria from their legs or bodies. They are a major nuisance in premises such as bakeries, during the late summer.

Cockroaches

The two species of cockroach widely distributed in the United Kingdom are the Oriental Cockroach and the German Cockroach.

The Oriental cockroach

The most frequently encountered cockroach species in the UK. Adults grow to about 24mm long and are shiny dark brown to black. They can climb rough vertical surfaces, such as brickwork, and are frequently found in cellars, kitchens, bakeries, hotels and drains.

The eggs are laid inside a case and take about two months to hatch at 25°C but this period is extended in cooler conditions. The female can produce over 150 eggs in its lifetime and it takes between six and 12 months to reach the adult stage in heated buildings with good food supplies.

The German cockroach (Steam Fly)

The adult grows to about 15mm long and is yellowish brown. It can climb smooth painted walls and prefers the warm moist conditions found in kitchens, bakeries and especially ships' galleys. The female can produce around 300 eggs in its life span of three to 12 months.

German cockroach.

Cockroach habits

Cockroaches live in groups and are omnivorous, nocturnal insects that give off an unpleasant characteristic odour. During the day they usually hide in cracks and crevices and their presence is usually detected by faecal pellets or their smell. Neither species fly. Over 40 pathogenic organisms have been isolated from cockroaches including food poisoning organisms.

Psocids or Booklice

Psocids are small (1mm to 2mm) cream, light brown or dark brown insects which are omnivorous and commonly infest flour, grain, nuts, chocolate, fish and meat products. They also feed on moulds and yeasts and infestations may be associated with packaging materials and pallets. The presence of booklice usually indicates conditions of high humidity.

Stored product insects

This is a large group of insects which attack foodstuffs in storage, transport and manufacture. It includes beetles, weevils, moths and their larvae. Dried products, cereals, flour, beans, and nuts may all be attacked.

Pharaoh's ant

Pharaoh's ants are light yellow and approximately 2mm in length. Infestations usually occur in permanently heated buildings, especially hospitals, bakeries, hotels and residential property where they are often found in seemingly impenetrable food containers. All kinds of food may be attacked, although there is a preference for sweet and high protein food. Nests are difficult to detect and destroy. Physical transmission of pathogens to food is possible as they may visit drains, excreta and soiled dressings.

Bird pests

Birds which commonly gain access to food premises are sparrows and feral pigeons, although starlings occasionally cause problems. Warehouses and large food factories are prime targets although bakeries and supermarkets may also be affected.

Reasons for control

- to prevent the contamination of food or equipment by droppings, bodies, feathers and nesting materials

- to prevent the transmission of food poisoning organisms

- to remove sources of insect and mite infestation provided by nests, excreta and the birds themselves

- to prevent blockages of gutters which may result in flooding and expensive maintenance

- to prevent defacement of buildings (bird droppings produce an acid which attacks stone)

- to prevent roosting on fire escapes and similar structures, which may result in a safety hazard for human occupants

- to prevent damage to food packaging.

Pest control

Every food business should carry out integrated pest management, i.e. a control programme involving a series of integrated measures to control pests. Pests require food, shelter and security. Denial of these factors is known as environmental control and is the first and most important control measure intended to prevent infestation.

Environmental control

may be considered as denial of:

- access – by design, maintenance and proofing of buildings

- food and harbourage – by good house-keeping.

Poor maintenance will allow pest entry.

Design, maintenance and proofing of buildings

Pests gain access to food premises in various ways. They may enter through open windows or doors, through gaps and cavities in the structure of the building or they may be brought in with food, packaging material or even laundry. Buildings must be designed and maintained to avoid undisturbed areas which can provide harbourage for pests. False ceilings, boxing, ducting, ovens and elevators must always be accessible for inspection and treatment. Cavities in internal walls or between surface finishes and walls must be eliminated or effectively sealed. Service pipes or conduits passing through walls should be cemented in position.

All structural damage which provides access for pests must be repaired immediately and gaps around pipework must be sealed. Defective drains should be made good.

All buildings should be adequately proofed; doors should be self-closing and provided with metal kick plates, ventilation stacks should be provided with wire balloons and all ventilation openings, including opening windows (where there is a risk of infestation) must be adequately proofed to avoid pests gaining access. If a pencil can pass through a gap so can a young mouse.

All sources of water, such as dripping taps, defective gutters and leaks should be repaired and puddles removed.

Good housekeeping

If a pest breaches the first stage of the defences, i.e. proofing and maintenance, as well as inspection of raw materials, then good housekeeping will reduce the risk of the lone invader becoming a major infestation. In particular, it is important to ensure that:

◆ premises are kept in a clean and tidy condition to reduce sources of food harbourage and nesting material

◆ cleaners do not remove or reposition bait trays

◆ spillages are cleared away promptly

◆ food is kept in pest-proof containers and lids are always replaced

◆ stock is stored and rotated correctly

◆ undisturbed areas of unused equipment are checked frequently

◆ adequate provision is made for the disposal of waste and areas are kept clean and tidy with tight-fitting lids being provided and used

◆ as far as practicable, areas around the premises are kept free of harbourage and pests

◆ all raw materials, including food, packaging and equipment, are checked to ensure they are not bringing pests in the premises

◆ storage areas are regularly inspected and cleaned. Goods should be stored off the floor in well-lighted and ventilated areas. Old stock and new stock should, as far as practicable, be segregated.

Physical and chemical control methods are necessary when environmental control has not succeeded.

Physical control methods

Physical control methods are usually preferred as the pest is caught, either dead or alive and consequently is not able to die in some inaccessible place and the dead body will not contaminate food. Furthermore, physical control methods can be used during food production. Examples of physical control include rodent traps which can be baited or unbaited, electronic flying insect killers which use ultra-violet light to attract insects which are then electrocuted

Catch trays must be emptied frequently.

on charged grids (catch trays for dead insects should be emptied frequently and units should never be positioned above food or food equipment), sticky fly papers (which should not be used in public areas), cockroach traps (useful for monitoring the extent of infestations and the success of chemical treatments), mist nets for birds and bird scaring devices.

Chemical control methods

Unfortunately, although physical control methods may catch the occasional invader, they are usually unsuitable for dealing with major pest infestations, which have to be destroyed as quickly as possible.

Rodenticides are used in bait trays and modern formulations can be provided in solid blocks or in a paste formulation to avoid problems from spillage and reduce the risk of food contamination.

The key to effective chemical control is to identify the insect and then determine which is the most vulnerable stage in its life cycle. Knock-down and residual insecticides of low toxicity can be used to control insects. Before use, all food and, where practicable, equipment should be removed and after treatment, work surfaces thoroughly cleaned and pests removed before food production commences. Particular care is necessary to avoid food contamination if aerosol fly spray is used by food handlers. (Indiscriminate control by food handlers is not good practice.)

A range of insecticidal dusts, baits, gels and sprays may be used to control most pests if care is taken to avoid contamination of food. Most treatments

rely on the insects walking over the formulation and ingesting or absorbing a lethal dose. Dichlorvos strips of residual insecticides are not recommended in food rooms because the continuous presence of insecticide during food production may result in dead insects in the food.

Fumigation of product is usually the only successful way to control infestations within commodities, although severe infestations may require the destruction of the product because of contamination with dead bodies.

Narcotizing of birds using alphachloralose, which is a stupefying substance, may be successful as any protected species can be released and the pest species collected and humanely destroyed.

It is essential that chemical control is undertaken by trained staff from either local authorities or specialist contractors. Safety precautions must be taken to comply with Health and Safety legislation. As soon as an infestation is discovered, immediate advice must be obtained.

The use of a pest control contractor

When selecting a pest control company, apart from the cost of the service, the following points should be taken into consideration:

◆ the type of pests you wish to control and the company's competency to deal with them

◆ the ability to give 24-hour cover and provide an emergency call-out service

◆ the use of suitably trained and discreet staff, with experience of the food industry

◆ the frequency of the visits

◆ the methods and materials to be used

◆ if the company is a member of an appropriate professional association

◆ the ability to provide a written report, including recommendations

◆ the adequacy of appropriate insurance cover regarding product, public and employees liability.

The employment of a contractor does not absolve the company from overall responsibility for the conditions of the premises and food. However, it would most likely assist if a "due diligence" defence was being relied upon.

It is important that the following points are actioned:

◆ staff should be trained to recognize and report signs of infestation

Brown rat

House mouse

Rodent teeth marks

Rodent damage

Rodent damage

Spillage resulting from rodent damage of sacks

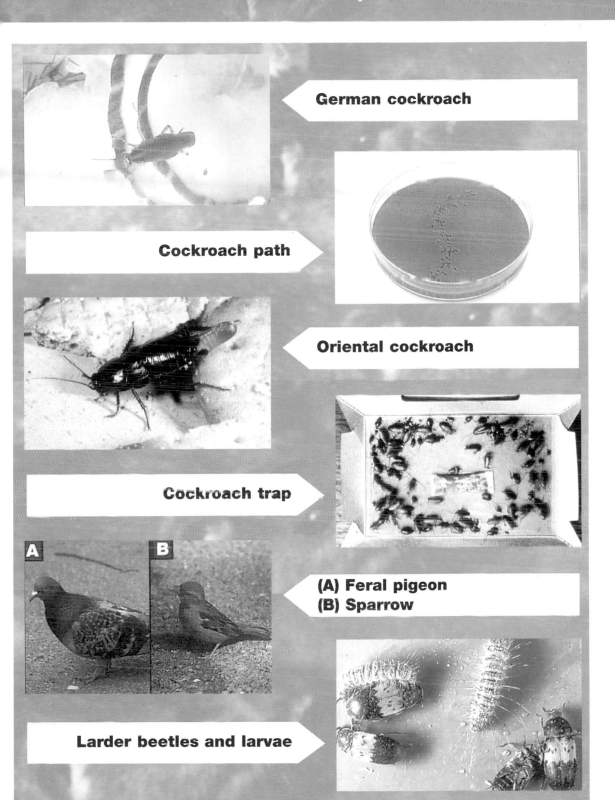

German cockroach

Cockroach path

Oriental cockroach

Cockroach trap

(A) Feral pigeon
(B) Sparrow

Larder beetles and larvae

Larva of flour beetle

(A) Grain beetle
(B) Grain weevil

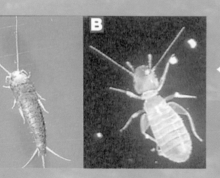

(A) Silver fish
(B) Book louse

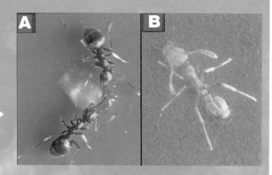

(A) Garden ant
(B) Pharaohs ant

Mill moth

Mill moth larva

- an effective notification system should be in place to summon the contractor

- the contractor should be accompanied during his/her visit

- any unsatisfactory housekeeping should be noted

- the position of bait boxes should be recorded

- recommendations should be carried out quickly

- regular inspections of bait boxes should be made by nominated personnel.

Key points

- rats, mice, flies and cockroaches are the most common pests of food premises

- pests can spread foodborne diseases

- infestations of pests may result in serious food complaints and the closure of the food business

- staff must be trained to identify evidence of pests which should be reported immediately

- environmental controls, i.e. preventing access and good housekeeping are the most cost-effective way of preventing infestations

- physical controls are preferred to avoid food contamination

- chemical controls should be applied by specialists.

*All pest photographs used in this book were provided courtesy of Anticimex (Sweden) and Rentokil Initial plc.

Supervisors and middle managers are an essential link in maintaining high standards of hygiene and preventing food poisoning. Their most important role is to ensure that food safety policies are implemented and the company's aims and objectives are achieved. Supervisors must communicate standards and ensure that staff are aware of their responsibilities. They should provide effective supervision, including motivation, instruction and on-the-job training to develop competency and control. Supervisors have a key role in the successful implementation of HACCP, hazard analysis or other food safety management systems. They must ensure that hazards are controlled, monitoring is effective and corrective action is taken in the event of failures. Supervisors should advise management when standards are being formulated and, in particular, ensure management are aware of the resources necessary to achieve the required standards.

Standards

Standards are necessary to ensure consistency and to provide a reference point to determine when a target has been achieved or a task, such as cleaning, has been completed satisfactorily. The term "standard" may be used in several different ways. Voluntary standards, for example, hygiene or cleanliness, may be arbitrary levels; legal standards, such as storage temperatures and bacteriological standards, are obligatory minimum levels and international standards such as HACCP and ISO 9000 are recognised by many countries. Standards can relate to premises, people or products and include labelling and packaging.

Standards may be set by an individual, a company, customers, Governments, trade associations and independent standards authorities. They are used to provide a uniform service or product which the customer expects. Premises with high standards develop a good reputation, which attracts new customers, with the minimum number of complaints. Food safety standards set above the minimum legal level will ensure compliance with the law, codes of practice and industry guides and the production of safe, wholesome food of acceptable quality and shelf-life. Standards are also essential to facilitate control, monitoring and auditing to assess compliance.

Specifications are documented standards which describe the safety and quality characteristics of the raw materials and the products obtained from suppliers. Specifications ensure uniformity and may include minimum standards for weight, size, colour, pH, a_w, absence or maximum numbers of microorganisms, processing requirements, delivery details, including temperature, absence of physical and chemical contaminants, packaging and labelling. They may also detail the action that will be taken, usually rejection, if the specification is not adhered to.

Food safety policies

When a company has determined its aim and objectives, the standards can be determined and incorporated into a food safety policy. The food safety policy can be used to attain good hygiene practice or good manufacturing practice which are essential pre-requisites to the effective implementation of HACCP or hazard analysis. This document is also very useful to support a due diligence defence and an effective way of communicating the required standards to staff and identifying training needs. To remain effective, the document should be reviewed regularly. A responsibility flow chart showing management structure and individual responsibilities with regard to hygiene should be included, together with the following:

◆ a commitment to produce safe food

◆ a commitment to observe all relevant legal requirements, industry guides to good hygiene practice and Government codes of practice

◆ a commitment to identify hazards and implement effective control and monitoring procedures, especially at points critical to food safety and to review the hazard analysis system periodically and whenever the food business operations change

◆ staff training and the implementation of a planned food hygiene training programme (training records should be maintained)

◆ procedures to ensure that all food and water suppliers are satisfactory/approved (suppliers should provide a copy of their food safety policy and customer references)

◆ a commitment to provide the necessary premises, equipment, facilities and maintenance to achieve high standards of hygiene, including personal hygiene

◆ satisfactory temperature control and monitoring systems for food ingredients and products during storage, preparation/processing, distribution and display. Procedures should be identified for safe alternatives if equipment is defective

◆ systems to ensure satisfactory cleaning and, where necessary, disinfecting of the premises, equipment and facilities (cleaning schedules will be required)

◆ adequate pest control measures, including proofing, the use of specialist contractors and maintaining records;

◆ procedures and systems for health screening and the reporting of staff illness, dealing with visitors, contractors, enforcement officers, food poisoning incidents, customer complaints, delivery of raw materials, product recall, hazard warnings and waste management

◆ effective quality assurance/control systems, including stock rotation, foreign body control, organoleptic assessment, sampling, food labelling and in-house audits. Procedures for removing unacceptable suppliers from the approved list

◆ a commitment to provide the resources for and training of managers to ensure the implementation, updating and enforcement of the policy throughout the business.

Quality assurance

Quality assurance may be considered as all the planned and systematic actions necessary to provide confidence that a product or service will satisfy the customer's requirements for quality over time. Many organizations have developed their own quality assurance systems and some of these may comply with the International Standards Organisation ISO 9000 series. Recognition for achieving the standard is through accredited certification bodies.

Quality control

Quality control is differentiated from quality assurance in that it is a series of techniques used to assess compliance with a standard specification by testing and product sampling. It is usually based on statistical criteria and often occurs on completion of production. In essence, it is a reactive process which identifies things that are wrong after the event and does not necessarily determine the cause of the problem.

Quality assurance is proactive and attempts to stop things going wrong in the first place. It is a continuous process of product assessment and fault correction throughout production and should be the responsibility of all staff. The effective implementation of quality assurance requires:

◆ the specification (what is to be done)

◆ documented instruction (how it is to be done)

◆ the recording system (to confirm it has been done)

◆ a monitoring system (to confirm recording and corrective actions are satisfactory).

Quality must be built into a food product, it cannot be inspected into it.

The inspection of food premises

An inspection of a food premises or operation will only be effective if the person undertaking the inspection has a clear understanding of the reason for inspection and they have the relevant technical knowledge, skills and experience. The inspection must be planned and sufficient time must be allowed to achieve their objective. Having completed the inspection, the data collected will need to be analyzed to determine the action to be taken to rectify any defects. A comprehensive report should be written and problems must be followed up to ensure compliance. An inspection involves careful observation and examination whereas an audit may be considered as comparing what you actually do with what you say you do. The two processes will usually overlap.

Knowledge required

The inspector must have a thorough understanding of:

◆ all technical aspects of the operation, for example, catering practice, cook-chill or canning

◆ the legal requirements and relevant codes of practice or industry guides

◆ the main causes of food poisoning and complaints associated with the type of operation

◆ all relevant aspects of HACCP

◆ the industry norm, i.e. standards expected for similar premises.

Purpose of the inspection

There are many different reasons for

inspecting a premises, including:
- to ensure that the premises/operation is capable of producing safe food

- to assess the effectiveness of HACCP/hazard analysis, especially in relation to critical control points

- to check that standards have been achieved

- to identify the training needs of staff;

- to provide advice

- to demonstrate management commitment to food safety

- to respond to a complaint

- to re-visit.

Stages in the inspection
(1) Planning and preparation
Having decided on the objectives of the inspection, the scope and depth can be determined. The inspection may consider microbiological, chemical and physical hazards and it may be a full or part inspection or very specific.

The equipment required will include a probe thermometer, torch, protective clothing, sample bags, a scraper and an A4 pad and clipboard. The inspector may need additional knowledge and training to develop inspection skills, including interviewing, simulation/reconstruction, measurement, analyzing and report writing.

Prior to undertaking the inspection, it is useful to have records of previous inspections, specifications, hazards, risks, relevant legislation, industry guides and codes of practice. Access to monitoring records relating to customer complaints, pests and cleaning, together with the HACCP plan and site layout, would also be beneficial.

To be effective, checklists should be designed specifically for the premises being inspected, although *aide-memoires* may be even more useful.

(2) Conducting the inspection
The timing of the inspection will be dictated by the objective. If undertaking a comprehensive inspection, it is necessary to examine each step in the production of food from the receipt of deliveries to the serving of customers. The hazards (contamination, multiplication and survival) controls, monitoring and corrective action at each stage (critical control point) should be considered.

Observations should be carried out as inconspicuously as possible and the inspection should be methodical. A typical routine involves starting at a defined point, such as the wash-hand basin, within a room, the progressive examination of all relevant items around the perimeter and then the same ordered examination of central fittings, installation or equipment.

The inspection should be thorough. Every aspect of the subject under examination should be covered. It may not be enough to look at a piece of equipment; it may need to be dismantled and/or moved from its position. Cupboards and refrigerators may need to be wholly or partially emptied and surfaces may need to be scraped or tapped to assess soundness. In this respect, full use should be made of the senses: sight, smell, hearing and touch.

(3) Analyzing the data

All of the raw data collected during the inspection will need careful analysis to provide meaningful information which can be presented in the report. For example, several cleaning defects in differing rooms may indicate inappropriate cleaning schedules. If staff are wearing dirty protective clothing this may result from poor communication and/or supervision or training. Several empty paper towel or soap dispensers may demonstrate ineffective monitoring as well as poor management commitment to achieving high standards of personal hygiene. Food hygiene certificates may be hung on the wall, but the staff may not be competent to undertake their activities and to produce safe food.

(4) Report

The report of the inspection should be more than just a list of faults. Good practice and achievements should be complemented. Faults should be grouped together, for example, personal hygiene or cleaning. The remedial work should be prioritized, for example, an unsafe process should be dealt with at the time of the inspection, some cleaning problems may need to be rectified within a day, whereas some decoration, structural items or replacement equipment may be dealt with in one to three months.

Recommendations and requirements should be clearly distinguished, and any solutions proposed should be cost-effective and practical.

Inspection by an enforcement officer

In the event of an inspection by an enforcement officer, the supervisor or manager should make the officer welcome and answer his/her questions accurately and honestly. A plan of the premises should be available, together with all relevant monitoring records. The officer will be interested in the food safety policy and any HACCP documentation provided.

It is usual for the officer to be accompanied throughout the inspection. If you do not understand the reason for a request or, for example, why a particular process is considered to be a risk, you should always ask for an explanation.

At the conclusion of the inspection, it is advisable to keep a record of any work that must be completed immediately and also the follow-up action, if any, the officer intends to take. Priorities and timescales for completing any remedial work should be noted.

Staff training

The objectives of hygiene training

The main objective of hygiene training is to change the behaviour and attitude of food handlers at work and so minimize the risk of food poisoning and food complaints. To achieve this objective, staff will need to be provided with the knowledge and skills to operate hygienically and then motivated and supervised to ensure that they implement what they have learned. Training should not be undertaken haphazardly but must be carefully planned. The most effective way of undertaking hygiene training is to develop and implement a training programme, the principles of which are applicable to all businesses, although the programme will be less formal for smaller businesses.

The benefits of hygiene training

Training contributes significantly to the profitability of a food business by:

◆ assisting in the production of safe food

◆ safeguarding the quality of the product and reducing food wastage

◆ reducing complaints

◆ generating a pride in appearance and practices, increasing job satisfaction and probably reducing staff turnover

◆ contributing to increased productivity

◆ ensuring that all the correct procedures, including cleaning, are followed

◆ complying with any legal provisions or the requirements of industry guides or codes of practice

◆ promoting a good company image which should result in increased business

◆ improving the supervisory skills of managers.

Training methods

There are many ways of ensuring that food handlers are effectively trained depending on the type of business, their level of hygiene knowledge and their literary skills. Continuous on the job instruction and control by a knowledgeable supervisor is essential. A large number of visual aids are available to enhance training sessions or reinforce important messages. Videos, overhead transparencies, books, leaflets, posters and computer-based training packages are all useful, especially if the audience finds them enjoyable. Humorous illustrations are more memorable then text. Interactive training packages and training sessions produce better results, for example, group exercises, quiz books, software, games and role playing.

The legal requirement for training

The Food Safety (General Food Hygiene) Regulations, 1995 state:

"The proprietor of a food business shall ensure that food handlers engaged in the food business are supervised and instructed and/or trained in food hygiene matters commensurate with their work activity."

The Catering Guide to Good Hygiene Practice suggests that in order to comply with this requirement,

"all food handlers must receive written or verbal instruction in the essentials of food hygiene before they start work and additional hygiene awareness instruction within four weeks of starting work."

Food handlers who prepare open high-risk foods or have a supervisory role should receive formal Level 1 training within three months of starting work. Level 1 training may be delivered in-house, if of the appropriate standard, or food handlers may attend a food hygiene course, of around six hours duration, accredited by:

◆ The Chartered Institute of Environmental Health

◆ The Royal Institute of Public Health

◆ The Royal Society for the Promotion of Health

◆ The Society of Food Hygiene Technology

◆ The Royal Environmental Health Institute of Scotland.

It is recommended that supervisors undertake Level 2 (12 to 24 hours) or Level 3 (24 to 40 hours duration) training, depending on their actual duties. Such training can be provided in-house or by attending courses accredited by the above organisations.

It must always be remembered that competency to undertake their activities and produce safe food are more important than an ageing certificate on the wall.

Training programme and records
It is good practice for food businesses to have a training programme which identifies the training needs of each food handler. Records of training, to include induction (hygiene essentials), hygiene awareness, Level 1, 2 or 3, any specific courses attended, such as HACCP, and refresher training, should be completed for each food handler to demonstrate compliance with the legal requirements and to assist in establishing a "due diligence" defence.

THE INVESTIGATION OF FOOD POISONING OUTBREAKS
The effective investigation of food poisoning outbreaks is essential to limit the spread of infection and to provide information:
◆ for the food industry on unsafe products and practices

◆ to improve the effectiveness of inspections by enforcement officers

◆ to use when formulating new legislation.

In the event of a serious or large outbreak, an outbreak control team is usually established. A food poisoning outbreak control team consists of several experts, including a consultant in communicable disease control, a microbiologist and an environmental health officer.

The objectives of an investigation are to:
◆ contain the spread of illness

◆ identify the outbreak location (place where food vehicle was prepared or served)

◆ identify the food vehicle (food eaten which gave rise to the illness) and prevent further sales

◆ identify the causative agent involved, for example, *Salmonella enteritidis,* Norwalk virus, a poisonous chemical or a toxic plant

◆ trace cases/carriers, especially food handlers

◆ trace the source of the causative agent

◆ determine the main faults that contributed to the outbreak, for example, food left at ambient temperatures for several hours
◆ make recommendations to prevent recurrence

◆ provide data for use in surveillance.

The role of the environmental health officer

In addition to his/her involvement with the outbreak control team, the environmental health officer uses his/her skills in tracing cases and persons at risk, organizing the collection of specimens and interviewing people involved to obtain information to assist with achieving the above objectives.

When the outbreak location has been identified, the investigating officer will undertake a comprehensive investigation and inspection of the operation to ascertain the faults in the food preparation and the management failures that resulted in the faults. If the evidence suggests the sale of unfit food and the absence of a due diligence defence, the officer may also collect evidence for use in legal proceedings.

The officer will need to secure the assistance of the manager and/or supervisor to assist in the investigation. In the event of a very recent outbreak, the officer will request the suspension of cleaning and disinfection and, perhaps, the termination of food production or even the closure of the food premises.

The officer will require details of:
◆ all food production staff and their functions

◆ staff sickness records, including staff with septic cuts or boils

◆ all relevant food production details.

The officer may require samples of food and meal or packaging remains. Swabs of surfaces and equipment may be taken. Staff will be interviewed and asked to provide faecal specimens.

The role of the supervisor

If a supervisor suspects the business may have been responsible for a food poisoning outbreak, he/she should advise the manager, who will probably require any further food sales to be suspended, if the outbreak is very recent, until the allegation has been investigated. Any staff with symptoms should be sent to the doctor and not resume food handling duties until medical clearance has been obtained. In the case of retail or manufacturing, recall procedures for suspect food may need implementing.

Supervisors will be responsible for assisting management to provide the necessary records and information for the environmental health officer. Records provided by management may be slightly out of date because of last minute changes and the supervisor will need to check the accuracy, especially of menus, supplier lists, staff work and sickness records, methods of preparation and persons at risk.

Supervisors will also be given the task of ensuring the premises are thoroughly cleaned and disinfected once the environmental health officer is satisfied that they are capable of producing safe food. In addition any recommendations from the environmental health officer on preventing future outbreaks will need to be implemented.

The role of the consultant in communicable disease control (CCDC)

CCDCs are public health doctors employed by the health authorities and who work for local authorities. They are responsible for controlling public health diseases, including food poisoning, and usually chair the outbreak control team. In addition to their medical skills, they often provide the epidemiological expertise and give advice on controlling infection and treatment required. They rarely get involved in enforcement matters or the inspection of premises.

The role of the Public Health Laboratory Service (PHLS)

The PHLS was established under the National Health Services Acts to provide for the surveillance and control of infectious diseases in England and Wales. There are 52 laboratories, usually in major hospitals, and the Communicable Disease Surveillance Centre at Colindale. The laboratories assist Environmental Health Departments investigating food poisoning incidents by providing epidemiological and microbiological expertise. Suspect food, water and faecal samples and swabs are examined at the laboratories in an attempt to isolate pathogens responsible for illness. Routine food and water samples are also sent to the laboratories for examination.

HACCP (HAZARD ANALYSIS CRITICAL CONTROL POINT)

Terminology associated with HACCP

Control measures: actions required to eliminate or reduce hazards to a safe level.

Corrective action: the actions to be taken when the results of monitoring indicate a control point is moving out of control.

Criteria: specified characteristics of a physical e.g. time or temperature; chemical e.g. pH; or biological e.g. sensory, nature.

Critical control point (CCP): a step in a process which must be controlled to eliminate or reduce a hazard to an acceptable level.

Critical limit: the value of a monitored action which separates acceptable from unacceptable.

Decision tree: a sequence of questions applied to each process step with a potential hazard to identify which process steps are critical to food safety.

Deviation: a measurement or an observation outside the critical limit.

Flow diagram/chart: the detailed sequence of operations involved with a particular product or process, usually from receipt of raw materials to the end-user.

HACCP: a structured and documented hazard analysis system based on specialist advice and applied to a standardized food production process with a view to ensuring cost-effective food safety.

Hazard: the potential to cause harm to the consumer and can be microbiological, chemical or physical.

Hazard analysis: any system which enables a food business to identify hazards, the steps at which they could occur and the introduction of measures to control them.

Microbiological hazards: the unacceptable contamination, the unacceptable multiplication, the unacceptable production or persistence of toxins and/or the unacceptable survival of pathogenic microorganisms in food. Including bacteria, viruses, parasites and moulds.

Monitoring: the planned observations and measurements of targets and tolerances of control points to confirm that the process is under control.

Prerequisites for HACCP: all the good hygiene practices that need to be in place before a satisfactory HACCP can be implemented.

Risk: the estimate of the probability of a hazard occurring.

Risk assessment: the process of identifying hazards, assessing risks and severity and evaluating their significance.

Severity: the magnitude of the hazard or the seriousness of possible consequence.

Target level: the predetermined value for the control measure which will eliminate or control the hazard.

Tolerance: the specified degree of latitude for a control measure which, if exceeded, requires immediate corrective action.

Verification: the procedures, other than those used in monitoring, designed to establish if the HACCP system is functioning as planned and is effective.

HACCP is a food safety management system developed in the early 1960s as a result of a joint effort by the Pillsbury Company and NASA to guarantee the safety of food intended for astronauts. HACCP shifts the emphasis of control from end-product testing and inspection to identifying current and predicted hazards and risks and removing them prior to or during production. However, the system was developed for manufacturing premises that were already operating to the highest possible standards of hygiene, which ensured minimal risk of contamination or abuse of temperature control.

HACCP is a complex, preventive system which requires a detailed scientific analysis of the ingredients, process and the processing environment. It involves analyzing hazards, and where they occur, risks, severity and introducing control measures. The work involved requires a team of experts and may take several months to implement if a large number of food products are produced.

Having decided on control points, the team then uses the "decision tree" to determine which points are critical to food safety. Critical limits are established at these points which are then closely monitored. Deviations from a critical limit involve taking corrective action which may require the destruction of the product. The system must be fully documented and requires comprehensive monitoring records. It must be verified and reviewed as and when necessary.

HACCP has proved reasonably effective in ensuring safe food production in large food factories. However, because of the lack of consistency in production techniques, the large number of products simultaneously handled and the lack of detailed scientific and microbiological knowledge relating to specific products and equipment, it is impractical to apply HACCP to most catering and retail businesses. However, an appropriate food safety management system based on the principle of HACCP can be implemented. In effect this is what the law requires and it is often referred to as hazard analysis.

Hazard analysis

Hazard analysis involves identifying any step in the food business which is critical to food safety and ensuring that adequate safety procedures are implemented on the basis of the following principles:

◆ analysis of the food hazards associated with the food business operation, including microorganisms and toxins, chemical contamination and physical contamination

◆ identification of the points in the operation where food hazards may occur. Food hazards should be identified at each step in the operation using a generic flow diagram. The particular hazards to consider at each step are

(a) the presence of the contaminant in the raw food or ingredient, for example, salmonella in raw chicken, pesticides on fruit or a foreign body in flour;

(b) the likely contamination of the food at a particular step, for example, storage of raw food and high-risk food together or contamination by glass;

(c) the multiplication of bacteria or toxin production, for example, because food is left at room temperature for too long;

(d) the ability of microorganisms to survive a particular process such as cooking or disinfection which should have killed them;

◆ deciding which of the points identified are critical to ensuring food safety (critical points). At each step there is likely to be several hazards and the points at which hazards must be effectively controlled to ensure food safety should be considered as critical control points

Bacterial contamination, of high-risk food, for example, from unhygienic practices, must be controlled, as must any steps which would allow multiplication of bacteria. Times and temperatures of cooking or processing and cooling are always likely to be critical points

◆ identification and implementation of effective control and monitoring procedures at critical points. Controls must be implemented to eliminate the hazard or reduce it to a safe level. Measurable target levels should be set and checks introduced to ensure targets are achieved. Temperature and times are two of the most important parameters as they are precise and relatively easy to monitor. For example, high-risk foods should be stored at or below 5°C and during preparation should never be left at ambient temperature for longer than 30 minutes. Records are necessary for managers to ensure that the appropriate monitoring has been undertaken. Written procedures on corrective action in the event of targets not being met are also essential

◆ review of the analysis of food hazards the critical control points and the control and monitoring procedures periodically and whenever the food business' operations change. A review of the system is necessary if:

(a) controls are ineffective or the product is unsatisfactory;

(b) the type of product, the raw materials, the recipe or ingredients alter, for example, cooked chicken is purchased instead of raw;

AN EXAMPLE OF A HACCP CONTROL CHART SHOWING STEPS IN THE OPERATION CRITICAL TO FOOD SAFETY

Step	Hazard	Control	Monitoring	Corrective Action
Purchase of raw materials	Presence of contaminants; microbiological, chemical or physical.	Select least hazardous ingredients. Only use approved suppliers. Specification for product quality and safety including delivery temperatures. Food safety systems.	Inspect supplier or request records to show that they follow good manufacturing practice. Historical check of deliveries. Absence of customer complaints. Bacteriological sampling.	Revisit/inspect supplier. Change supplier. Review product specification.
Delivery of raw materials	Presence of contaminants. Multiplication of food poisoning bacteria.	Specify delivery requirements, especially time and temperature. Minimize time for unloading/placing in storage. Deboxing area. Food protected/covered.	Check delivery vehicles and drivers, date codes, time for unloading and temperature and condition of food (as per specification).	Refuse to accept delivery. Change supplier if it is a persistent problem. Review product specification.
Storage (chilled, frozen, dry)	Multiplication of food poisoning bacteria. Contamination due to poor hygiene practices.	Store at correct temperature (alarmed units). Cover/wrap food. Stock rotation/date codes. Separate raw/high-risk foods.	Check air/food temperature, date codes, and food complaint records. Audits and visual checks of food. Check condition of food and packaging	Adjust temperatures. Repair/replace equipment. Use food immediately. Discard food.
Preparation	Multiplication of food poisoning bacteria. Contamination due to poor hygiene practices and poor personal hygiene.	Prepare minimum amount of food. Minimize time at room temperature. Separate raw/high-risk foods and use of separate equipment. Colour coding. Food protected/covered.	Check time/temperature. Audits/visual checks. Bacteriological swabbing of hands and surfaces.	Reduce time at ambient. Discard food. Review systems to prevent contamination.
Cooking/ baking/ heating (or reheating)	Survival of food poisoning bacteria. Contamination and multiplication also possible.	Centre temperature at least 75°C. (Reheat to 82°C). Ensure frozen poultry/joints completely thawed. Stir liquids. Protect from contamination. Cook just before eating.	Check time/temperature. Audits/visual checks.	Raise temperature. Increase time.Discard food. Repair/replace equipment.
Cooling	Multiplication of surviving food poisoning bacteria, or germination of spores. Contamination.	Minimise weight/thickness of joints. Cool rapidly (blast chiller). Cool in shallow trays. Keep covered. No contact with raw food. Refrigerate immediately after cooling.	Check time/temperature. Audits/visual checks.	Discard food. Repair/replace equipment(blast chiller). Review systems to prevent contamination.
Addition of fillings/ toppings	Contamination. Multiplication of food poisoning bacteria.	Use clean and disinfected equipment and work surfaces. Use separate equipment to avoid cross-contamination. Minimise time at ambient.	Audits/visual checks. Check time at ambient.	Discard food. Review systems to prevent contamination.
Service/ display	Contamination due to poor hygiene practices. Multiplication of food poisoning bacteria.	Minimise handling. Keep <5°C or >63°C. Keep food covered. Stock rotation. Separate raw/high-risk foods. Sell within shelf-life. Prevent customer contamination. Colour coding. Minimise time at room temperature.	Check time/temperature and date codes. Condition of food. Audits/ inspections.	Adjust temperatures/times. Discard food. Repair/replace equipment. Review systems to prevent contamination.

(c) the method of preparation changes, for example, a microwave oven replaces conventional cooking;

(d) staff numbers and/or responsibilities change;

(e) new equipment is introduced, for example, a new refrigerator or oven.

Documentation of the system is not a legal requirement but effective documentation and monitoring records may assist a defence of due diligence in the event of prosecution. It is also extremely difficult to apply controls and checks consistently if there is no documentation.

Prerequisites for HACCP

Prior to the implementation of HACCP the premises should be designed and operated to minimise the risk of contamination, and be well maintained. Equipment should be in good condition and be subject to satisfactory maintenance agreements. Where necessary equipment must be calibrated. The prerequisites for the implementation of HACCP include:

◆ the adherence to good hygiene/manufacturing practices competent staff with high standards of personal hygiene
◆ effective cleaning and disinfection and the use of cleaning schedules

◆ effective pest management and electronic flykillers sited to prevent food contamination

◆ effective waste management

Although the above items will be omitted from the HACCP control chart they remain important. An assessment of hazards controls, monitoring and corrective action should be made for each of them.

This approach enables critical control points to be centred on the food product and also reduces the number of critical control points to a more manageable level.

Monitoring

Monitoring of critical control points is an integral part of all hazard analysis systems and will also ensure:
◆ expected standards are being achieved

◆ compliance with legislation and will assist in the due diligence defence

◆ problems are identified, for example, sources of contamination

◆ safe food production that minimizes complaints

◆ commitment of staff and improved motivation

◆ effectiveness of control systems.

Organoleptic assessment of food

The appearance, smell, texture, taste and other physical characteristics of food are valuable for obtaining a rapid assessment of food standards (quality, taint and spoilage). However, food contaminated by pathogenic bacteria may appear in all respects fit to eat and suspect food should not be tasted. Specific indicators include:
◆ *Smell* – good food should smell fresh, pleasant and natural. Unusual, stale,

musty or rancid smells should invite suspicions. Chemical smells may indicate chemical contamination. Ammonia smells in some fish are an early sign of decomposition

◆ *Taste* – unusual bitterness, sweetness, a soapy taste or any untypical flavour may indicate unfitness

◆ *Appearance* – food should be visibly free from signs of spoilage, fungal growth, slime, darkening or other change in colour, untypical wetness and mechanical damage. Absence of foreign objects and dirt in finished goods, including pests, pest debris and parasites, is important. Meat, poultry and fish should be free from signs of disease or other pathological conditions. In frozen food excessive ice can be an indicator of mishandling, as can large ice crystals within the texture; loose foods such as peas should not be welded together. A final judgement of frozen food can only be made after defrosting

◆ *Sound* – many packed foods, especially canned goods, emit a characteristic sound on being tapped or shaken. Any such food or pack emitting an untypical sound is suspect

◆ *Texture* – unusual softness, hardness, brittleness or change in texture may be indicative of unfitness. Meat, fish and certain other products, such as cheese, should display a springy texture. Light pressure from a finger that causes an indentation to remain can be significant.

Bacteriological monitoring

Bacteriological monitoring can be used to assist the verification of HACCP or hazard analysis, but is also commonly used in manufacturing premises to:

◆ build up a profile of product quality

◆ indicate trends in product quality

◆ ascertain whether handling techniques are satisfactory

◆ indicate product safety and the absence of specific organisms or pathogens

◆ determine effectiveness of cleaning and disinfection

◆ determine effectiveness of processing

◆ confirm that legal standards or customer's specifications are being met.

However, bacteriological monitoring has the following disadvantages:

◆ it is usually retrospective and cannot be used to verify product safety where there is a short time between production and consumption, for example, in conventional catering or for products with short shelf-lives

◆ it is relatively expensive

◆ considerable expertise may be needed to interpret results and relate them to product age

◆ the non-uniform distribution of bacteria in foods and the effect of different laboratory techniques and sampling methods significantly affect the results

◆ the operation is being controlled by a laboratory technician who may be remote from the food production

◆ only a limited number of samples can be taken

◆ not all hazards are identified

◆ only a small section of the workforce assumes responsibility for product safety.

Monitoring of food handlers

Monitoring of food handlers by supervisors is essential to identify failures in personal hygiene or hygiene practices and to identify training needs. Monitoring can involve observation, for example, to ensure staff wash their hands properly when entering the food room and to ensure protective clothing is clean, put on and worn correctly. More formal monitoring can involve bacteriological swabbing of fingers, competency testing and annual medical checks by medical staff to reinforce rules relating to illness.

Monitoring documents

Comprehensive and accurately completed monitoring records are an integral part of hazard analysis and are essential when investigating breakdowns in hygiene, including customer complaints and food poisoning. Monitoring records are also extremely useful to assist in a successful due diligence defence.

Records that are recommended include:
◆ supplier assessment and assurance forms

◆ pre-employment medical questionnaires

◆ staff hygiene training

◆ goods received check lists

◆ refrigerator and freezer temperatures

◆ cooking/processing/reheating/cooling (time and temperature)

◆ equipment maintenance

◆ cleaning and disinfection

◆ pest sightings/control

◆ customer complaint forms

◆ allegation of illness

◆ enforcement officer visits

◆ internal audit forms

◆ product traceability and recall

◆ bacteriological monitoring/swabbing of surfaces (mainly manufacturing).

Corrective Action

Corrective action is necessary when monitoring indicates that a CCP is moving out of control. Procedures for corrective action should specify: the action to be taken; who should take action; who should be notified; whether or not production/ sales should continue; whether product should be recalled; how the product be dealt with; and who can authorise the restart of production or sales. Manufacturers, wholesalers and retailers should ensure that all products are clearly labelled and traceable in the event of a recall being necessary.

Verification

After the implementation of the HACCP system it should be verified to ensure it is working effectively. Verification may involve auditing against the HACCP plan to ensure the correct implementation and control of hazards. Random sampling, including microbiological tests. All scientific data, on which the system was based, can be re-examined to ensure it is still applicable. Monitoring records, deviations and complaints can also be examined.

Key points

◆ supervisors and managers have an essential role in producing safe food and preventing food poisoning

◆ standards ensure consistency and customer satisfaction. They are essential to facilitate control and monitoring

◆ food safety policies should demonstrate the commitment of the company to operate to high standards and produce safe food

◆ quality assurance is proactive, quality control is reactive

◆ persons undertaking inspections or audits of food premises must have the relevant technical knowledge, skills and experience

◆ training of food handlers should be carefully planned as part of a comprehensive food safety training programme

◆ the effective investigation of food poisoning is essential to limit the spread of infection and provide information to assist in surveillance

◆ HACCP or hazard analysis are food safety management systems which predict hazards and risks, enabling their removal prior to food production.

The law is a complex subject and most acts and regulations affecting the food industry are difficult to interpret. However, ignorance of the law is no defence in the event of a prosecution and supervisors must make a special effort to become conversant with legislation which affects their work.

This chapter includes an outline of the most important legislation relating to food and food hygiene in England and Wales, and Scotland; Northern Ireland has its own legislation, although any differences are usually minor. Should information or advice be required regarding the interpretation of a particular section, or the current legislation applicable, the local environmental health officer or a solicitor should be consulted.

Legislation consists of: Acts of Parliament which are concerned with principles of legislation; regulations and orders which normally deal with specific premises or commodities in much greater detail than acts; and local acts or bylaws which are made or adopted by local authorities and are legally binding only within the area of the particular authority.

Scotland has a different legal system than England, being founded on principles originating from Roman law. In the event of any legal query, it is always best to consult someone conversant with the specifics of both the legal system and the subject matter in question.

Acts and regulations applicable to the food industry are concerned with:

◆ preventing the production or sale of injurious, unsafe or unfit food

◆ preventing the contamination of food and food equipment

◆ the hygiene of food premises, equipment and personnel (including training)

◆ hygiene practices, including temperature control and the control and monitoring of hazards at points which are critical to food safety

◆ the provision of sanitary accommodation, water supplies and washing facilities

◆ the control of food poisoning

◆ the importation of food

◆ the composition and labelling of food

◆ the registration and licensing of food premises and vehicles.

The European Community

Since the United Kingdom joined the Common Market, several hundred regulations have been introduced to secure compliance with the requirements of EC directives.

The Food Safety Act, 1990

This is the most important Act relating to the sale of food for human consumption and as such is applicable to all food premises in England, Scotland and Wales.

Section 1. "Food" includes water which is bottled for sale or used as an ingredient (water supplied to the premises is excluded). It excludes live animals, birds or fish, animal feeding stuffs or drugs.

"Food business" means any business in the course of which commercial operations in respect of food or food sources are carried out (whether for profit or not). This would include businesses giving food away as part of a promotion.

"Premises" includes any place, vehicle or stall.

Section 2. Extends the meaning of sale to include food which is offered as a prize or reward or given away in connection with any entertainment for the public.

Section 3. Food, or ingredients, commonly used for human consumption are presumed, until the contrary is proved, to be intended for sale for human consumption.

Section 7. It is an offence to treat food so as to render it injurious to health with the intent that the food will be sold in that state. Regard shall be had to the cumulative effect of foods consumed over a long period.

Section 8. It is an offence to sell, offer for sale or have in possession for sale food intended for human consumption which fails to comply with the **food safety requirements,** i.e. food which has been rendered injurious to health, is unfit for human consumption or is so contaminated (whether by extraneous matter or otherwise) that it would be unreasonable to expect it to be used for human consumption in that state.

Section 9. An authorized officer of a food authority may seize or detain food (for up to 21 days) which fails to comply with **food safety requirements** or which is likely to cause food poisoning or a foodborne disease. Food which is seized has to be dealt with by a Justice of the Peace. Any person liable to be prosecuted in respect of such food is entitled to make representations to the Justice of the Peace. If the food is not condemned, or detained food is cleared, compensation can be claimed. Any expenses incurred in the destruction of condemned food must be paid by the owner of the food.

Section 10. An authorized officer can serve an **improvement notice** on the proprietor of a food business for failing to comply with regulations relating to hygiene or to the processing or treatment of food. The **notice** must state the grounds for non-compliance, the contraventions and measures necessary to secure compliance, and the time (not less than 14 days) allowed. Failure to comply is an offence.

Section 11. If a proprietor of a food business is convicted of an offence under the regulations **and** the court is satisfied that the business, any process/treatment, the construction or condition of any premises or the use or condition of any equipment involves a risk of injury to health, they shall impose a **prohibition order**. A **prohibition order** can apply to the use of a process/treatment, the premises (or part thereof) or any equipment. A copy of the **prohibition order** must be conspicuously fixed on the premises and contravention of the order is an offence.

The **prohibition order** ceases to have effect when the enforcement authority issues a certificate which states that there is no longer a health risk. The court may also impose a prohibition on the proprietor or manager participating in the management of any food business. This prohibition applies for at least six months.

Section 12. If an authorized officer of an enforcement authority is satisfied that there is an imminent risk of injury to health he may issue an **emergency prohibition notice.** An application for an **emergency prohibition order** must then be made to the court within three days of serving the notice.

The **emergency prohibition notice** and **emergency prohibition order** must be served on the proprietor and conspicuously displayed on the premises. Any contravention is an offence. An **emergency prohibition notice/order** ceases to have effect when the enforcement authority issues a certificate which states that there is no longer a health risk.

Section 14. It is an offence to sell, to the prejudice of the purchaser, any food which is not of the nature (different kind or variety) or substance (not containing proper ingredients) or quality (inferior, for example, stale bread) demanded by the purchaser.

Section 20. Enables proceedings to be taken against another person when the offence was due to his act or default.

Section 21. It is a defence for a person to prove that he took all reasonable precautions and exercised all due diligence to avoid the commission of the offence, by himself or by a person under his control.

In the case of persons not involved with the preparation or importation, for example, a retailer, charged with an offence under Sections 8, 14 or 15, it is a defence to prove:
(a) the offence was due to another person;

(b) that he carried out all reasonable checks or it was reasonable to rely on checks carried out by his supplier; and

(c) he did not know or suspect his act or omission would amount to an offence.

Sections 29 & 30. Empower an authorized officer to purchase or take samples of food, food sources, contact materials or any article or substance required as evidence.

Section 32. Empowers an authorized officer, on production of an authenticated document showing his authority, to enter any premises within his area at all reasonable hours to carry out his duties under the Act. In the case of a private dwelling-house entry cannot be demanded unless 24 hours' notice has been given to the occupier. An enforcement officer is also empowered to enter any business premises outside his area for the purpose of ascertaining whether or not there are any contraventions of the Act or regulations/orders made thereunder. Warrants may be issued by a Justice of the Peace authorizing entry, by force if necessary, if entry is refused.

Authorized officers can inspect, seize and detain records, including computer records, required as evidence. Improper disclosure of information so obtained is an offence.

Section 33. It is an offence to obstruct persons executing the provisions of the Act, including the failure to assist or provide information (unless it incriminates them) or the furnishing of false information.

Section 35. The penalty for most offences is:
◆ on conviction on indictment to an unlimited fine and/or up to two years' imprisonment

◆ on summary conviction to a fine not exceeding the relevant amount and/or imprisonment for up to six months. (In the case of Sections 7, 8 or 14 the relevant amount is £20,000, the amount for the other sections is £5,000).

Section 40. This section empowers ministers to issue codes of practice to guide food authorities on the enforcement of food safety legislation. This is intended to assist in uniform standards of enforcement. The codes of practice are not legally binding but food authorities must have regard to them.

The Food Premises (Registration) Regulations, 1991 as amended 1997

It is a requirement for most premises used for food businesses, for five or more days within any five consecutive weeks, to be registered with the local, or port health, authority in whose area they are situated. New businesses must apply for registration at least 28 days before they open. There is no charge for registration and it cannot be refused. Failure to register may result in a fine not exceeding level 3, (£1,000) however, any person providing false information may be fined

up to level 5 (£5,000) on the standard scale.

The Food Safety (General Food Hygiene) Regulations, 1995

These Regulations apply to most food businesses in England, Scotland and Wales. The Regulations cover all stages of food production, except primary production and businesses carrying on activities covered by regulations implementing product specific directives (for example, manufacturers of meat, meat products, fishery products, dairy and egg products). The main objective of the Regulations is to protect human health.

Reg.4. A proprietor of a food business shall ensure that the preparation, processing, manufacturing, packaging, storing, transportation, distribution, handling and offering for sale or supply of food are carried out hygienically. The proprietor shall identify any step in the activities of the food business which is critical to ensuring food safety and ensure that adequate safety procedures are identified, implemented, maintained and reviewed on the basis of the following principles:
(a) analysis of the potential food hazards in a food business operation;

(b) identification of the points in those operations where food hazards may occur;

(c) deciding which of the points identified are critical to ensuring food safety ("critical points");

(d) identification and implementation of effective control and monitoring procedures at those critical points; and

(e) review of the analysis of food hazards, the critical control points and the control and monitoring procedures periodically, and whenever the food business' operations change.

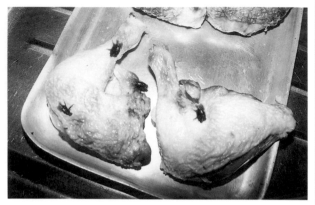

Food should not be exposed to risk of contamination.

Reg.5. A person working in a food handling area who:

(a) knows or suspects they are suffering from or may be a carrier of a foodborne disease or

(b) has an infected wound, a skin infection, sores, diarrhoea or any similar condition which may result in food contamination by pathogens shall report the condition or his suspicion to the proprietor of the food business.

Offences and penalties

Reg.6. Any person guilty of an offence against the Regulations shall be liable:

(a) on summary conviction, to a fine of up to £5,000; or

(b) on conviction on indictment, to an unlimited fine or imprisonment for a term not exceeding two years, or both.

Enforcement and execution

Reg.8. These Regulations shall be enforced by the food authority which must:

(a) ensure that food premises are inspected with a frequency which has regard to the risk associated with those premises;

(b) ensure that inspectors include a general assessment of the potential food safety hazards associated with the business and pay particular attention to critical control points identified by food businesses to assess whether the necessary monitoring and verification controls are being operated; and

(c) give due consideration to whether the proprietor of a food business has acted in accordance with any relevant guide to good hygiene practice.

Schedule 1 (Rules of hygiene)
Chapter I (General requirements for food premises)

◆ Food premises must be kept clean and maintained in good repair and condition

◆ The layout, design, construction and size of food premises shall:
(a) permit adequate cleaning and/or disinfection

(b) be such as to protect against the accumulation of dirt, contact with toxic materials, the shedding of particles into food and the formation of condensation or undesirable mould on surfaces

(c) permit good food hygiene practices, including protection against cross-contamination between and during operations, by foodstuffs, equipment, materials, water, air supply or personnel and external sources of contamination such as pests

(d) provide, where necessary, suitable temperature conditions for the hygienic processing and storage of products.

◆ An adequate number of wash basins must be available, suitably located and designated for cleaning hands. An adequate number of flush lavatories must be available and connected to an effective drainage system. Lavatories must not lead directly into rooms in which food is handled

◆ Wash basins for cleaning hands must be provided with hot and cold (or appropriately mixed) running water, materials for cleaning hands and for hygienic drying. Where necessary, the provisions for washing food must be separate from the handwashing facility

◆ There must be suitable and sufficient means of natural or mechanical ventilation. Mechanical air flow from a contaminated area to a clean area must be avoided. Ventilation systems must be so constructed as to enable filters and other parts requiring cleaning or replacement to be readily accessible

◆ All sanitary conveniences within food premises shall be provided with adequate natural and/or mechanical ventilation

◆ Food premises must have adequate natural and/or artificial lighting

◆ Drainage facilities must be adequate for the purpose intended; they must be designed and constructed to avoid the risk of contamination of foodstuffs

◆ Adequate changing facilities for personnel must be provided where necessary.

Chapter II (Specific requirements in rooms where foodstuffs are prepared, treated or processed)

(1) (a) Floor surfaces must be maintained in a sound condition and they must be easy to clean and, where necessary, disinfect. This will require the use of impervious, washable and non-toxic materials, unless the proprietor of the food business can satisfy the food authority that other materials used are appropriate. Where appropriate, floors must allow adequate surface drainage.

(b) Wall surfaces must be maintained in a sound condition and they must be easy to clean and, where necessary, disinfect. This will require the use of impervious, washable and non-toxic materials and require a smooth surface up to a height appropriate for the operations, unless the proprietor of the food business can satisfy the food authority that other materials used are appropriate.

(c) Ceilings and overhead fixtures must be designed, constructed and finished to prevent the accumulation of dirt and reduce condensation, the growth of undesirable moulds and the shedding of particles.

(d) Windows and other openings must be constructed to prevent the accumulation of dirt. Those which can be opened to the outside environment must, where necessary, be fitted with insect-proof screens which can be easily removed for cleaning. Where open windows would result in contamination of foodstuffs, windows must remain closed and fixed during production.

(e) Doors must be easy to clean and, where necessary, disinfect. This will require the use of smooth and non-absorbent surfaces, unless the proprietor of the food business can satisfy the food authority that other materials used are appropriate.

(f) Surfaces (including surfaces of equipment) in contact with food must be maintained in sound condition and be easy to clean and, where necessary, disinfect. This will require the use of smooth, washable and non-toxic materials, unless the proprietor of the food business can satisfy the food authority that other materials used are appropriate.

(2) Where necessary, adequate facilities must be provided for the cleaning and disinfecting of work tools and equipment. These facilities must be constructed of materials resistant to corrosion, and must be easy to clean and have an adequate supply of hot and cold water.

(3) Where appropriate, adequate provision must be made for any necessary washing of the food. Every sink or other such facility provided for the washing of food must have an adequate supply of hot and/or cold potable water as required, and be kept clean.

Chapter III Requirements for market stalls or mobile sales vehicles, premises used primarily as a private dwelling house, premises used occasionally for catering purposes and vending machines)

Premises and vending machines must be sited, designed and constructed, kept clean and maintained in good repair and condition to avoid risk of food contamination and pest harbourage, so far as is reasonably practicable. Where necessary, there must be facilities to maintain adequate personal hygiene and for the cleaning of equipment and food to avoid contamination.

Chapter IV (Transport)

Conveyances and/or containers used for transporting foodstuffs must be kept clean and maintained in good repair and condition, and must, where necessary, be designed and constructed to permit adequate cleaning and/or disinfection. Foodstuffs must be placed and protected to minimize the risk of contamination.

Chapter V (Equipment requirements)

Articles, fittings and equipment with which food comes into contact shall be kept clean, and be so constructed, be of such materials and be kept in such good order, repair and condition, as to minimize any risk of contamination of food and enable them to be kept thoroughly cleaned and, where necessary, disinfected. They must be installed so as to allow adequate cleaning of the surrounding area.

Chapter VI (Food waste)

Food waste and refuse must not be allowed to accumulate in food rooms unnecessarily. Waste must be deposited in closeable containers (unless the food authority agree otherwise) which, if necessary, are easy to clean and disinfect. Adequate provision must be made for the removal and storage of waste. Refuse stores must be designed and managed to enable them to be kept clean, to prevent access by pests and prevent contamination of food, drinking water, equipment or premises.

Chapter VII (Water supply)

An adequate supply of potable water must be provided and used to ensure foodstuffs are not contaminated. If used, ice must also be from potable water, if it could contaminate the food. It must be stored to protect it from contamination.

Chapter VIII (Personal hygiene)

Persons working in food handling areas must maintain a high degree of personal cleanliness and wear suitable clean and, where appropriate, protective clothing. Persons suspected or known to be suffering from a foodborne disease or condition which could contaminate food with pathogens must not be permitted to work in food handling areas where there is a likelihood of directly or indirectly contaminating food.

Chapter IX (Provisions applicable to foodstuffs)

Contaminated or decomposed raw materials must be rejected unless normal sorting and hygienic preparation will ensure their fitness for human consumption. All food must be protected against contamination during handling, storage, packaging, display and distribution. Effective pest control procedures must be implemented. Hazardous and/or inedible substances, including animal food, must be labelled and stored in separate and secure containers.

Chapter X (Training)

The proprietor of a food business shall ensure that food handlers engaged in the food business are supervised and instructed and/or trained in food hygiene matters commensurate with their work activities.

The Food Safety (General Food Hygiene)(Butchers' Shops) Amendment Regulations 2000.

Schedule 1A-Licensing of Butchers' Shops.

The Regulations require butchers' shops in England involved with the sale of both raw meat and ready-to-eat food to be licensed annually by the food authority for a charge of £100. To obtain a licence, the following conditions must be satisfied:

◆ The business complies with the Food Safety (General Food Hygiene) and the

Food Safety (Temperature Control) Regulations, 1995.

◆ All food handlers are satisfactorily trained.
◆ At least one person in the shop is trained in food hygiene to enable him to supervise effectively and ensure that all HACCP procedures are followed.

◆ HACCP procedures are in place. (Procedures include verification that the HACCP system is working effectively and relevant documentation including training records.) Records may be written or electronic.

The Food Safety (Temperature Control) Regulations, 1995

Chill holding requirements

Food which supports the growth of pathogens must not be kept above 8°C unless:

◆ it is hot food on display

◆ there is no health risk

◆ it is canned or dehydrated

◆ it is raw food intended for cooking or further processing.

Chill holding tolerance periods

Food may be kept above 8°C if the manufacturer has undertaken a scientific assessment confirming there is no risk and the shelf-life is not exceeded.

Food on display, or for service, may be kept above 8°C for up to four hours on a single occasion. Food may also be kept above 8°C for unavoidable reasons, such as defrosting equipment or breakdowns,

provided this is consistent with food safety.

Hot holding requirements

Hot food on display must not be kept below 63°C. Food may be kept below 63°C if a scientific assessment has indicated there is no health risk.

Hot food for service or display may be kept below 63°C for up to two hours on a single occasion.

Part III Temperature Control Requirements in Scotland

Chill and hot holding offences

Food should be kept in a refrigerator or a cool ventilated place or above 63°C unless:

(a) it is undergoing preparation for sale;

(b) it is exposed for sale or has been sold;

(c) it is being cooled under hygienic conditions as quickly as possible to a safe temperature immediately following cooking or the final processing stage;

(d) it may be kept at ambient temperatures with no risk to health.

Reheating of food

Food which is to be reheated before being served for immediate consumption or exposed for sale shall be raised to a temperature of not less than 82°C. Unless this would result in a deterioration in its qualities.

◆ Gelatin used for bakers' confectionery filling, meat or fish products shall, immediately before use, be brought to the boil or kept at a temperature of not less than 71°C for 30 minutes

- Any gelatin remaining, other than waste, shall be cooled as quickly as practicable and refrigerated or stored in a cool ventilated place.

Cooling of food

Food intended for cold storage must be cooled as quickly as possible after heat processing.

Voluntary industry guides to good hygiene practice

The industry guides provide food businesses with a practical guide to complying with the regulations and must be given due consideration by enforcers. They will also assist in achieving consistency of enforcement. The guides may be used in courts to illustrate good practice. However, food businesses do not have to follow the advice in any guide as they may wish to comply with the regulations in some other way. Several industry guides have been, or are being, produced including guides for:

- the catering industry

- the baking industry

- the retail industry.

The Food Labelling Regulations, 1996

These Regulations apply in England, Scotland and Wales and require most food, sold for human consumption, to be labelled with:

- the name of the food

- a list of ingredients

- a "best-before" date which provides an indication of minimum durability (shelf-life) or in the case of food which, microbiologically, is highly perishable and in consequence likely, after a short period, to constitute an immediate danger to human health, a "use-by" date

- any special storage conditions or conditions of use

- the name and address of the manufacturer or packer or of a seller.

NORTHERN IRELAND

The food safety legislation applicable to Northern Ireland includes:

The Food Safety (NI) Order, 1991
The Food Premises (Registration) Regulations (NI), 1992, amended 1997
The Food Premises (General Food Hygiene) Regulations (NI), 1995
The Food Premises (Temperature Control) Regulations (NI), 1995

The enforcement of food safety legislation in the United Kingdom

In the United Kingdom, Central Government has given the responsibility for protecting public health and ensuring food businesses comply with food hygiene legislation to local authorities. Officers with a wide range of qualifications, experience and expertise are employed to enable authorities to carry out the significant range of food hygiene and food safety controls that now exist. The most common local authority official involved in food hygiene control is an environmental health officer (EHO). Authorities may also appoint technical officers with specialist food qualifications. These officers are authorized to enforce the various acts and regulations.

The functions of EHOs and other authorized officers include:

◆ ensuring product safety and fitness for consumption

◆ reducing possible sources of contamination entering the food environment

◆ monitoring conditions and hygienic operations within the food environment

◆ ensuring compliance with relevant legislation

◆ establishing the integrity of management and effectiveness of control procedures

◆ offering professional guidance, including preventive advice, particularly when legislation is changing.

EHOs and other officers undertake the above functions:

◆ during routine visits to and inspections of food premises

◆ whilst investigating food poisoning outbreaks and incidents

◆ whilst investigating food complaints

◆ by lecturing on hygiene courses and seminars and giving related talks

◆ by using the media, for example, press releases, committee reports and hazard warnings

◆ whilst dealing with planning and licence applications

◆ by developing partnerships with businesses' decision-making bases in the local authority's area (often referred to as the "Home Authority Principle")

◆ by developing local business forums for the exchange of information and the provision of advice.

Inspections of food premises by enforcement officers

Code of Practice No. 9 states that food hygiene inspections have two main purposes:

◆ to identify risks arising from the food businesses' activities and determine the effectiveness of the businesses' own assessment of hazards and controls

◆ to identify contraventions of food legislation and seek to have them corrected.

Before carrying out a food hygiene inspection, EHOs will take account of a number of issues. These will include:

◆ reviewing the premises' previous history – including information on its operations and systems, previous complaints and responses to earlier inspection outcomes

◆ timing of inspection – generally unannounced, although advance notice may occasionally be appropriate to ensure relevant persons are present

◆ equipment availability, for example,

calibrated temperature recording equipment

◆ appropriate protective clothing

◆ assessing the need for additional expertise, for example, food examiners.

Frequency of inspections

Effective inspection programmes recognize that the frequency of inspection will vary according to the type of food business, the nature of the food, the degree of handling and the size of the business. Code of Practice No. 9 details an inspection rating scheme for assessing premises for this purpose. The frequency of visits is determined by the hazards associated with the business, including the current level of compliance with food safety legislation, the confidence of the enforcement officer in management, the history of compliance and the control systems in place. Essentially, those premises posing potentially a higher risk should be inspected more frequently than those premises with a lower risk.

Businesses handling low-risk foods, with few customers, that comply with food hygiene legislation and are managed effectively may only be inspected every five years. Businesses processing high-risk food or at risk from *E coli* O157 or *Clostridium botulinum*, or supplying vulnerable consumers, are likely to be inspected at least every six months.

Action taken as a result of an inspection

During an inspection, an EHO may identify contraventions of food hygiene legislation and/or poor or unsafe food handling practices. Several options exist to remedy the contraventions and detailed guidance is found in a number of the Food Safety Act, 1990, Codes of Practice as to the most appropriate action. The options available and potential outcomes for all food hygiene inspections include:

◆ verbal advice/warnings or informal written advice/warnings where the EHO is confident the work will be carried out. Letters should clearly differentiate between legal requirements and recommendations

◆ an improvement notice, for contraventions of food hygiene legislation, allowing not less than 14 days to comply

◆ the detention or seizure of unsafe food where food does not comply with the food safety requirements

◆ an emergency prohibition notice, where there is an imminent risk of injury to health, requiring closure of the premises or prohibition of processes or use of equipment (a court will issue a prohibition order if the proprietor is convicted and there is a risk of injury to health)

◆ a formal caution where an offence exists but it is not considered in the public interest to prosecute through the courts

◆ prosecution, where it is considered in the public interest.

The reference in the Food Safety Act, 1990 to the defence of "due diligence" with regard to food related offences is worthy of specific note. The Act creates a number of offences known as "strict liability". In such a case, it does not matter that the person accused did not intend to break the law. The mere fact that there is clear evidence that the statute has been contravened is sufficient for a conviction. This regime of strict liability was perceived as causing injustice if a person was held to have committed an offence for which he had no responsibility at all, or because of an accident or some cause completely beyond his control. In order to create a balance of fairness, a defence was included which has become known as the "due diligence defence".

The Act specifically states that it is a defence to prove that all reasonable precautions were taken and all due diligence exercised to avoid the offence. Through legal precedent, various principles have been confirmed as necessary if a defence is to succeed. Some positive steps will always be required. Taking reasonable precautions involves the setting up of a system of control having regard to the nature of the risks involved. Due diligence involves securing the proper operation of that system. Where there is a reasonable precaution then it should be taken. Written records are not a legal requirement, however, satisfactory records may be useful to assist a due diligence defence.

The Food Standards Agency

The Food Standards Agency was established on 1 April 2000. Its role is 'to protect public health from risks which may arise in connection with the consumption of food and otherwise to protect the interest of consumers in relation to food'.

The core values of the Agency are to:

◆ Put the consumer first.

◆ Be open and accessible.

◆ Be an independent voice.

The Agency's functions are to:
◆ Provide advice and information to the public and to the Government on food safety from farm to fork, nutrition and diet.

◆ Protect consumers through effective enforcement and monitoring

◆ Support consumer choice through promoting accurate and meaningful labelling.

The Food Standards Agency is led by a Board and accounts to Parliament through Health Ministers. The headquarters are based in London. Scottish, Welsh and Northern Irish Executives of the Agency are responsible for implementing policies on food issues specific to each country within the Agency's framework.

The Agency has responsibility for:
◆ Food Safety, contaminants, nutrition, additives and labelling.
◆ Animal feed and veterinary public health.
◆ The performance of Local Authority enforcement.
◆ The Meat Hygiene Service.
◆ Research.

Website: www.foodstandards.gov.uk

Acute disease	A disease which develops rapidly and produces symptoms quickly after infection. Patients soon recover, or die.
Aerobic	Requiring oxygen.
Algae	Simple plants capable of photosynthesis and most commonly found in aquatic environments or damp soil, for example, sea weed and spirogyra (forms bright green slimy masses in ponds).
Ambient temperature	The temperature of the surroundings. Usually refers to the room temperature.
Anaerobic	Requiring the absence of oxygen.
Antiseptic	A substance that prevents the growth of bacteria and moulds, specifically on or in the human body.
Aseptic	Free from microorganisms.
A_W (water activity)	A measure of the water available to microorganisms in food.
Bactericide	A substance which destroys bacteria.
Binary fission	Asexual method of reproduction by the division of the nucleus into two daughter nuclei, followed by similar division of the cell body. The method of reproduction used by bacteria.
Biodegradable	Chemicals and materials which can be broken down by bacteria or other biological means (usually during sewage treatment).
Carrier	A person who harbours, and may transmit, pathogenic organisms without showing signs of illness.
Chronic disease	A disease which usually develops slowly and symptoms last for a prolonged period.
Chronic poison	A substance which is used at low concentration and relies on repeated intake by the target pest to ensure elimination.
Cleaning	The process of removing soil, food residues, dirt, grease and other objectionable matter.
Clean surface	A surface which is free from residual film or soil, has no objectionable odour, is not greasy to touch and will not discolour a white paper tissue wiped over it.
Contamination	The occurrence of any objectionable matter in the food or food environment.
Controlled atmosphere packing	The packaging of food in an atmosphere that is different from the normal composition of air, the gases being precisely adjusted to specific concentration which are maintained throughout storage.
Critical control point (CCP)	A step in a process which, if controlled, will eliminate or reduce a hazard to an acceptable level.
Danger zone	The temperature range within which the greatest multiplication of pathogenic bacteria is possible, i.e. from 5°C to 63°C.

Detergent	A chemical that facilitates the removal of grease and food particles and promotes cleanliness.
Disinfectant	A chemical used for disinfection.
Disinfection	The reduction of microorganisms to a level that will not lead to harmful contamination nor spoilage of food. The term disinfection normally refers to the treatment of premises, surfaces and equipment, but may also be applied to the treatment of skin.
Epidemiology	The study of disease of people and animals, including incidence, sources, causes, mode of spread, distribution and control.
First aid materials	Suitable and sufficient bandages and dressings, including water-proof dressings and antiseptic.
Food handling	Any operation in the production, preparation, processing, packaging, storage, transport, distribution and sale of food.
Food hygiene	All measures necessary to ensure the safety and wholesomeness of food during preparation, processing, manufacture, storage, transportation, distribution, handling and offering for sale or supply to the consumer, i.e. at all stages of the food chain.
Food poisoning	An acute illness of sudden onset caused by the recent consumption of contaminated or poisonous food.
Fungi	Plants unable to synthesize their own food and usually parasitic or saprophytic. Include single-celled microscopic yeasts, moulds, mildews and toadstools.
Fungicide	A substance that kills fungi and mould.
Galvanized metal	Iron or steel which has been coated with zinc for protection against corrosion.
Gastroenteritis	An inflammation of the stomach and intestinal tract that normally results in diarrhoea.
Grease trap	A device fitted into a drainage system to prevent fat and grease entering the sewer.
HACCP	Hazard analysis and critical control point. A structured and documented hazard analysis system based on seven principles and applied to a standardized food production process with a view to ensuring cost-effective food safety. Critical control points are determined and then monitored. Specified remedial action is taken if any measurements deviate from safe limits.
Hazard	The potential to cause harm to the consumer (the safety aspect of the product) and can be microbiological, chemical or physical.

Hazard analysis	Identifying hazards, the steps at which they could occur and the introduction of measures to control them.
High-risk foods	Ready-to-eat foods which, under favourable conditions, support the multiplication of pathogenic bacteria and are intended for consumption without treatment which would destroy such organisms.
Incubation period	The period between infection and the first signs of illness.
Infective dose	The number of a particular microorganism required under normal circumstances to produce clinical signs of a disease.
Moulds	Microscopic plants (fungi) that may appear as woolly patches on food.
Mycotoxin	A toxin produced by some moulds.
Neurotoxin	A toxin that affects the nervous system.
Onset period	The period between consumption of the food and the first signs of illness. (Where incubation of microorganisms within the body does not take place.)
Optimum	Best.
Pathogen	Disease-producing organism.
Pest	Any living creature capable of directly or indirectly contaminating food.
Pesticide	A chemical used to kill pests.
pH	An index used as a measure of acidity or alkalinity.
Primary production	Those stages in the food chain up to and including, for example, harvesting, slaughtering, milking and fishing.
Quats	A popular name for quaternary ammonium compounds.
Residual insecticide	A long-lasting insecticide applied in such a way that it remains active for a considerable period of time.
Risk	The likelihood that the hazard will be realized.
Risk assessment	The process of identifying hazards, assessing risks and evaluating their significance.
Safe food	Food which is free of contaminants and will not cause illness or harm
Sanitizer	A chemical agent used for cleansing and disinfecting surfaces and equipment.
Spores	A resistant resting-phase of bacteria which protects them against adverse conditions.
Sterile	Free from all living organisms.

Sterilization	A process that destroys all living organisms.
Total viable count	The total number of living cells detectable in a sample. The number of cells is assessed from the number of colonies which develop on incubation of a suitable medium which has been inoculated with the sample of bacteria.
Toxins	Poisons produced by pathogens.
Viruses	Microscopic pathogens that multiply in living cells of their host.
Wholesome food	Sound food, fit for human consumption.
Yeast	A single-celled fungus which reproduces by budding and grows rapidly on certain foodstuffs, especially those containing sugar. Yeasts are the chief agents of fermentation. (Sugar converted to alcohol and carbon dioxide.)

Index

A

Accelerated freeze drying, 63
Acetic acid, 64
Acid foods, 6,10,31,45,61
Acid fermentation, 58, 64
Acidification, 64
Acute disease, 125
Aerobes, 10, 64
Aerobic, 125
Aerosol fly spray, 90
Air-blast freezing, 59
Alcohols, 81
Algae, 125
Allergy, 6
Alpha-amylase test, 60
Alphachloralose, 91
Ambient temperature, 125
Anaerobes, 10, 57, 64
Anaerobic, 125
Animals, 36, 86
Antibiotics, 64
Antimony, 31
Antiseptic, 125
Aprons, 41
Aquatic biotoxins, 32
Artificial drying, 62
Aseptic, 125
Authorized officer, 113, 114
Autolytic enzymes, 57
Automatic roller towel
   cabinets, 38
Aw, 125

B

Bacillary dysentery, 34
Bacilli, 8
Bacillus cereus, 11, 27
Bacteria, 8, 9, 15, 24
Bacterial contamination, 14,
   15, 106
Bacterial multiplication, 9
Bactericide, 125

Bacteriological monitoring,
   108
Bacteriology, 8
Bains marie, 55
Bait trays, 22, 89, 90
Bakery products, 12
Barrier creams, 38
Benfits of high standards of
   hygiene, 5
Benzene, 31
Best-before date, 46, 121
Binary fission, 9, 125
Biodegradable, 125
Bird pests, 88
Bivalves, 6, 33
Blanching, 59, 62
Blast chillers, 50
Blast-freezing, 54
Bleach, 12, 81
Blowflies, 87
Boils, 8, 39, 42
Bolts, 19
Booklice, 88
Botulinum cook, 61
Botulism outbreak, 30
Brining, 63
Bristles, 21, 79, 80
Brown rat, 85
Brushes, 75, 79, 80
Building, 66, 89

C

Cadmium, 31
Campylobacter enteritis, 34
Campylobacter jejuni, 34
Canned foods, 6, 14
Canned goods, 45
Canning, 61
Caramelization, 60
Carriers, 6, 15, 16, 34, 38, 41,
   102, 116, 125
Catering Guide to Good

   Hygiene Practice, 15, 101
Causal factors, 28
Causative agent, 24
Caustic soda, 78
Ceilings, 66
Cell wall, 9, 11
Cereals, 44
Chemical additives, 31
Chemical contamination, 14,
   22
Chemical control methods,
   90
Chemical disinfection, 81
Chemical energy, 79
Chemical food poisoning, 31
Chemical preservation, 63
Chemical store, 78
Chill holding, 120
Chilled display cabinets, 49
Chlorinated water, 62
Chronic disease, 125
Chronic poison, 125
Clean surface, 125
Cleaning, 21, 125
   benefits, 78
   chemicals, 23
   energy, 79
   equipment, 79, 81
   facilities, 70
   of equipment, 76
   problems, 78
   procedures, 81
   schedules, 83
Cling film, 45
Cloakrooms, 70
Clostridium botulinum, 11,
   27, 30, 61, 62, 123
Clostridium perfringens, 10,
   11, 25, 30, 64
Cloths, 15, 21, 79, 81
Cocci, 8
Cockroaches, 87

Code of Practice No. 9, 122
Codes, 46
Codes of Practice, 96, 97, 115
Colonies, 8
Colour coding, 76, 79
Coloured waterproof dressing, 39
Commensals, 8
Commercially sterile, 60, 61
Compactors, 71
Competition, 11
Condensation, 19, 44, 47, 69, 82, 118
Construction of premises, 66
Consultant in communicable disease control, 103
Contact time, 79
Containers, 18
Contamination, 14, 17, 48, 76, 125
Contamination control, 16
Control measures, 18, 34, 35, 104, 107
Controlled atmosphere packing, 125
Controlled atmospheres, 64
Controls, 25, 26, 27, 107
Convalescent carriers, 6
Cook-chill, 48, 53, 54
Cooked meat slicing machine, 83
Cook-freeze, 55
Cooking, 10, 12, 49, 60
Cooling, 49, 50, 121
Copper, 31
Corrective action, 104, 107, 110
Craft knives, 14
Cream, 44
Criteria, 104
Critical control point, 104,125

Critical limit, 104
Critical points, 106, 115
Cross-contamination, 15, 35
Cryogenic freezing, 59
Curing, 63
Customer complaints, 12, 17, 109
Customer contamination, 22
Cut-out switches, 68
Cuts, 39
Cutting boards, 76
Cytoplasm, 9

D

Damaged stock, 46
Danger zone of bacterial growth, 125
Data loggers, 49
De-boxing, 66
Decision tree, 104
Dehydration, 10, 44, 62
Deliveries, 16, 43, 49, 51
Dental sepsis, 42
Design of premises, 66
Destruction of bacteria, 11
Detergent, 126
Deviation, 104
Dichlorvos strips, 22, 91
Diffusers, 20
Disinfectant, 12, 81, 126
Disinfection, 80, 126
Disinfection frequency, 81
Distribution, 4, 50
Documentation, 106
Doors, 67
Drainage, 69
Drip, 15, 48
Drivers, 16
Dry-goods stores, 47
Due diligence, 18, 22, 43, 46, 91, 96, 102, 103, 106, 109, 114, 123, 124

Duration of illness, 25, 26, 27, 34, 36
Dustbins, 71
Dysentery, 34

E

E. coli O157, 35, 36, 38, 86
Ears, 39, 42
Eggs, 44
Electrical supplies, 68
Electronic fly killers, 22, 90
Emergency prohibition order, 114
End product testing, 105
Endotoxins, 10
Enforcement, 121
Enforcement officer, 100, 114, 122
Engineers, 19, 21
Enteric fever, 33
Enterotoxins, 10
Environmental control, 88
Environmental Health Department, 42, 46, 52
Environmental health officer, 42, 102, 103
  functions of, 122
Enzymes, 51, 52, 57, 58, 59, 65
Epidemiology, 126
Equipment, 72, 74, 118
Equipment design, 72
Equipment surface, 75
Escherichia coli O157, 35
European Community, 112
Exclusion of food handlers, 37, 41
Exotoxins, 10, 11
Extraneous matter, 17, 18, 113

F

Faecal specimens, 103
Faecal-oral route, 36, 37
Failure of management, 29, 30
False ceilings, 89
Fermentation, 64,
Fingernails, 38
First aid, 40, 126
Flagella, 9
Flaking paint, 19
Flexible connections, 68
Flies, 86
Floors, 44, 68
Flow diagram, 104
Fluctuating temperatures, 52
Fluidized-bed freezing, 59
Food, 112
Food business, 113
Food handlers, 20, 101
Food handling, 126
Food hygiene, 4, 126
Food hygiene inspections, 122
Food Labelling Regs.1996, 121
Food poisoning, 4, 6, 7, 8, 9, 24, 112, 126
Food poisoning bacteria, 9, 10, 85
Food poisoning organisms, 24
Food poisoning outbreaks, 29, 30, 102
Food premises, 116
Food Premises (General Food Hygiene) Regs (NI) 1995, 121
Food Premises (Registration) Regs. 1991, 115
Food Premises (Temperature Control) Regs (NI) 1995, 121
Food Safety Act 1990, 18, 22, 112, 123
Food Safety (General Food Hygiene) (Butchers' Shops) Amendment Regs. 2000, 119
Food Safety (General Food Hygiene) Regs. 1995, 115
Food Safety (NI) Order 1991, 120
Food Safety (Temperature Control) Regs. 1995, 120
Food safety policies, 96
Food safety requirements, 113
Food Standards Agency, 124
Food storage, 43
Food vehicles, 15, 16, 24, 25, 26, 27, 28, 31, 36
Food waste, 119
Foodborne diseases, 33
Footwear, 41, 70
Foreign bodies, 14, 17, 18
Foreign body detection, 22
Freezer breakdown, 52
Freezer burn, 51, 57, 59
Frozen poultry, 53
Fruit, 44
Fruit flies, 87
Fumigation, 91
Fungi, 12, 126
Fungicide, 31, 126

G

Galvanised metal, 31, 126
Gas supplies, 68
Gastroenteritis, 6, 126
Generation time, 9
Generic controls, 28
German cockroach, 87

Glass, 20
Good housekeeping, 89
Good hygiene practice, 72, 96, 97, 106, 116
Grease, 19, 126
Grease trap, 69, 126
Greenhouse effect, 46

H

HACCP, 18, 96, 104, 105, 126
Haemolytic uraemic syndrome, 35
Hair, 40
Hairnets, 40
Hand disinfection, 81
Hand drying,38
Hand-contact surfaces, 16
Hands, 38
Handwashing, 38
Handwashing facilities, 70
Haricot beans, 32
Hazard, 14, 18, 30, 37, 40, 55, 76, 104, 106, 107, 126
Hazard analysis, 104, 105, 127
Healthy carriers, 6
Heat disinfection, 80
Heat resistant, 60
Hepatitis A, 36
High-risk food, 5, 8, 46, 50, 127
Hot cupboards, 56
Hot food, 48, 120
Hot holding, 55
Hot plates, 56
House mouse, 85, 86
Hydrogen gas, 32
Hygiene training, 100
Hypochlorite, 82

I

Ice crystals, 52, 53, 54, 59

Ice-cream, 44
Improvement notice, 113, 123
Incidence of food poisoning, 7
Incubation period, 24, 33-36, 127
Infective dose, 33, 36, 127
Infestation, signs of, 86
Infested food, 21
Infrared thermometer, 49
Injurious to health, 113
Insects, 21, 57, 86
Inspection belt, 18
Inspection by an enforcement officer, 100
Inspection of food premises, 98, 122
Investigation of food poisoning, 102
Irradiation, 12, 65, 80
ISO 9000, 96, 98

J

Jewellery, 20, 40
Justice of the Peace, 113, 114

K

Kinetic energy, 79
Kitchen design, 71

L

Lactic acid, 64
Lacto bacillus, 60
Lead, 31
Level 1 training, 101
Lighting, 69
Lipases, 58
Liquid egg, 60
Liquid soap, 38, 81
Listeria monoctygenes, 35
Listeriosis, 35

Living cells, 33
Lockers, 70
Low-acid canned foods, 60
Low-acid foods, 61
Low-risk food, 5

M

Main clean, 81
Maintenance operatives, 21
Manual dish washing, 82
Meat pies, 44
Mechanical dishwashing, 82
Mechanical equipment, 80
Medical questionnaire, 42
Mesophiles, 10
Metallic food poisoning, 31
Microbiology, 8
Microorganisms, 8
Milk, 44, 60
Minded to notice, 122
Modified atmosphere packaging, 64
Modified atmosphere packs, 45
Monitoring, 104, 107, 108
Monitoring documents, 110
Monitoring food handlers, 110
Monitoring temperatures, 49
Mould inhibitors, 12
Moulds, 12, 57, 59, 127
Mouldy food, 14
Mouth, 8, 39
Multi-deck units, 47
Mussels, 33
Mycelium, 12
Mycotoxins, 57, 127

N

Nail biters, 38
Nail brushes, 38
Nail varnish, 38

Narcotizing, 91
Negligent cleaning, 78
Neurotoxin, 127
Nisin, 64
Non-potable water, 69
Norwalk virus, 33
Nose, 8, 39
Notice boards, 20
Nuclear material, 9
Nutrients, 9
Nuts, 19, 21

O

Obstruction, 115
Oil, 19, 20, 71
Olive oil, 32
Onset, 27, 127
Onset period, 24-27, 31, 33, 36, 126
Optimum, 9, 127
Optimum temperature, 10, 79
Organoleptic assessment, 108
Oriental cockroach, 87
Outbreak control team, 102
Outbreak location, 102
Outbreaks of food poisoning, 28
Out-of-date, 16, 48, 103
Overloading of refrigerators, 48
Oxygen, 10, 45, 57, 58, 64
Oysters, 5, 6, 33

P

Packaging, 18, 19, 43, 45, 51, 52, 54, 60, 66, 89
Packing, 18, 59, 64
Paper sacks, 19
Paper towels, 21, 38, 82
Parasites, 36, 57, 59, 65
Paratyphoid, 33

Index

Pasteurization, 60
Pasteurized canned foods, 62
Pathogens, 8, 86, 88, 104, 127
Penalties, 115, 116
Perfume, 40
Perimeter areas, 71
Personal hygiene, 119
Person-to-person spread, 33, 36
Pest control, 85, 88
Pest control contractor, 91
Pesticide, 31, 32, 127
Pest, 127
pH, 10, 57, 61, 63, 64, 127
Pharoah's ants, 88
Physical contamination, 14, 17
Physical control methods, 90
Pickling, 64
Pillsbury Company, 105
Plate freezing, 59
Poisonous fish, 32
Poisonous plankton, 32
Poisonous plants, 32
Polypropylene, 75, 76, 79, 83
Power of entry, 114
Pre-clean, 81
Premises, 113
Preparation surfaces, 75
Prerequisites (for HACCP), 105, 108
Preservation, 57, 58, 64
Preservatives, 57, 58
Prevention of contamination, 15
Price tickets, 44
Primary production, 127
Prohibition order, 113, 123
Proofing of buildings, 89
Propionates, 64
Protective clothing, 37, 41,

119
Psocids, 88
Psoriasis, 42
Psychrophiles, 10
Public Health Laboratory Service, 104
Puffer fish, 32
Purulent gingivitis, 42

Q

Quality assurance, 97
Quality control, 98
Quaternary ammonium compounds, 81, 127
Quats, 127

R

Radiant heat, 49
Rancidity, 51, 58, 59, 64, 65
Rats, 85
Raw foods, 6, 43
Raw materials, 17, 18, 19, 43, 66, 119
Raw meat, 43
Raw poultry, 6, 35, 43, 57
Red kidney beans, 32
Red whelk, 32
Refrigerators, 47, 58
Refuse, 66, 71, 119
Regeneration, 53, 54, 55
Registration, 115
Reheating, 55, 120
Report, 100
Reservoir, 36
Residual insecticide, 127
Review of hazard analysis, 106
Rinse aid, 82
Risk, 105, 127
Risk assessment, 105, 127
Rodenticides, 90
Rodents, 21, 85

Roller drying, 62
Rope, 57
Routes, 15, 16, 38
Rust, 19

S

Safe food, 4, 127
Salmonella, 7, 25, 30
Salmonella paratyphi, 33
Salmonella typhi, 33
Salt, 63
Samples of food, 114
Sanitary conveniences, 70
Sanitizer, 82, 127
Satellite kitchens, 53
Scientific assessment, 120
Scombrotoxic fish poisoning, 32
Seams, 62
Seizure, 113, 114, 123
Septic spots, 39
Services, 68
Severity, 105
Sewage, 15, 33, 34, 35
Shelf-life, 43, 45, 48, 60, 64, 120, 121
Shellfish, 5, 33, 36, 43
Shellfish poisoning, 32
Shigella sonnei, 34, 38
Sinks, 70
Site selection, 66
Siting of equipment, 75
Skin infections, 8, 37, 39, 42
Smoking, 40, 64, 65
Sodium nitrate, 31, 63
Sodium nitrite, 32, 63
Sources, 15, 16, 24, 25, 26, 27, 35, 102
Specifications, 18, 96
Spillages, 49
Spirochactes, 8
Spoilage, 8, 10, 44, 45, 51,

57-59

Spores, 11, 12, 25, 27, 49, 57, 59, 60, 62, 63, 65, 80, 127

Spray drying, 62

SRSVs, 33

Staff responsibilities, 48

Staleness, 58

Standards, 96

Staphylococcus, 8

Staphylococcus aureus, 26, 30, 37, 39, 40

Staples, 19

Steam, 12, 60, 67

Steam cleaners, 80

Steam disinfection, 80

Sterile, 127

Sterilization, 60, 80, 128

Sterilizing sinks, 70

Sterilizing units, 80

Sticky fly papers, 90

Stock control, 46, 51

Stock rotation, 44, 46, 51

Storage times, 51

Stored product insects, 88

String, 19, 21

Sugar, 63

Sulphur dioxide, 63, 64

Sun drying, 62

Suppliers, 18, 19, 96, 97

Supply of Machinery (Safety) Regs.1992, 74

Symptoms, 24, 25, 26, 27

T

Taenia saginata 36

Taint, 23, 40, 43, 44, 45, 57

Tapeworms, 36

Target level, 105

Thawing, 51, 52, 53, 59

Thermal energy , 79

Thermometer, 49, 50, 51, 54

Thermophiles, 10

Tin, 32

Tobacco, 40

Tolerance, 105

Total viable count, 128

Toxins, 6, 10, 12, 32, 55, 59, 60, 65, 128

Training, 37, 96, 97, 100, 101, 119, 120

Training methods, 101

Training programme, 102

Training records, 102

Transport, 118

Typhoid, 33

U

Ultra heat treatment, 60

Unfit food, 10, 12, 16, 46, 113

Unloading, 43

Unpacking, 18

Unsafe foods, 123

Use-by-date, 45, 46, 121

V

Vacuum packs, 12, 14, 45, 64

Vegetables, 6, 43, 44, 47, 49, 52, 57, 59, 61, 62

Vegetative bacteria, 11, 12

Vegetative state, 9

Vehicles, 9, 27

Ventilation, 69,

Verification, 105, 111

Vibrios, 8

Viral gastroenteritis, 33

Viruses, 13, 15, 31, 128

Visitors, 97

W

Walls, 67

Warm-air dryers, 38

Waste disposal systems 70

Waste food, 66, 71

Water supply, 68, 119

Waterproof conduits, 68

Waterproof dressings, 39

Weedkillers, 31

Weil's disease, 85

Wholesome food, 128

Windows, 67

Wood splinters, 19

Workflow, 66

Y

Yeasts, 12, 13, 57, 59, 128

Z

Zinc, 31